Ford/Southampton Studies in North/South Security Relations

Managing editor: Dr JOHN SIMPSON
Executive editor: PHILIP WILLIAMS

Nuclear non-proliferation: an agenda for the 1990s

*Ford Foundation Research Project 'North/South Security Relations', University
of Southampton*

Principal Researchers:
Professor P. A. R. CALVERT
    Dr J. SIMPSON
    Dr C. A. THOMAS
    Mr P. WILLIAMS
    Dr R. ALLISON

*While the Ford Foundation has supported this study financially, it does not necessarily
endorse the findings. Opinions expressed are the responsibility of their authors.*

Nuclear non-proliferation:
an agenda for the 1990s

Edited by
JOHN SIMPSON

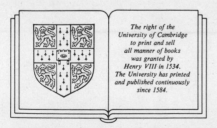

The right of the
University of Cambridge
to print and sell
all manner of books
was granted by
Henry VIII in 1534.
The University has printed
and published continuously
since 1584.

CAMBRIDGE UNIVERSITY PRESS
CAMBRIDGE
NEW YORK   NEW ROCHELLE   MELBOURNE   SYDNEY

Published by the Press Syndicate of the University of Cambridge
The Pitt Building, Trumpington Street, Cambridge CB2 1RP
32 East 57th Street, New York, NY 10022, USA
10 Stamford Road, Oakleigh, Melbourne 3166, Australia

First published 1987

Printed in Great Britain at the University Press, Cambridge

British Library cataloguing in publication data

Nuclear non-proliferation: an agenda for
the 1990s.
1. Nuclear non-proliferation
I. Simpson, John, *1943 July 26-*
355.8′25119   JX1974.73

Library of Congress cataloguing in publication data

Nuclear non-proliferation. I. Simpson, John,
1943-
JX1974.73.N76   1987   327.1′74   87–362
ISBN 0 521 33308 3

Contents

Contents

Contents

Inside the black box
Applications
A word on public debate
Conclusions

Part 4
Extending the nuclear non-proliferation regime beyond 1995:
issues and prospects

        Introduction – setting the stage for 1995
        The rules of procedure and the mechanics of voting at
        the 1995 Conference
        The nature of any extension proposals
        A 1995 Review and Amending Conference?
        Preparing for the 1995 Conference

        Introduction
        The effects of a collapse of the NPT on the Non-
        Proliferation Regime
        International security without the NPT
        The effects on international relations of a collapse of the
        NPT
        The emerging suppliers and the demise of the NPT
        Conclusions

        Introduction
        How NPT termination could affect international
        safeguards
        Technical constraints and denial
        Conclusions

        Introduction
        The management of nuclear armaments in the 1990s

Notes on contributors

Charles N. van Doren Former Assistant Director, United States Arms Control and Disarmament Agency. Alternate United States Representative to the 1975 and 1980 NPT Review Conferences. Member of IAEA Safeguards Committee and of the US delegation to the Nuclear Suppliers' Group.

Lewis A. Dunn Assistant Director, United States Arms Control and Disarmament Agency. Alternate US Representative to the 1985 NPT Review Conference.

Dennis Fakley Former Assistant Chief Scientific Adviser (Nuclear) in the UK Ministry of Defence. Member of the British delegation to the CTBT negotiations, 1977 to 1978.

David Fischer Assistant Director-General for External Relations at the International Atomic Energy Agency, 1957 to 1982.

Norman (Ned) Franklin Professor of Nuclear Engineering, Imperial College, London (1984–6). Chief Executive, British Nuclear Fuels Limited and its predecessor 1969–1975; Chief Executive, National Nuclear Corporation (UK) 1975–1984; Board Member UKAEA 1969–86.

Jozef Goldblat Head, Arms Control and Disarmament Programme, Stockholm International Peace Research Institute, Sweden.

Philip Gummett Chairman, Department of Science & Technology Policy, University of Manchester.

Peter Lomas Research Student, University of Southampton: Research Assistant to SIPRI Non-Proliferation Workshop, 1984–5.

Ronald Mason Chief Scientific Adviser at the UK Ministry of Defence 1977–1983. Former Professor of Chemistry at the Universities of Sheffield and Sussex. Chairman of Hunting Engineering Limited.

Harald Müller Senior Research Fellow, Hessiche Stiftung Friedens-und

Konfliktforschung, Peace Research Institute Frankfurt; formerly Senior Research Fellow, Centre for European Policy Studies, Brussels.

Joseph Pilat   Member of Strategic Analysis Division, Los Alamos National Laboratory, USA. Formerly Philip Moseley Fellow at Georgetown's Centre for Strategic and International Studies, 1978–81; Senior Research Associate, Congressional Research Service, 1981–3.

Aswini K. Ray   Chairman, Centre for Political Studies, School of Social Studies, Jawaharlal Nehru University, Delhi.

Mohamed I. Shaker   Ambassador, Deputy Permanent Representative of Egypt to the United Nations. President, Third Review Conference of the Non-Proliferation Treaty, 1985; Representative of Director General of IAEA, 1982–83.

John Simpson   Senior Lecturer in Politics and Deputy Director, Centre for International Policy Studies, University of Southampton. Coordinator of Ford Foundation Research Project.

Ian Smart   Assistant Director, International Institute for Strategic Studies, 1969–73; Director of Studies, Chatham House, 1973–83; Chairman, International Consultative Group on Nuclear Energy (ICGNE), 1977–80.

Steve Smith   Senior Lecturer in Politics, University of East Anglia.

William Walker   Senior Fellow, Science Policy Research Unit, University of Sussex. Secretary to the International Consultative Group on Nuclear Energy, (ICGNE) 1978–1980.

Preface

In the autumn of 1983, the Ford Foundation of the United States awarded the University of Southampton a multi-year grant to enable a team of researchers in its Department of Politics to investigate the problems likely to be encountered in North–South security relations in the 1990s and the policy options relevant to them. One area singled out for intensive investigation was nuclear non-proliferation, for if additional states were to acquire nuclear weapons it would drastically alter the future context of global security relationships.

When research work commenced in mid-1984 the international community was starting to make preparations for the Review Conference on the Non-Proliferation Treaty (NPT) scheduled for September 1985. One component of the Southampton research effort was a national seminar on non-proliferation problems which met several times in London in the months preceding the Conference. This seminar involved a mixed group of academics, officials and industrialists and the idea of holding an international symposium in the immediate aftermath of the Review Conference on problems of nuclear non-proliferation in the 1990s arose from it. Such a symposium could be given a clear empirical focus because the NPT provides for a conference in 1995 to discuss how the treaty will be extended beyond that date.

I was fortunate enough to be able to both attend the NPT Review Conference in Geneva as part of my Ford Foundation funded research activities and discuss the proposal for a symposium with many delegates and observers. This led to some changes in the proposed structure for the meeting and to several of those present in Geneva agreeing to write papers for it. The meeting itself, called the Sarnia Symposium after the Roman name for the Channel Islands, was held in the Old Government House Hotel on the island of Guernsey from 17–20 March 1986. The chapters which follow are derived both from papers prepared for it and ideas which arose out of it.

I owe a debt of gratitude to many people for their assistance and unstinting support in both preparing for the symposium and producing this volume. Ian Forbes, Mary Hendy, Elizabeth Schlamm, Freida Stack, Angela Wilkinson and Jane Tsabet were largely responsible for the detailed organisation of the symposium and typing and copy editing drafts of the chapters in this volume. Darryl Howlett acted as rapporteur for the symposium and prepared the final manuscript for publication. William Walker was particularly helpful in discussing possible papers in the formative period of the enterprise, as were some of the British government officials responsible for this policy area.

All the contributors gave generously of their time and expert advice in both the preparation and running of the symposium and in responding to my many suggestions for revisions to their papers prior to publication. My colleagues at Southampton, especially Roy Allison, Mark Hoffman and Caroline Thomas gave me invaluable support, whilst without the financial assistance and encouragement of the Ford Foundation and particularly its International Relations Programme Officer, Enid Schoettle, this volume could never have been created.

J.S.
Southampton, October 1986

Abbreviations

ABM	Anti-Ballistic Missile
ALCM	Air Launched Cruise Missiles
ASAT	Anti-Satellite (weapon)
ASW	Anti-Submarine Warfare
BARC	Bhabba Atomic Research Centre
C^3I	Command, Communication, Control and Intelligence
CAS	Committee on Assurances of Supply (International Atomic Energy Agency)
CEP	Circular Error Probable
CEPS	Centre for European Policy Studies (Brussels)
CIRUS	Indian Research Reactor
CIVEX	Project to develop a new type of reprocessing system
CMEA	Council for Mutual Economic Assistance (Eastern Europe)
CORTEX	System developed in the United States for on-site monitoring of the yield of nuclear weapon tests
CTBT	Comprehensive Test Ban Treaty
DHRUVA	Indian Research Reactor
EURATOM	European Atomic Energy Community
FBR	Fast Breeder Reactor
FBS	Forward-based Nuclear Weapon Systems
FSS	Full Scope Safeguards
GCD	General and Complete Disarmament
GW	Gigawatt
HEU	Highly Enriched Uranium
HEXAPARTITE	Project to develop safeguards system for gas centrifuge enrichment plants
IAEA	International Atomic Energy Agency
ICBM	Inter-Continental Ballistic Missiles

ICF	Inertial Confinement Fusion
IISS	International Institute for Strategic Studies
INF	Intermediate Range Nuclear Forces
INFCE(P)	International Nuclear Fuel Cycle Evaluation (Progamme)
INFCIRC	IAEA Information Circular
IPEN	Instituto de Pesquisas Energéticas e Nucleares
IRR	Israel Research Reactor
MARV	Manoeuvering Re-entry Vehicle
MIRV	Multiple Independently-targetable Re-entry Vehicle
MX	United States Heavy Ballistic Missile
NATO	North Atlantic Treaty Organisation
NNPA	United States Nuclear Non-Proliferation Act (1978)
NNWS	Non-Nuclear Weapon States
NPT	Non-Proliferation Treaty
NSG	Nuclear Suppliers Group
NWFZ	Nuclear Weapon Free Zone
OECD	Organisation for Economic Cooperation and Development
PINSTECH	Pakistan Institute for Nuclear Science and Technology
PNE	Peaceful Nuclear Explosions
PTBT	Partial Test Ban Treaty
PUNE	See UNCPICPUNE
PWR	Pressurised Water Reactor
SAARC	South Asian Association for Regional Cooperation
SDI	Strategic Defence Initiative
SIPRI	Stockholm International Peace Research Institute
SLBM	Submarine Launched Ballistic Missiles
SWU	Separative Work Unit (Unit for measuring uranium enrichment work)
TASTEX	Tokai Advanced Safeguards Technology Exercise (IAEA project)
UNCPICPUNE	United Nations Conference on Promoting International Cooperation in the Peaceful Uses of Nuclear Energy
URENCO	United Kingdom-Netherlands-West Germany Centrifuge Enrichment Company

Introduction

There are few more evocative sights than an old film clip of an atmospheric nuclear explosion. There is a flash which turns night into day, an orange globe of fire and then an expanding, brown cauldron of smoke against a back drop of diagonal white lines produced by the exhausts of sampling rockets. The cloud gradually forms a mushroom shape as it rises thousands of feet into the air, taking its radioactive debris with it. Yet those who have witnessed such an explosion at short range tell us that its visual impact is minor compared to actually experiencing its effects: the heat on the back of the neck; the X-ray picture of the bones of hands placed over the eyes to protect them from the flash; the shock of the blast and the overall impression of awesome and uncontrollable forces having been unleashed.

It is an old film clip because the United States, United Kingdom and USSR agreed to stop testing nuclear devices above ground in 1963, France followed their lead in 1974 and China has recently done the same. Nuclear testing now goes on underground and out of sight and its very lack of physical and political visibility has reduced pressures to stop it entirely.

Concerns over nuclear non-proliferation have been ameliorated in a similar fashion by the fact that almost a quarter of a century has elapsed since the last nuclear weapon state, China, exploded its first nuclear device. Yet the threat of the spread of nuclear weapons to additional states, a problem that has been termed horizontal proliferation, may prove just as significant for the future of global security as vertical proliferation, the continued competitive development and expansion of nuclear weapon arsenals by the nuclear weapon states.

This threat of horizontal proliferation, coupled with the fear of the catastrophic consequences of the use of nuclear weapons, provides the

I

impetus behind this volume. Its more specific objective is to help to ensure that no additional states acquire nuclear weapons. A central role in this process is played by those international arrangements designed to deter nuclear proliferation, often termed collectively the non-proliferation regime, and in particular the Treaty on the Non-Proliferation of Nuclear Weapons (NPT).

The NPT was signed in 1968 and came into force in 1970. It comprises eleven articles, of which only the first seven are substantive (see Appendix 1 for full text). The first two involve promises by nuclear weapon states not to transfer their weapons to any other state or to assist non-nuclear weapon states to acquire nuclear weapons and commitments by non-nuclear weapon states not to seek these weapons. The third requires all non-nuclear weapon state parties to the Treaty to subject their national nuclear activities to IAEA safeguards and requires all parties to make acceptance of such safeguards a condition of export. The fourth guarantees non-nuclear weapon states access to nuclear energy for peaceful purposes, while the fifth outlines procedures to gain access to the nuclear weapon states' nuclear explosives for civil engineering purposes. The sixth is an undertaking by the nuclear weapon states to negotiate disarmament agreements 'in good faith', whilst the seventh guarantees the right of all parties to negotiate regional nuclear free zone treaties. The eighth lays out general procedures for amending the Treaty and holding conferences every five years to review its operation. The ninth deals with signature and ratification, the tenth with withdrawal from the Treaty and the last with the authenticity of texts. In addition, the tenth also states that:

Twenty-Five Years after the entry into force of the Treaty, a Conference shall be convened to decide whether the Treaty shall continue in force indefinitely, or shall be extended for an additional fixed period or periods. This decision shall be taken by a majority of the Parties to the Treaty.

The first conference convened under the terms of Article 8 to review the operations of the NPT met in Geneva in 1975. This succeeded in agreeing a final declaration and consensus document on the operation of the Treaty, although considerable conflict occurred between the superpowers and certain Third World states over nuclear disarmament. At the next conference in 1980, however, a consensus document of this type could not be agreed and the conference broke up in disarray. Several explanations were offered for this failure, including lack of detailed preparation, the legacy of the negotiations among suppliers in the mid-1970s for a more restrictive trading regime, the hostile influence of states such as India that had stayed outside the NPT and the lack of progress in super-power disarmament negotiations, particularly upon a Comprehensive Test Ban Treaty (CTBT).

The lack of consensus displayed during this second Review Conference led many observers to fear that the non-proliferation regime was starting to crumble, despite the slow rise in the number of states party to the NPT. This gave the third Review Conference in 1985 special significance, as a second failure to agree a consensus document or the withdrawal of one or more parties would have marked a further decline in the regime. In ad-dition, although controversy over the trading regime had subsided over the previous five years, superpower arms control negotiations had only just been restarted, while the United States refused to engage in negotia-tions on a CTBT as it argued that reductions in nuclear warheads had a higher priority.

The experience of the 1980 Review Conference led to major efforts being made by the United States and other countries to lobby capitals in advance of the 1985 Conference and to ensure that effective preparations were made for it. Many delegations came to the 1985 conference deter-mined to agree a consensus document even if compromises had to be accepted. The result was agreement on a document which offered a de-tailed review of the state of the Treaty and regime, even though procedural problems and disagreements between Iran and Iraq made a final consen-sus difficult to achieve.

The next NPT Review Conference will be held in 1990 and the period between Review Conferences has tended to see foreign offices turn their attention to issues other than non-proliferation. Yet it is during these periods that the opportunity exists to prepare proposals for changes in the regime and to examine methods of overcoming obstacles that lie ahead. The most obvious of these is that in 1995 there is to be a conference to discuss extending the Treaty. All the guidance that exists on its nature is contained in the short paragraph quoted in full above. The 1990 Review Conference will thus be a forum where rules for handling this Extension Conference and mechanisms to resolve difficulties that might be encoun-tered during it could be agreed well in advance of 1995.

The NPT Extension Conference is one of the few fixed points in the diplomatic calender of the 1990s. It will have a major bearing on North–South security relations in that period and will play a significant role in their evolution over the decade. For the NPT and its linked regime are key elements in sustaining security in the Third World and its collapse would have catastrophic effects on global security. The initial task, however, is to identify the nature and substance of the problems likely to be encountered in 1995 and start an extended search for policy options which would be relevant to resolving them.

It was against this background that diplomats and scholars from some ten countries met in March 1986 to consider the issues likely to confront governments as they approached the Extension Conference in 1995. Considerable thought was given to the structure of both the papers prepared for this meeting and the chapters for this volume in order that the resulting product might be much more than the sum of their parts. As a consequence, the two chapters in Part 1 and the five in Part 2 represent an attempt to present a coherent picture of the likely environment in which non-proliferation policies will be operating in the 1990s. In Part 3 there are three chapters evaluating methods for strengthening the regime in the 1990s, including initiatives designed to reinforce constraints within states and amend the Treaty. Finally in Part 4 there are four chapters which examine the procedural problems likely to be encountered in 1995, the possible consequences of any degradation of membership and collapse in the NPT and the probable nature of the debates both at and surrounding the 1995 Conference.

Looking into the future is always a risky business. But unless we consciously seek to identify the problems that may face us as this century draws to a close and seek solutions to them while there is yet time for action, the world may become a much more insecure and dangerous place. After superpower nuclear war, nuclear proliferation is one of the major threats to the future of mankind. It is hoped that this preliminary reconnaissance into the agenda of issues in this area in the 1990s may be of some assistance to those governments, politicians, statesmen and researchers who seek to sustain the international non-proliferation regime through to the end of the century.

Part 1: Non-proliferation in the late 1980s

Overview

The non-proliferation regime in the mid-1980s comprises several elements. These include the Non-Proliferation Treaty (NPT), the safeguards system administered by the International Atomic Energy Agency (IAEA), the guidelines underpinning interstate trade in nuclear materials and technology and related national export controls, the existence of nuclear weapon free zones (NWFZs) in at least one region and the existence of a general international sentiment that in peacetime circumstances a public declaration of nuclear weapon status is unlikely to offer a net gain in security and is therefore an act of last resort. The regime itself has been moving in a universalist direction, with some 130 states having become parties to the NPT by the middle of the decade and rather more states being members of the IAEA. Several key states remain outside certain of the formal elements of the regime, however, including two of the nuclear weapon states and six others who possess nuclear facilities not covered by IAEA safeguards.

A common assessment of the state of the regime as the decade moves towards its close is one of cautious optimism. Although technical options for the manufacture of nuclear weapons appear to be slowly increasing, a fragile yet visible international consensus on the undesirability of doing so has been sustained. In addition, detailed analysis appears to suggest that states with technical options to move to overt nuclear weapon status have little political or military incentive to do so. Yet public controversy still remains over the alleged unequal nature of the regime, stemming from disagreements over whether its prime aim is to prevent additional states acquiring nuclear weapons or is to assist in achieving a world in which they have been totally eliminated.

The two chapters which follow reflect this cautious optimism. Mohamed Shaker offers an authoritative account of events at the 1985 NPT Review

7

Conference. In contrast to its predecessor in 1980, this conference was able to agree a consensus final document. He identifies a number of factors that accounted for this and describes the issues which dominated the debates. Although the document upon which the conference reached agreement contained many substantive points, its main significance was probably the manner in which the consensus was obtained. The fact that all the states assembled in Geneva were prepared to compromise their positions was a sign of the value they placed upon the NPT and its related regime, as well as an indication of their common desire to signal to the world that support for the regime was stronger in 1985 than in 1980.

Although a failure to reach consensus at a review conference is an indicator of a weakening of the non-proliferation regime, the emergence of new nuclear weapon states would be an even greater blow to it. Jozef Goldblat and Peter Lomas analyse this latter possibility in their chapter, basing themselves on information on known and planned unsafeguarded facilities for producing fissionable materials and possible motives for the states possessing such facilities to acquire nuclear weapons. Their conclusion is that while each case is different and heavily dependent on the individual regional context, only a radical change in a state's security position is likely to cause it to convert options into overt capabilities.

The message from the present to the future is that a series of international structures and processes exist to dissuade states from proliferating, but that there are major political disagreements over their objectives and functioning. A consensus to sustain this regime has been difficult to obtain and its strength is not easy to gauge. States contemplating proliferation are likely to do so for localised rather than global and universalist motives, however, and a major challenge confronting the international regime will be how it can deal with these regional and particularist challenges.

I The legacy of the 1985 Nuclear Non-Proliferation Treaty Review Conference: the president's reflections

Mohamed Ibrahim Shaker

INTRODUCTION

A few months before the Third Review Conference of the parties to the Non-Proliferation Treaty (NPT) convened in Geneva on 27 August 1985 the prospects for a successful conclusion of its deliberations were not considered to be very bright by many analysts. Progress on disarmament, more particularly nuclear disarmament, had been negligible since the convening of the Second NPT Review Conference in 1980 and it had been this issue which had led to an impasse at that conference over the adoption of a Final Declaration. The fear of a recurrence of the same result in 1985 led the Treaty's three nuclear-weapon state depository governments to consider whether there was any need for a Final Declaration to be part of the 1985 review of the operation of the Treaty. This idea gained little support, however, and an overwhelming majority of delegates came to Geneva intent on negotiating such a declaration.

In these inauspicious circumstances, the prospective president of the conference was occasionally asked by some of his colleagues, once his candidature was known, why he sought such a responsible position in a conference which was doomed to experience the same fate as its predecessor. He was concerned about the prospects of failure, but was not pessimistic. As the start of the conference neared, a number of factors gave him cause for optimism and as the conference proceeded it became clear that they were greatly assisting the smooth review of the operation of the Treaty. These factors were: the ongoing Geneva negotiations on nuclear and space arms and the November Geneva summit; the good preparatory work undertaken by the parties to the Treaty; the organisation and procedural aspects of the conference itself; and the determination by all parties to prevent the 1985 conference repeating the failure of the 1980 one.

9

This chapter will analyse these four major factors in turn, and then examine the major results of the conference and the lessons to be drawn out of it for the 1990 and 1995 conferences.

FACTORS CONTRIBUTING TO THE SUCCESSFUL OUTCOME OF THE REVIEW CONFERENCE

The ongoing Geneva Nuclear and Space Arms Talks and the November 1985 Geneva summit

The Geneva negotiations were initiated in March 1985 while the parties to the Treaty were engaged in preparatory work for the Review Conference. There was much hope that these negotiations would lead to some fruitful results, but in view of their complexity and the length of time needed to draft such agreements, it was not expected that concrete results would be easy to achieve in a short time. However, the superpowers appeared to be pursuing the negotiations with all seriousness and this helped to create an atmosphere of hope and expectation within the international community. The announcement of a summit meeting between the two leaders, Gorbachev and Reagan, led many of the participants at the Review Conference to believe that success in reaching a final substantive declaration would enhance the prospects for a productive summit. While far-reaching arms limitations agreements were not expected to emerge from this first summit between the two leaders, it was hoped it could lead later to some concrete results in the field of arms control and disarmament.

The preparatory phase of the conference

The 1985 conference was preceded by meetings of a preparatory committee which held three sessions. Although these meetings concentrated mainly on organisational issues and the preparation of documents for the conference, they enabled an extended exchange of views on a number of substantive issues to take place. It was apparent during the third and last session of the preparatory committee in April–May 1985 that the parties to the Treaty were very keen to undertake a constructive and objective review of its workings, free from polemics and recriminations.

The organisational aspects tackled by the preparatory committee were also very important in enabling the conference to be conducted in an orderly manner. First, it was accepted by almost all the parties present that a Final Declaration would be the goal of the Review Conference and the general mood in the preparatory committee was very favourable not only to issuing such a declaration but also to making it a substantive one.

Second, agreement was reached on the nature of the main committees to be created during the conference. In previous review conferences there had been two main committees. Committee I had focused upon Articles I, II, III, VI and VII of the Treaty and their corresponding preambular paragraphs, as well as Security Assurances. Committee II was also responsible for reviewing Article III as well as Articles IV and V. A problem arose at the third session of the preparatory committee because the Group of Eastern European Countries wanted one of their delegates to chair a main committee rather than the drafting committee as at previous review conferences. In these two conferences the drafting committee had had a negligible role, and at the Second Review Conference it had not met at all. By contrast, the Group of 77 had provided the chairman for committee I and the Western Group and Others had chaired committee II.

After long and arduous negotiations during the last session of the preparatory committee in April 1985, it was agreed to establish three main committees, each to be chaired by a delegate from one of the three groups. Main committee I was to be responsible for reviewing Articles I, II, VI and VII, as well as Security Assurances. Main committee II was to focus on Articles III and VII. Main committee III was to deal with Articles IV and V. It was also agreed to retain a drafting committee and assign its chairmanship to a delegate from the Group of Non-aligned and Neutral States.

This agreement was reached despite pressures to leave the establishment of the three main committees and the division of labour among them for settlement by the conference itself. The president believed that the decision to settle this matter before the conference was a crucial one for its successful proceedings, for if it had been left open it would have prevented the conference from embarking upon early consideration of substantive issues. As it was, the Rules of Procedure of the conference had to be amended at an early stage in the deliberations to legitimise the establishment of the three main committees. Their creation and the decisions on the division of labour among them proved to be crucial to the efficient handling of the different agenda items at the conference.

The presidency of the conference was discussed at an early phase of the preparatory committee proceedings, and some states parties suggested that there should be an informal agreement on this matter prior to the convening of the conference. This would allow the prospective president to prepare himself thoroughly for the responsibilities of his office by becoming familiar with the different issues and by obtaining the views of a great number of the parties on the conduct, content and outcome of the conference. General acceptance of this procedure was reached before the second session of the preparatory committee in October 1984. An informal agreement emerged that the conference president should be the person nominated by those members of the Group of Non-aligned and Neutral States attending that session. This understanding was confirmed at the third session of the preparatory committee in April–May 1985 and greatly assisted the president in preparing himself for the conference.

Organisational and procedural aspects of the conference

During the week preceding the convening of the conference, it was clear from the consultations the president had with a number of delegations that a group of 'friends of the president' should be convened to help him in the conduct of the conference and advise him on the proceedings. This informal group of delegates, who acted either in their capacities as officers of the conference or as leaders of their respective groups, met with the president frequently. It included the chairmen of the three main committees, the chairman of the drafting committee, representatives of the three depository governments and the chairman of the Group of Non-aligned and Neutral States.[1] Invaluable assistance was also provided by the secretary-general of the conference, a further participant in the meetings of this group.

One of the most important agreements reached among the 'friends' was that each main committee should prepare a report on its deliberations, which should reflect both points of agreement and disagreement. Each report would be factual and describe the results achieved at the committee level. At the First and Second Review Conferences, the reports of the main committees had been 'procedural' reports, and lacked substantive content. At the First Review Conference, the Final Declaration was forged and drafted by the able and determined president, Inga Thorson. The Declaration drew from elements of the two main committees' work but not from these 'procedural' reports. At the Second Review Conference, which failed to agree a Final Declaration, the main committees' reports were again void of any substantive material, although consensus was reached as far as the work of committee II was concerned.

Most of the conclusions in the reports of the three main committees in 1985 were agreed upon by consensus, and the Review Conference was then in possession of substantive results which many felt should not be lost because of lack of agreement on the outstanding issues. There was no way back after the success achieved by the three main committees, and solutions had to be found for what had been left unresolved.

Another organisational aspect which proved to be instrumental in the successful conclusion of the 1985 Review Conference was the efforts of the drafting committee, chaired by Ambassador Rolf Ekeus, in synthesising the reports of the three main committees. The drafting committee had played little part in the First and Second Review Conferences, and it was suggested during the informal consultations in preparation for the 1985 Conference that the president should undertake the task of preparing and drafting the Final Declaration, as had happened in the First Review Conference. The president and others disagreed with this proposal, however, as they believed that the drafting committee and its chairman should be active in the proceedings and that all the institutions of the conference should be given every opportunity to contribute to its conclusions.

The successful work of the three main committees allowed the drafting committee to participate fully in the final outcome of the conference. The chairman of the drafting committee, the president and the chairman of the main committees favoured a Final Document that would consist of a brief solemn declaration prepared by the chairman of the drafting committee, followed by an Article by Article review which synthesised the consensus texts agreed by the main committees. It was feared that an elaborate and analytical draft declaration might reopen discussions on issues which had already been settled in the main committees. The strategy of a simple declaration followed by a review was successfully implemented and the president believed that this was one of the most advantageous understandings reached at the conference.

Avoidance of the failure of the 1980 Review Conference

In the preparatory phase of the conference and in the informal consultations, as well as during the conference itself, it was clear that there was a determination on the part of almost every participant to avoid repeating the experience of 1980. It was felt that the parties to the Treaty had an interest in keeping it alive as it was serving their national interest. As a consequence, suggestions for resorting to voting during the conference were strongly resented, as it was felt that if the conference was to be seen as a success and its conclusions respected and implemented, then they had to be reached by consensus. Moreover, it was feared that a vote might not settle the issues being voted upon and could lead to an impasse similar to that experienced in 1980. This determination to succeed surprised and disappointed many of the representatives of non-governmental organisations and of states attending the conference as observers. Some of these had worked out possible scenarios for forcing votes on key issues, to be followed by the convening of a resumed session of the conference during the following year.

MAJOR SUBSTANTIVE RESULTS OF THE 1985 REVIEW CONFERENCE

The substantive work of the conference, the results achieved by each main committee and the issues which were resolved later by the drafting committee or by the group of 'friends of the president' can best be analysed by examining briefly the deliberations of each of the three main committees, their reports and the unresolved issues at the committee level. The latter can be divided into two sets of problems: Article VI and the issue of a multilateral Comprehensive Test Ban Treaty (CTBT) and what could be called 'the regional issues'. These included the issues of nuclear cooperation with South Africa and Israel, the Israeli military attack on the Iraqi nuclear reactor and alleged attacks on Iranian nuclear facilities by Iraq.

Main committee I

Main committee I was chaired by Ambassador Jayantha Dhanapala of Sri Lanka. The committee discussions highlighted the resolve of the states parties to the Treaty to avoid the devastation that a nuclear war would bring. They reaffirmed their conviction that any proliferation of nuclear weapons would seriously increase the danger of a nuclear war. By contrast, it was concluded that the objective of Article VI, the elimination of all nuclear armaments, had not been achieved.

As regards Articles I and II, the committee's discussions resulted in the conference's confirming that one of the primary objectives of the Treaty, the prevention of further horizontal proliferation of nuclear weapons, had been achieved. Nevertheless, deep concern was expressed that the national nuclear programmes of some states not party to the Treaty might result in their obtaining a nuclear weapon capability.

Main committee I was able to arrive at language reflecting the position of all concerned on most of the items which were before it. It had very sensitive and contentious issues on its agenda but managed to sustain the common interest of all the states involved in strengthening the Treaty. It proved difficult at the committee level to reach a consensus on language related to a CTBT, however, and therefore both the report of committee I and that of the drafting committee contained the following bracketed words:

The Conference deeply regrets that until now a comprehensive multilateral Nuclear Test-Ban Treaty has not been concluded and therefore calls on the nuclear-weapon States Party to the Treaty to take the lead in (working for)(negotiations and) conclusion of such a Treaty in the context of the Conference on Disarmament.

In parallel to the language in these reports, the Group of Non-aligned and Neutral States placed before the conference three resolutions drafted by Mexico. The first urged the three depository states of the NPT to undertake negotiations to draft and adopt a CTBT in the course of 1985. The second called upon the same states to institute an immediate moratorium on all nuclear weapon tests as a provisional measure. The third called upon them to agree to a complete freeze on the testing, production and deployment of all nuclear weapons and their delivery vehicles, and to begin negotiations for substantial reductions in their existing stockpiles of nuclear weapons and delivery vehicles. The chairman of the drafting committee and a number of delegates from the states principally involved had extensive discussions on these resolutions and the relevant part of the drafting committee's Report, at the end of which they succeeded in drafting a compromise text, the key part of which read as follows:

The Conference except for certain States whose views are reflected in the following subparagraph deeply regretted that a comprehensive multilateral Nuclear Test-Ban Treaty banning all nuclear tests by all States in all environments for all time had not been concluded so far and, therefore, called on the nuclear-weapon States Party to the Treaty to resume trilateral negotiations in 1985 and called on all the nuclear-weapon States to participate in the urgent negotiation and conclusion of such a Treaty as a matter of the highest priority in the Conference on Disarmament.

At the same time, the Conference noted that certain States Party to the Treaty, while committed to the goal of an effectively verifiable comprehensive Nuclear Test-Ban Treaty, considered deep and verifiable reductions in existing arsenals of nuclear weapons as the highest priority in the process of pursuing the objectives of Article VI.

The 'certain States' referred to in the text were understood to be the United Kingdom and the United States.

The Group of Non-aligned and Neutral States considered that the objective sought by the first resolution was achieved by this consensus language on a CTBT. With regard to the other two resolutions, the Group placed on record its decision not to press them to a vote, and obtained agreement that this statement, together with the text of these resolutions, should be attached as an Annex to the Final Declaration of the conference. Without the tireless efforts of the chairman of the drafting committee and the cooperation and understanding of all interested and concerned parties, a consensus on this issue would not have been possible. Its achievement meant that only the so-called 'regional problems' stood in the way of a successful outcome to the conference.

Main committee II

Main committee II was chaired by Ambassador Milos Vejvoda of Czechoslovakia. It achieved near-consensus on its report covering international safeguards. This recognised the key role played by IAEA safeguards in providing assurances that states were complying with their non-proliferation undertakings and noted that the IAEA had not detected any diversion of safeguarded nuclear materials. It urged that Full Scope IAEA Safeguards (FSS) should be extended to all states and urged that states not party to the Treaty should accept them. There was an initial failure to reach consensus within the committee on language urging exporting states to make FSS a condition of supply, but West Germany, Belgium and Switzerland later accepted milder language urging exporting states to take effective steps towards achieving a commitment to FSS from all their trading partners.

Another important conclusion of committee II was that IAEA safeguarding activities had not hampered the economic, scientific or technological development of safeguarded states. It also recognised the value of the voluntary offers by the nuclear-weapon states to accept IAEA safeguards on some of their civil installations, and recommended further study both of ways of extending this to additional plants and of separating the civil and military facilities in those states. The committee also made several detailed recommendations for improving the effectiveness and efficiency of IAEA safeguards.

Main committee II also gave detailed consideration to the establishment of NWFZs, as envisaged in Article VII of the Treaty, and concluded that this process should be encouraged. The continued successful operation of the Treaty of Tlatelolco and the signing of the South Pacific Nuclear Free Zone Treaty were both welcomed.

The issue which remained unresolved in main committee II was a proposal by Iraq to condemn Israel for its attack in 1981 upon the safeguarded Iraqi nuclear installation. This had also been tabled in main committee III. These proposals did not gain consensus support in either committee, and their chairmen proposed that they be remitted to the president of the conference for resolution at a later stage.

Main committee III

Main committee III was chaired by Ambassador Ryukichi Imai of Japan. Its report strongly reaffirmed the undertakings of Article IV of the Treaty, including the inalienable right of any party to engage in research and development, production and use of nuclear energy for peaceful purposes. Specific recommendations were made for removing obstacles to the international exchange of equipment, materials, information and services in the nuclear field, these recommendations covering supply assurances. The work of the IAEA's Committee on Assurances of Supply was commended and encouraged, as were measures to assist developing countries. Main committee III recognised the difficulties facing developing countries in obtaining finance for their nuclear power programmes. Its report recommended steps that could be taken within the IAEA to ameliorate these difficulties. Several specific recommendations were addressed to the IAEA, particularly in the areas of nuclear power planning and development and regional cooperation agreements. It also dealt with protection of safeguarded nuclear facilities and formulated a strong statement about the negative effects on the development of the peaceful uses of nuclear energy of any armed attacks on such facilities, including proposals for national and international action in response to such attacks.

Three issues were not settled by this committee. They were the suspension of nuclear cooperation with South Africa and Israel until they joined the NPT and accepted FSS, the Israeli military attack against the safeguarded Iraqi nuclear facilities and allegations by Iran regarding attacks on its nuclear facilities by Iraq. The report of main committee III highlighted these disagreements and emphasised that attempts were being made to resolve them.

The outstanding issues

Continuous negotiations then took place from the morning of 20 September until the early hours of the morning of 21 September, the last day of the Review Conference, and resulted in all of these matters being resolved. The text which was under negotiation when committee III adjourned demanded that all nuclear cooperation with South Africa and

Israel be suspended until they joined the NPT, accepted IAEA safeguards and pledged not to manufacture or acquire nuclear weapons. The president of the conference invited interested and concerned parties, including the representatives of the United States, the United Kingdom, Nigeria, Cameroon and Senegal, to meet with him to discuss this matter. In the course of these consultations, a text which was previously agreed upon by committee I expressing its concern about the nuclear weapon capability of South Africa and Israel was reconsidered and slightly modified. The committee III text was then modified to reflect the great and serious concerns expressed by the conference about the nuclear capability of the two countries, rather than to articulate demands to suspend any nuclear cooperation with them. This resolved the issue in a manner acceptable to all interested parties.

The second outstanding issue concerned the Israeli attack on Iraq's safeguarded nuclear reactor. Sensing that this was a thorny issue and might jeopardise the chances of adopting a Final Declaration by consensus, the president convened a relatively large negotiating group to deal with it, comprising the 'friends of the president' and representatives of Iraq and other interested parties. When it met, it had before it two alternative formulations produced by the president in consultation with the United States and Iraqi representatives. This meeting proved inconclusive, so the president then convened a smaller group.

After a mixture of long hours of discussions in the smaller group, negotiations with the Arab representatives and bilateral consultations with the parties directly concerned, it was possible to agree a text which both expressed profound concern about the Israeli attack and, *inter alia*, recalled Security Council Resolution 487 of 1981 which strongly condemned it. This text was followed immediately by three paragraphs on the protection of safeguarded nuclear facilities, which made it easier for Iraq to accept a text on the Israeli attack which was weaker than the ones originally proposed. These early formulations had required the conference to condemn Israel for 'deliberate' or 'premeditated' military aggression.

The president, after settling the Iraq–Israel problem, then turned his attention to the third issue which involved Iran's allegation of an Iraqi attack on its nuclear facilities. By now it was moving towards the early hours of the morning of 22 September, and the whole membership of the conference had been waiting patiently since 9.0 p.m. on the 21st for the final plenary meeting of the conference to begin. This had originally been scheduled for 4.0 p.m. on the afternoon of the 21st, and once that time had passed it had been rescheduled for 9.0 p.m.

The president had to act swiftly in view of the time factor, and had bilateral meetings with the Iraqi and Iranian representatives. The text remitted by committee II for further negotiations on this topic read as follows:

The Conference notes that the Islamic Republic of Iran states its concern regarding attacks on its nuclear facilities.

The Iraqi representatives insisted that no mention be made of the Iranian allegations in the Final Declaration; the Iranians were adamant that reference be made to the attack on their nuclear facilities but without mentioning its source. The president was later joined by Jan Martenson, the Under-Secretary heading the United Nations Department of Disarmament Affairs, whose efforts to assist in settling the issue were also of no avail.

The president then decided that he would open the final plenary session of the conference and try to deal with the problem there, in the hope that the pressure building up in the Conference Room in the early hours of 22 September for a rapid conclusion to the proceedings would facilitate a solution. He reported to the conference on the impasse, and eventually suggested that he had no choice but to resort to a vote on whether or not to make a reference in the Final Declaration to the Iranian allegations. At this juncture, the representative of Belgium called for a fifteen-minute recess. This provided an opportunity to try once more to settle the issue without resorting to a vote, something which none of the key delegations at the conference favoured.

After almost two hours of shuttling between the Iraqi and the Iranian representatives, the president, with the assistance of a number of delegates, particularly the representative of Australia, Ambassador Richard Butler, succeeded in negotiating a compromise. This involved the Iranian delegation dropping any reference to the attack on their nuclear facilities in the review section of the Final Declaration, and the Iraqi representative allowing statements made by him and his Iranian colleague at the final plenary meeting to be reproduced in full after the Declaration. It was also agreed that after the adoption of a consensus Final Declaration, the Iraqi and Iranian representatives could make further statements which would be incorporated in the summary records of the meeting and, as with all other summary records, these would form part of the Final Document of the Conference. This understanding enabled the conference to adopt the Final Document, including the Final Declaration, by consensus.[2]

THE AFTERMATH AT THE UNITED NATIONS

The consensus reached on the Final Document was a fragile one, achieved only through the determination and will of all participants. This was demonstrated a few weeks after the conference when its former president, acting as a delegate of Egypt at the United Nations, invited all the NPT parties to a meeting to discuss both the tabling of a resolution at the United Nations General Assembly acknowledging the successful conclusion of the conference and the distribution of either its Final Declaration or the Final Document by the United Nations.

Four separate meetings were required before a consensus could be negotiated on a draft resolution which simply noted with satisfaction that the Third Review Conference had adopted a Final Document by consensus. The difficulties arose from two sources. Two of the depository governments, the Soviet Union and the United States, were reluctant initially to support any United Nations General Assembly resolution on this topic, fearing that it might be opposed by some of the non-NPT states and thus weaken the impact of the consensus document. Many others considered an elaborate resolution both very risky and difficult to draft. They feared it might open up all sorts of issues that had been settled with great difficulty at the Review Conference. In the event, the consensus Resolution was adopted by the United Nations General Assembly with a large majority, although a number of states not party to the Treaty did abstain.

The circulation of either the Final Document or the Final Declaration as a United Nations document proved to be even more contentious than the submission of a draft resolution. The United States representative wanted to avoid the impression that the Final Declaration and the annexed Declaration by the Group of Non-aligned and Neutral States on a CTBT, the Nuclear Test Ban Moratorium and the Nuclear Arms Freeze were of equal status. This interpretation of the structure of that document was not acceptable to many representatives, especially the one from Mexico, who considered the annexed Declaration to be an integral part of the compromise reached at the Review Conference.

A second alternative was to circulate the three volumes of the Final Document, including all the papers and summary records of the conference. This would have been expensive and difficult to organise, not least because at that point in time it had not yet been completed. This proposal was opposed by those delegations who feared that it would not allow the Final Declaration and the annexed Declaration to receive enough recognition. In addition, the Iraqi representative questioned informally the understanding reached at the conference that the two statements made by Iraq and Iran at the last plenary meeting of the Review Conference would be reproduced in full after the Final Declaration and the annexed Declaration.

As a result of these two major difficulties, the delegate of Egypt found that it was impossible to reach an agreed compromise position on circulating the Final Declaration or the Final Document as a United Nations Document. The impasse was eventually resolved by the representative of Mexico unilaterally requesting the circulation of the Final Declaration and the Declaration by the Group of Non-aligned and Neutral States in his capacity as a representative of a United Nations member state.

LESSONS TO BE DRAWN FOR THE 1990S

These attempts to bring the results of the Third Review Conference to the attention of United Nations members demonstrated how fragile the consensus reached in the Final Declaration really was. This fragility will certainly be put to the test at the next NPT Review Conference in 1990, if not before.

The organisational and procedural aspects of the Third Review Conference allowed every party to the NPT participating at the conference to contribute to its final conclusions. The Final Declaration was the product of intensive deliberations in the three main committees under the able guidance of their chairmen, of the work of the drafting committee and more particularly its tireless chairman, and finally of the informal consultations on a number of issues carried out by the president with a considerable number of interested concerned parties. The conference was not a 'one man show', but required concentrated effort and cooperation. This is one of the most important lessons to be drawn for 1990 and even for the Extension Conference in 1995. A more elaborate preparatory phase will certainly be required before the latter than took place in 1985. It will have to examine not only procedural and organisational issues, but also a variety of substantive ones. It is too early to make any suggestions in this respect, except to observe that the main contemporary problem with the NPT is not so much with its provisions as with their implementation.

The concrete results of the Review Conference included a substantive Final Declaration, whose language is quite different from the rhetoric found in most United Nations Resolutions. It contained a number of bold ideas which, although not completely new, enhanced its credibility and respectability. These included proposals on both the financing of nuclear power projects in the developing countries and the protection of nuclear facilities from attacks and threats of attacks. In addition, it reaffirmed the objective of applying FSS to the non-nuclear weapon states not parties to the NPT, which if it could be realised would reinvigorate the nuclear non-proliferation regime and render it more effective. This in turn would greatly assist the 1990 Conference in its review of the operation of the Treaty, and encourage it to come forward with fresh initiatives to reinforce the regime before the crucial 1995 Conference.

The Declaration also urged a continuation of the useful work of the IAEA Committee on Assurance of Supply (CAS), and the pursuit of efforts to achieve success at the 1987 United Nations Conference on the Promotion of International Cooperation in the Peaceful Uses of Nuclear Energy (UNCPICPUNE). The establishment of NWFZs was also advocated as a method of strengthening the nuclear non-proliferation regime. Such zones may offer advantages not provided by the NPT, such as special inspections and undertakings on both non-use of nuclear weapons and the complete absence of nuclear weapons in the territories of states parties to the zone. The newly concluded South Pacific NWFZ Treaty was therefore welcomed by the Review Conference as an important addition to the zones created by the Treaty of Antarctica and the Treaty of Tlatelolco. Hope was also expressed that before 1990 other zones of the world, such as Africa and the Middle East, might move towards nuclear weapon free status.

The NPT regime is still in troubled waters over nuclear arms control and disarmament and the implementation of Article VI of the Treaty, in spite of the compromise reached on a CTBT in 1985. The future of the NPT regime hinges upon the achievement of real and genuine progress in disarmament and more particularly nuclear disarmament. In 1985, the convergence of a number of factors helped the Review Conference in reaching a substantive Final Declaration despite lack of progress in this area. However, in 1990 the most powerful guarantee for a successful review would be the conclusion of concrete agreements on disarmament. A CTBT would be an ideal agreement both to ensure this and to facilitate negotiations at the 1995 Conference, provided that further agreements were reached before then.

The most important impact of the 1985 Review Conference may, however, be its effect on the non-parties to the Treaty, especially the so-called threshold or near nuclear states. These are not expected to accede to the Treaty in the near future as they are still opposed to it for a variety of reasons. But as one analyst has recently observed, 'an international regime does not need perfect adherence to have a significant constraining effect any more than domestic laws require an end to deviant behaviour in order to be effective'. However, he went on to say that 'there is a tipping point beyond which the accumulated weight of violations will upset today's balance of nuclear incentives and disincentives'.[3] The participation of a great majority of the states party to the NPT in the successful 1985 Review Conference and full and effective implementation of its recommendations should, in principle, create barriers and nurture inhibitions against further proliferation of nuclear weapons. Events prior to 1990 and 1995 will demonstrate whether these barriers and inhibitions are fictitious or real.

NOTES

1. The other groups at the conference were already represented among the 'friends of the president' by their chairmen. The Czechoslovak chairman of the Group of Eastern European Countries was there by virtue of his role as chairman of committee II: the chair of the Group of Western States and others was held by the United Kingdom, a depository state.
2. For the substance of this Final document see NPT/CONF.III/64/I.
3. Joseph S. Nye Jr, 'NPT: The Logic of Inequality', *Foreign Policy*, no 5 (Summer 1985), 130–1.

2   The threshold countries and the future of the nuclear non-proliferation regime

Jozef Goldblat and Peter Lomas

INTRODUCTION

When the conference to extend the NPT convenes in 1995, two of the key issues which will determine its outcome may well be which states are parties to the Treaty at that date and whether there exist any additional nuclear weapon countries beyond the original five. By 1 January 1986, as many as 134 states had joined at least one of the two main pillars of the non-proliferation regime, the NPT and the 1967 Treaty of Tlatelolco proscribing nuclear weapons in Latin America. This number included three nuclear weapon powers, the United Kingdom, the United States and the Soviet Union, as well as almost all the highly developed, industrialised and militarily significant non-nuclear weapon states. The two nuclear weapon powers which were not parties to the NPT, France and China, were nevertheless firmly committed to upholding its principles.

Most of the remaining forty or so non-parties to the NPT or the Treaty of Tlatelolco had no nuclear facilities and lacked the industrial infrastructure necessary for an indigenous nuclear programme. About half a dozen countries, however, were so-called threshold countries. Their attributes were that they both conducted significant nuclear activities and refused to accept international control over their indigenously produced nuclear material or equipment. In most cases they also operated unsafeguarded plants capable of making weapon-usable material such as plutonium or highly enriched uranium, claimed the right to carry out nuclear explosions for peaceful purposes, involving devices similar to those used in nuclear weapons, and could provide themselves with a reasonably effective nuclear weapon delivery capability. The countries belonging to this category were Argentina, Brazil, India, Israel, Pakistan and South Africa. A list of major unsafeguarded nuclear facilities in these countries is given in Table 1.

Table 1. *Major unsafeguarded nuclear facilities in threshold countries (operating, under construction, and planned)*

Country	Facility	Location	Remarks
Argentina a,b,c,d,e	Pilot uranium enrichment plant	Pilcaniyeu, Rio Negro province	Decision to build taken 1978; operation first announced Nov 83
	Uranium enrichment production plant	Pilcaniyeu	Start-up projected for 1986–7
	Pilot reprocessing plant	Ezeiza Atomic Centre, Buenos Aires	Start-up projected for 1987; a labatory scale plant was in operation here 1967–71
	Uranium dioxide plant	Córdoba	Due to commence production 1988
	Uranium hexafluoride plant	Pilcaniyeu	
	Pilot heavy water plant	Zárate (Atucha), Buenos Aires province	Due to come into operation 1984; start-up delayed
Brazil a,b,c,f,g,h	Laboratory scale uranium enrichment plant	Instituto de Pesquisas Energéticas e Ncleares (IPEN), São Paulo	Experimental operation has begun; this institute, on São Paulo University campus, is under the joint control of the Brazilian Navy & the state government of São Paulo, with finance from the Navy and the National Security Council
	Laboratory scale reprocessing plant	IPEN	First operational 1983
	Laboratory scale uranium hexafluoride plant	IPEN	First operational 1982
	Pilot uranium hexafluoride plant	IPEN	Possibly already in operation
Israel a,b,c,l,m	Israel Research Reactor 2 (IRR-2)	Negev Nuclear Research Centre, Dimona, Negev	First operational 1963
	Reprocessing plant	Dimona	No official data available; the plant has been mentioned by the IAEA; its existence is contested by some analysts
	Fuel fabrication plant	Dimona	Not confirmed
	Pilot heavy water plant	Weizmann Institute of Science, Rehovoth	In operation by 1954

Country	Facility	Location	Status
India a,b,c,i,j,k	Kalpakkam I & II power reactors	Kalpakkam, Madras	Commissioned 1983 and 1985; heavy water/natural uranium; 8 identical reactors are planned between now and mid-1990s
	Fast Breeder Test Reactor	Kalpakkam	Critical October 1985
	DHRUVA (R-5) Research Reactor	Bhabha Atomic Research Centre (BARC), Trombay, Bombay	Critical Aug. 1985; designated as replacement for CIRUS research reactor (plutonium source for India's 1974 nuclear explosion)
	Reprocessing plant	BARC	First operational 1964; being expanded to process spent fuel from CIRUS and DHRUVA
	Reprocessing plant	Kalpakkam	Start-up projected for 1986; will have separate stream for reprocessing fast breeder spent fuel
	Heavy water plant	Nangal, Punjab	First operational 1962
	Heavy water plant	Baroda (Vadodára) Gujarat	First operation 1977
	Heavy water plant	Tuticorin, Tamil Nadu	First operational 1978
	Heavy water plant	Talcher, Orissa	First operational 1982
	Heavy water plant	Kota, Rajasthan	First operational 1984
	Heavy water plant	Manuguru, Andhra Pradesh	Start-up projected for 1987
	Heavy water plant	Thal-Vaishet, Bombay	Start-up projected for 1987
	Heavy water plant	Not yet decided	Start-up not yet known
	Fuel fabrication plant	BARC	First operational 1955
	Fuel fabrication plant	BARC	First operational 1959
	Fuel fabrication plant	BARC	First operational 1959
	Fuel fabrication plant	Hyderabad	First operational early 1970s; safeguards apply only to handling of enriched uranium
Pakistan a,b,c	Pilot uranium enrichment plant	Sihala, Rawalpindi	Enrichment announced Feb 1984
	Uranium enrichment plant	Kahuta, Rawalpindi	First operational 1960
	Laboratory scale reprocessing plant (hot cell)	Pakistan Institute for Nuclear Science & Technology (PINSTECH), Rawalpindi	
	Pilot reprocessing plant	Rawalpindi	First operational 1981
	Reprocessing plant	New Labs, Rawalpindi	Known to be completed; not yet under safeguards
	Reprocessing plant	Chashma Barrage, Dera Ismail Khan	At least partially constructed; not yet under safeguards

Table I (*cont.*)

Country	Facility	Location	Remarks
	Fuel fabrication plant	Chashma Barrage	First operation Sept 1980
	Uranium hexafluoride plant	Multan	First operational 1982
	Heavy water plant	Karachi	First operational 1976
	Heavy water plant	Multan	First operational 1980
South Africa a,b,c,n	Pilot uranium enrichment plant	Valindaba, Pretoria	First operational 1975 (testing module); full scale module operational 1977
	Uranium enrichment production plant	Valindaba	Due to begin production 1987; safeguards negotiations under way with the IAEA for several years
	Fuel fabrication plant	Pelindaba, Pretoria	First operational 1981; 45% enriched fuel has already been produced
	Pilot uranium hexa-fluoride plant	Pelindaba	First operational 1975
	Uranium hexafluoride production plant	Pelindaba	Due to come into operation 1986
	Metallurgical hot cell complex	Pelindaba	For post-irradiation examination of nuclear fuel elements

SOURCES

a   Jozef Goldblat (ed.), *Non-Proliferation: the Why and the Wherefore* (London: Taylor and Francis, for SIPRI, 1985), Appendix VI.

b   Leonard S. Spector, *Nuclear Proliferation Today*, (New York: Vintage Books, for the Carnegie Endowment for International Peace, 1984).

c   Leonard S. Spector, *The New Nuclear Nations* (New York: Vintage Books, for the Carnegie Endowment for International Peace, 1985).

d   Mario H. Orsolini, 'Plan Nuclear. Un modelo de accon estratégica', *Estratega: Revista Argentina des Estudios Estratégicos* (Buenos Aires) I (1), July–Sept. 1984, 44–54.

e   Pedro H. Stipanicic, 'Origen y desarrollo de la industria del uranio en la Argentina', *Estratega* (Buenos Aires) I (1), July–Sept. 1984, 55–7.

f   *Folha de São Paulo* 28 April 1985, translated in *Foreign Broadcast Information Service: Latin America*, 1 May 1985, pp. 40–1.

g   *International Herald Tribune*, 4 February 1983.

h   David J. Myers, 'Brazil: reluctant pursuit of the nuclear option', *Orbis* 27 (4), Winter 1984, 881–911.

i   'Power reactors 1985', *Nuclear Engineering International* 30 (372), August 1985 supplement.

j   K. S. Jayaraman, 'New reactor 'not for bombs'', *Nature* 316, 29 August 1985, 758.

k   *International Herald Tribune*, 9 August and 19–20 October 1985.

l   Peter Pry, *Israel's Nuclear Arsenal* (Boulder, Colo.: Westview Press, 1984).

m   United Nations Institute for Disarmament Research, *Israeli Nuclear Armament*, General Assembly Document A/40/520, 9 August 1985.

n   'Indigenous Nuclear Programme Thrives Under Sanctions', *Nuclear Engineering International* 31 (381), April 1986, 10–11.

This chapter will examine the reasons why these hold-outs from the non-proliferation regime keep the nuclear weapon option open and then attempt to determine whether in the foreseeable future any of these states can be expected to cross the threshold and join the nuclear club.

INDIA/PAKISTAN

Of the six hold-outs India is the only one in which a nuclear explosion has been conducted. Although the device used in the explosion is believed to have been crude and not easily 'weaponised', the event constituted a crossing of the formal threshold used in the NPT to separate nuclear from non-nuclear weapon states. The intention was presumably to demonstrate to the world India's ability to make the bomb. Since then successive Indian governments have reiterated the peaceful nature of their nuclear programmes and this, coupled with a policy of refraining from further testing, has put India back in the class of non-nuclear weapon states. Nevertheless, India maintains a complete nuclear fuel-cycle, refuses IAEA safeguards on the indigenously developed elements of the cycle, is expanding its capacity to reprocess spent reactor fuel, continues to accumulate unsafeguarded plutonium, possesses advanced aircraft and has shown an interest in acquiring long-range dual-purpose surface-to-surface missiles.[1] India thereby preserves, and is developing, the capacity to build in a relatively short time an arsenal of nuclear weapons and to deliver them against possible targets in Pakistan or China, its only rivals in Asia.

Some influential Indian personalities have contended that without nuclear weapons the country is not in a position to defend itself against China, despite the formal Chinese commitment not to use or to threaten to use nuclear weapons against non-nuclear weapon states under any circumstances. This commitment is unlikely to be revoked by any Chinese government, given China's possession of the largest conventional forces in the world in terms of manpower and considering that China's most plausible reason for maintaining its nuclear forces is to provide a counterweight for Soviet nuclear might, not for India's conventional forces. It is also alleged that nuclear weapons may be needed to respond to the Pakistani nuclear threat. However, it is a matter of historical record that India had already laid the foundations for a nuclear weapon capability when Pakistan embarked upon the construction of its sensitive nuclear facilities.

The Pakistani nuclear programme, unlike that of India, is not linked to a significant effort to produce energy for peaceful purposes. Moreover, whereas India followed the plutonium route to first-generation nuclear weapons, Pakistan is exploring both the plutonium and the uranium routes. The Pakistani authorities have gone to great lengths to acquire installations for the separation of plutonium from spent reactor fuel and used data purloined from foreign plants and clandestine purchases of relevant equipment from industrialised states in their uranium enrichment project. Pakistani attempts to obtain non-nuclear components of nuclear weapons are also public knowledge.[2] In addition, Pakistan has legally acquired potential nuclear weapon delivery systems in the form of advanced fighter-bombers and is said to have been seeking dual-purpose ground-to-ground missile systems.[3]

The Pakistani unwillingness to join the NPT and to accept Full Scope Safeguards (FSS) over its nuclear activities has little or nothing to do with threats to national security from any of the recognised nuclear weapon powers. It is motivated by fear of the nuclear weapon potential of its principal enemy, India, with which Pakistan has been at war three times, the last occasion being in 1971. In the late 1960s Pakistan had a sympathetic attitude towards United Nations efforts to check the proliferation of nuclear weapons. It made frequent declarations of willingness to forego these weapons were India to reciprocate and to have the nuclear facilities in each of the two countries internationally inspected, either under the NPT or a South Asian nuclear weapon free zone (NWFZ). All of this suggests that its position is basically a reflection of that of India. It should, of course, also be borne in mind that the gradual growth of the Pakistani nuclear establishment, the creation of links with those Middle Eastern countries financing some of Pakistan's nuclear efforts and fear of the perceived Indian superiority in conventional arms may now have become significant factors in their own right.

It is sometimes asserted that by demonstrating its ability to manufacture a nuclear weapon, India has reaped political dividends. But whatever prestige it gained was short-lived and has not been translated into the international political currency of influence in world organisations or in the Third World. Nor did the demonstration of nuclear prowess enhance India's security. Instead, it has given successive Pakistani regimes, fearful of Indian nuclear blackmail, a justification for increased efforts to acquire a nuclear capability.

Pakistan's nuclear activities may have enhanced its prestige, at least in those parts of the Arab Middle East where there appears to be an interest in the development of an 'Islamic bomb'. Moreover, by implying that the momentum towards a nuclear explosive capability can be slowed down if its security and economic needs are satisfied, Pakistan has reinforced its leverage *vis-à-vis* the United States and succeeded in obtaining considerable military and economic aid. All these advantages, however, are of a short-term nature.

More broadly, there can be little doubt that the open acquisition of nuclear weapons, or the testing of any nuclear explosive device by one of these countries, would now provoke a response in kind from the other. The resulting proliferation would weaken the security of both, and by imposing a heavy economic burden over and above their present substantial military expenditures would probably give rise to increased domestic political unrest.

ARGENTINA/BRAZIL

The declared aim of Argentina's nuclear policies since the 1950s has been to build a self-sufficient capacity in the production of nuclear energy and to be a major nuclear supplier to other developing countries. Argentina has acquired considerable expertise in the construction of certain nuclear facilities and has signed export contracts with a number of states. By adding the recently mastered uranium enrichment capability to its plutonium reprocessing potential, Argentina has achieved a high degree of self-sufficiency and autonomy and can now produce unsafeguarded weapon-grade material in significant quantities. With its sophisticated air force providing potential nuclear delivery systems, only a political decision stands in the way of the country becoming a nuclear weapon state.

The public position of Argentina in rejecting the NPT and in preserving a nuclear explosive option is ostensibly based on national security considerations. However, the precise targets of Argentine nuclear weapons have never been clearly identified; the country is already militarily powerful compared to most other Latin American countries. The unofficial justification for Argentine nuclear ambitions during the 1970s was the claim that in Brazil, Argentina's neighbour and rival, important groups were advocating the use of the national nuclear energy programme for military purposes, thus setting off a race in which Argentina must not be left behind.[4] Despite this claim, a nuclear arms race with Brazil has never become a substantial public issue in Argentina, and with the improvement of relations between the two countries in the 1980s this excuse is losing its *raison d'être*. The policy of rejecting international control over Argentina's nuclear programme thus appears to be aimed at inflating the country's international prestige rather than safeguarding its security.

The ambitious Brazilian nuclear programme, based on the multibillion dollar deal of 1975 with West Germany to acquire a full fuel-cycle, has suffered serious economic and technical setbacks. Out of the eight reactors planned only one is in operation (functioning at less than half its capacity) and the construction of several others has been suspended indefinitely. Satisfactory operation of the enrichment plant has been considerably delayed, while the mastery of reprocessing technology is now only a distant possibility. A far-reaching government inquiry into the future of nuclear energy was announced in 1985.[5]

Apart from this 'official' programme, which is to be carried out under IAEA safeguards, there reportedly exists an indigenously constructed, unsafeguarded, laboratory-scale uranium enrichment plant under joint military/civilian control.[6] Furthermore, research into various military applications of nuclear energy is believed to be going on at different Brazilian institutions. Brazil lags behind Argentina in the development of an indigenous, unsafeguarded capacity to produce nuclear weapons but is ahead in developing missile delivery systems as its air force is engaged in an important rocketry programme.[7] Against, this, one should note that in Brazil, by contrast with Argentina, there is little public support for the nuclear energy programme in general or for a nuclear weapon programme in particular. The influence of the military on nuclear matters in Brazil has never been very strong and appeals have recently been made by several prominent Brazilians, including scientists, for the scrapping of the entire nuclear programme.[8]

The nature of future Brazilian nuclear activities will nevertheless be influenced by developments in Argentina. The aspirations of the military in Brazil have partly been fuelled by competition with their counterparts in Argentina, and Brazil's refusal to be fully bound by the Treaty of Tlatelolco is mainly a product of Argentina's declining to ratify the Treaty. Yet from a national security perspective there seems to be no justification for a Brazilian nuclear bomb, for at no time during the continuous political and social turmoil of the past few decades has the country's territorial integrity been at risk from external forces.

As regards economic aspects, the claim that acquisition of a full nuclear fuel-cycle could reduce the technological gap between underdeveloped and industrialised states has no basis in the economic realities of either country. Both would do better to try to exploit rationally their substantial non-nuclear energy resources than to build uneconomic nuclear power stations. Moreover, the possibility of improving their balance of payments and reducing foreign indebtedness through exports of nuclear plant and technology is very remote, given the competition for markets experienced by established nuclear suppliers.

More to the point, desires for nuclear independence can hardly explain policies of rejecting non-proliferation measures if these desires are inherently peaceful. The contention by the pro-nuclear lobby in Brazil that renouncing nuclear weapons reduces a country to a quasi-colonial status *vis-à-vis* the great powers is apparently not shared by the 131 non-nuclear parties to the NPT. Meanwhile, acquisition of all the elements of a nuclear weapon programme free of international control is bound to give rise to misgivings regarding motives. Having said this, continued democratisation in Argentina and Brazil, the inevitable financial restrictions on their nuclear programmes and the participation of political leaders from both countries in international arms control and disarmament initiatives and negotiations may in time soften their opposition to the non-proliferation regime.

ISRAEL

Israel has probably not tested a nuclear explosive device, but is widely assumed to have at its disposal at least a dozen nuclear weapons, either assembled or ready for assembly. This supposition is based on the existence of an unsafeguarded nuclear reactor, in operation since 1963, and of a spent-fuel reprocessing plant capable of producing plutonium. Those who believe that Israel is already a nuclear weapon state base their belief on reports that both uranium and essential components of nuclear explosives have been clandestinely acquired. There have also been reports of the development of surface-to-surface missiles capable of being fitted with nuclear warheads.[9]

No Israeli government has either admitted or denied possession of nuclear weapons. The policy, as it has evolved, has been repeatedly to assert that Israel 'would not be the first' country in the Middle East to introduce such weapons into the region. This assertion, however, may mean only that Israel will not formally reveal the existence of weapons it already possesses unless another country in the region either acquires them or allows them to be stationed on its territory.

The situation of Israel is exceptional among the threshold countries, because the very existence of the state has been under constant threat since its foundation. Nuclear weapons may well be considered by many Israeli leaders to be decisive for the nation's survival. However, given the geopolitical circumstances in the Middle East, nuclear deterrence is hardly likely to be a trump card over the long term. The appearance of another nuclear weapon state in the region, in direct response to Israeli nuclear armament, would inevitably nullify the advantages of Israel's initial monopoly. It would reduce the security of all the countries in the region, but Israel's security would be particularly affected because, owing to its small land-area and the density of its population, Israel would have more to lose from a nuclear exchange than any neighbouring Arab state.

It would seem, therefore, that a formalised and fully guaranteed absence of nuclear weapons, both indigenous and foreign, in the entire Middle East region would serve the security interests of the countries concerned. This would best be achieved by accession of all the states in the region to the NPT and full implementation of the Treaty's provisions. However, the Israeli authorities are opposed to joining the Treaty, claiming that it would be used to focus hostile pressures against their country. Their counter-proposal is for a nuclear weapon free zone in the Middle East on the pattern of the Treaty of Tlatelolco.

SOUTH AFRICA

South Africa has very substantial uranium reserves, and raw uranium has long been one of its major export commodities. Partly through indigenous research, and partly using imported equipment and know-how, South Africa has succeeded in acquiring a uranium enrichment capability. A pilot plant began operating in 1975, while a larger, semi-commercial plant, with the declared purpose of producing enriched uranium for export, is set for commissioning in 1987. Neither of these installations is under international control, although negotiations with the IAEA for safeguarding the commercial plant have been going on for some time. It is estimated that enough weapon-grade uranium may already have been accumulated for twenty or so nuclear explosive devices.[10] It is not known, however, whether weapons have actually been manufactured, nor have reports alleging nuclear testing been confirmed.

Support for the acquisition of nuclear weapons has been expressed intermittently and with varying degrees of explicitness by South African politicians, military officers and executives of the national nuclear authorities. A number of aircraft possessed by the South African forces would be adequate for nuclear weapon delivery, especially in view of the limited air defences of neighbouring states. On the other hand, South Africa is under no threat of external aggression and in any event its armed forces are stronger than those of its likely regional adversaries, its military equipment is substantial and sophisticated and its conventional arms industry well developed. There is of course the ever-present danger of mass internal insurgency, possibly supported by neighbouring countries, but nuclear weapons would hardly be useful in dealing with this threat.

The official South African attitude towards non-proliferation is, like that of Israel, deliberately ambiguous. But unlike Israel, South Africa has no need of nuclear weapons for deterrence. Rather, its policy is to seek to capitalise on the country's advanced position in the nuclear field and to use the nuclear weapon option as a bargaining chip to remove, or to alleviate, international boycotts or embargoes imposed by the United Nations and other international organisations or by individual states. The fact remains, however, that these goals are not achievable as long as the apartheid regime is maintained. At this stage accession to the NPT would do very little to improve the country's image in the outside world and certainly would not affect the explosive internal situation there.

SUMMARY AND PROSPECTS

None of the threshold countries has formally claimed a military nuclear capability, but neither are they likely to give up their potential in the nuclear weapon field. Nevertheless, the probability of these countries becoming nuclear weapon states is, for the foreseeable future, low. It could be reduced even further if the present regional disputes and conflicts which feed their nuclear ambitions were definitively settled. Specifically, the prospects seem to be that India and Pakistan, though busily engaged in building up their nuclear weapon capability, are interlocked in a relationship which may deter either side from crossing the nuclear threshold by testing a nuclear device (for the second time in the case of India). A competition in arms, as distinct from a competition in capabilities, would not only endanger the security of both countries, but would also prove economically ruinous, among other reasons because of the almost certain withdrawal of a good part of their foreign assistance. India and Pakistan will, therefore, almost certainly continue to declare a policy of not aiming at the acquisition of nuclear weapons and can fairly be expected to do so in less ambiguous terms than hitherto. Something of a thaw in their relations, including a somewhat greater openness in nuclear matters, was noticeable in 1985. The announcement in December of that year by the Pakistani and Indian leaders that they had agreed to prohibit attacks on each other's nuclear facilities is significant in this respect. The South Asian Association for Regional Cooperation (SAARC), which includes India and

Pakistan, may also be instrumental in settling disputes between them. Yet despite such hopeful signs, these two powers' nuclear competition is the primary contemporary challenge to the non-proliferation regime.

Argentina and Brazil are in the kind of economic straits which should rule out nuclear weapon programmes unwarranted by security needs. Moreover, internal political changes have increased the chances that both countries might eventually fully accede to the Treaty of Tlatelolco and thus accept FSS. Such action would be the practical equivalent of NPT adherence. As in South Asia, there is evidence of a rapprochement which may soften political rivalry. An expansion of cooperation between Argentina and Brazil in the peaceful use of nuclear energy, through the creation of jointly owned, managed and supervised facilities, might help to remove suspicion and provide both countries with an assurance that neither is directing its nuclear activities to military purposes. Furthermore, it could provide an impetus for wider regional nuclear cooperation in which both would play a central role as suppliers, and thereby eliminate residual incentives to embark on military programmes.

In the remaining two threshold countries, Israel and South Africa, there appears to be little willingness to dissipate the doubts generated about their nuclear status, for by fostering these doubts down the years these states have sought to deter enemies and to extract concessions from allies. For the same reasons, however, it is highly unlikely that either will proceed to nuclear testing.

One way of attracting Israel and South Africa into the non-proliferation regime often mentioned in United Nations debates would be to set up NWFZs in the respective regions. However, the denuclearisation of Israel is conceivable only as part of an overall political settlement in the Middle East, and this is still far away. Equally, in the present situation of tension and open hostility in the southern part of the African continent, a regional agreement providing for the denuclearisation of South Africa appears to be unlikely. Nevertheless, the prospect of losing the last vestiges of support from the West and of being subjected to mandatory United Nations sanctions may yet deter the present South African regime from moving further towards a nuclear weapon capability.

The existence of nuclear threshold countries and the consequent threat of their becoming nuclear weapon states creates an atmosphere of uncertainty in international relations. Moreover, it has to be acknowledged that the arsenals of the 'established' nuclear powers and their manipulation for political purposes provide fertile ground for such a threat. In the long run, it is only in conditions of a sustained process of dismantling these arsenals, and of de-emphasising the role of nuclear weapons in foreign policy, that the imperative of non-proliferation of nuclear weapons can firmly entrench itself among the generally accepted norms of international conduct. This imperative would then be valid even for states not party to formal non-proliferation agreements.

NOTES

1. See Rodney W. Jones, *Proliferation of Small Nuclear Forces* (Washington, DC, Georgetown University Center for Strategic and International Studies, 1984), Appendix C, 145; and Chris Smith, 'The Pokharan Test Ten Years After', *ADIU Report* 6 (3) (May 1984), 8.
2. 'Three Pakistanis accused in US court of trying to buy atomic arms parts', *International Herald Tribune*, 23 July 1984.
3. Jones, *Proliferation of Small Nuclear Forces*; and Richard P. Cronin, 'Prospects for Nuclear Proliferation in South Asia', *The Middle East Journal* 37 (4) (Autumn 1983), 602.
4. See, for example, the polemic by Gral. de Div. (R.) Juan R Guglialmelli, *Argentina, Brasil y la Bomba Atomica* (Buenos Aires: Tierra Nueva, 1976).
5. *Latin American Newsletter, Regional Reports: Brazil*, RB-85–07 (9 August 1985), 7.
6. *Folha de Sao Paulo*, 28 April 1985, translated in *Foreign Broadcast Information Service: Latin America*, 1 May 1985, 40–1.
7. For details, see Max G. Manwaring, 'Nuclear Power in Brazil', *Parameters* 14 (4) (Winter 1984), 44.
8. The late President-elect Tancredo Neves was apparently of their number. *Latin American Newsletter Special Report* SR-85–02, (April–June 1985), 5; and note 5.
9. *Aerospace Daily*, 1 May 1985, 5. A recent full-scale assessment of the putative Israeli nuclear arsenal is Peter Pry, *Israel's Nuclear Arsenal* (Boulder, Colo., Westview Press, 1984).
10. Leonard S. Spector, *Nuclear Proliferation Today* (New York, Vintage Books for the Carnegie Endowment for International Peace, 1984), 304.

Part 2: The world in 1995

Overview

The world of 1995 will be one of continuity and change. One method of understanding how it might affect the context of the NPT Extension Conference is to identify likely changes in areas of international activity that will directly affect non-proliferation policies. These are likely to include the probability that further states will have publicly declared their nuclear weapon status by 1995, the scope for global and regional policies to combat proliferation at that point in time, the state of the international nuclear industry and its related trading system, the evolution of weapon-related technologies and the state of United States–Soviet Union strategic relations and arms control negotiations.

Josef Goldblat and Peter Lomas tackled the first of these questions in Chapter 2 and concluded that the likelihood of any of the existing 'threshold' states publicly declaring their nuclear weapon status was low, unless they perceived themselves to be in a very grave security situation. The current structure of incentives and disincentives appears to favour publicising a state's *capability* to make weapons, but not actual possession of them. Although the existence of additional overt nuclear weapon states cannot be ruled out by 1995, the indications are that what is more likely is the development by a number of states of a capability to make several fission bombs within a period of days or weeks rather than years.

Any decision to move to overt possession of nuclear weapons will probably be linked to the regional security situation rather than the global one, and it is the relationship between globalism and regionalism that is central to Chapter 3 by Ian Smart and Chapter 4 by Aswini Ray. Smart concludes that the predominant change over the period to 1995 will be a move away from universalism and globalism in international relationships towards regionalism, whilst Ray feels that from a Third World viewpoint the bipolar structure of the global system arising from the Cold War gives such states little opportunity for indigenous development. In addition, he suggests that in an insidious way Western priorities and modes of thought about security are gaining hold among military elites in the Third World and warns of the consequences of this for nuclear proliferation.

The common element in these analyses appears to be that for Smart the *trend of events* will be in the direction of more regionalism, while for Ray the *policies* of Third World states will move in this direction, though their outcomes are likely to be determined by global political and economic structures. Both of the chapters, therefore, point to the need for more effective international action at the regional level in the 1990s to prevent proliferation, while sustaining the global framework of nuclear regulation that already exists. This links in with the analysis of Mohamed Shaker in Chapter 1, which highlighted the difficulties posed by regional problems in reaching agreement on the Final Document at the 1985 NPT Review Conference.

The state of the international nuclear industry and nuclear trade in 1995 can be predicted with some certainty because investment in many nuclear facilities has to be made on the basis of a ten-year construction cycle. William Walker analyses the demand and supply situation for nuclear plant and materials in Chapter 5 and concludes that it will be a buyers' market through to 1995. Moreover, the main contracts in the 1990s are likely to be for the refurbishment of existing facilities rather than the construction of new ones. Lack of finance, among other things, is going to make it unlikely that any new nuclear projects will be started in Third World states during this period.

Walker concludes that the relative absence of trade and new markets will ease the problems of sustaining the Nuclear Suppliers Group guidelines in the 1990s and ameliorate conflicts over them. He believes that the reliance of the French industry upon the United States market will make it more open to pressure to conform to these guidelines and that the leaders of the trading regime in the 1990s will be these two countries. At the same time, he recognises that a number of new sources for the supply of nuclear plant will exist in states which are not parties to the NPT and highlights the problems of assimilating them into the non-proliferation regime. His message is, therefore, that acute conflict over international nuclear trade is unlikely in the 1990s, especially in view of events such as the Chernobyl accident, but that problems will remain over how to bring new entrants to the market into the existing supplier arrangements.

In the two final chapters in Part 2, Dennis Fakley and Ronald Mason review the future evolution of weapon-related technologies, while Steve

Smith examines the superpower strategic relationship in the 1990s. Fakley and Mason discuss in Chapter 6 both the Strategic Defence Initiative and the impact of new conventional technologies upon European defence strategies, and conclude that the linkages between these areas of activity and nuclear proliferation is uncertain and indirect. They also examine the effect of new technologies upon fissile material production and suggest that there might be a need to try to restrict the diffusion of information on these technologies in the 1990s. Additionally, they conclude that the adaption by the IAEA of EURATOM's civil/military division as the basis for IAEA safeguards might be a useful initiative for strengthening the non-proliferation regime.

Steve Smith discusses the indirect nature of the links between the superpower strategic relationship and nuclear non proliferation in Chapter 7, before going on to examine a number of alternative scenarios for that relationship in the 1990s. He suggests that the key factor determining the nature of the relationship is probably going to be the state of the political linkages between the two superpowers, which in turn will be crucially dependent on the policies of the new incumbent of the White House in 1989, particularly his attitude to the SDI. Smith warns of the impact of qualitative changes in nuclear arsenals upon crisis stability and accepts that arms control is an inherently difficult process. Although changes in the United States–Soviet Union political relationship at the turn of the decade could enable significant arms control agreements to be negotiated, it seems unlikely that the superpowers will be able to demonstrate convincingly to the rest of the world in 1995 that they are moving towards nuclear disarmament.

These chapters have almost inevitably omitted certain events and trends that will loom large at the 1995 Conference. They do suggest, however, that the environment in 1995 is more likely to be akin to that found prior to the 1985 NPT Review Conference than the 1980 one. In particular, the conflicts over nuclear trade seem likely to remain dormant, whilst the superpowers will continue to be attacked for their lack of progress on nuclear disarmament. The major new development will be the increasing prominence of regional issues, linked to the existence of states with nuclear weapon production capabilities. A major challenge to the future of the non-proliferation regime will thus be how to deal with these matters.

3 The international system in the 1990s

Ian Smart

INTRODUCTION

Decades pass quickly. A week may be a long time in politics, but ten years represent a very short fragment of history. Looking forward to the middle of the 1990s, the first impulse to be wary of, therefore, is a natural inclination to exaggerate the likely scale and scope of changes in either the economic or the political environment. Setting aside the real but small possibility of cataclysm, the world of 1995 will resemble the world of 1986 much more than it will differ from it.

In the first place, a decade really is a brief period in relation to the secular groundswell of international politics: enough for finding clues to the major factors of change, but not for sifting or testing them. In the second place, short-term alterations may well be reversed within a ten-year span, restoring the superficial situation to its *ante bellum* status.

A view of 1985 taken from 1976 would have illustrated both phenomena. The same basic questions about North–South or East–West relations, for instance, stand before us now as they stood before us then. Superpower arms control negotiations were high on the international agenda in 1976, as they were again ten years later. Then, as now, a successful Non-Proliferation Treaty Review Conference was fresh in our memories. Yet the economic outlook, at least for the industrial market economies, has performed a striking somersault in the interim, only to recover something of its previous character. Oil prices are falling today, as real if not nominal oil prices were falling in 1976. Economic output was rising then as well, especially in the United States and Japan. And the second 'oil shock' of 1979–80, with the consequent economic relapse, had yet to be imagined, experienced or forgotten. The fact remains that few of us in 1976 would have predicted either the similarity of the present or the particular turbulence of the interim. Reaching through the future fog towards 1995, therefore, we must be careful that we neither quicken artificially the drumbeat to which history marches nor forget the frequency with which history steps aside from its true route, only to return.

In the circumstances, we must choose to concentrate either on the large probability that the international environment will undergo relatively little change by 1995 or on the smaller but clearly present chance of some major and unreversed discontinuity. The latter cannot be ruled out or ignored. But the former should surely prevail. That said, however, the most important purpose of all must always be not to predict what changes will in reality occur by 1995 or thereafter, but rather to pick out the tendencies and expectations of change, the plausible flow of the tide, by which the minds of those shaping policy in 1995 are likely to be influenced.

THE BALANCE BETWEEN GLOBALISM AND REGIONALISM

Internationally or nationally, politically or economically, the state of what we call too glibly the 'system' is always mirror to a balance between centrifugal and centripetal forces peculiar to that moment in that place. That is the unvarying essence of politics as a process or economics as a field of action: to combine or compete; to campaign or compromise; to assimilate or insulate. And the only thing rendering some specific movement in either direction tolerable is contrary, compensating movement on a different but related level of activity. Separate forces of political association and dissociation must always off-set and, as it were, license each other.

Because that is a constantly shifting affair, never marked by perfect equilibrium or by a persistent preference for, say, association, another error when trying to look forward in the international environment is to suppose that trends towards 'internationalism' are irreversible. It is often suggested, or assumed, that international trade and communications expand inexorably under the pressure and by the leave of advancing technology. Fine phrases about the growing interdependence of nations are bandied about with little thought. Yet the tendency towards 'globalism', to coin a conventional shorthand, has not been unremitting in the past and is most unlikely to be so in the future. Indeed, it already seems that the next ten years will witness something of a remission.

One reason is that, contrary to popular belief, technical, economic and social progress do not always militate in favour of political globalism. At

43

least for a time, progress on one or more of those fronts may instead
conspire to shift the balance of advantage in favour of a narrower focus in
politics and thus of dissociation as against association. To pick a special
but telling example, rising relative use of natural gas and increasing elec-
trification, elements of energy supply that have a regional or even national
flavour for both technical and economic reasons, are already beginning to
erode parts of the truly worldwide energy market formerly created and
perennially served by oil. The moral is that the world energy economy in
1995 is likely to be rather less 'global' than it is today, or was in 1975.

A larger reason for suspecting some remission of globalism in the coming decade has to do less with the benefits of technological progress than
with its costs. Technology has helped to make our world increasingly
interdependent, but interdependence hurts as well as heals. More efficient
trade and economic communication make it impossible to contain the
social and economic consequences of any one national government's policies within its national borders. Industries or financial markets in other
countries are affected and potentially threatened. So is employment and,
over time, the social structures in those other countries. And so in consequence are the reputation and, dare one say it, the self-esteem of those
other governments. Meanwhile, communications technology in another
form disseminates and synthesises idioms, ideas and standards in a manner calculated to challenge just that sense of ultimately independent identity on which both governments and citizens then seek to fall back for
consolation. And eventually there comes the point at which the pain of
full exposure in an interdependent world is thought intolerable: at which
moment politics is called in to combat globalism itself.

Hence, in part, the sort of pressures towards trade protectionism of
which we are increasingly aware. Hence also, a growing tendency to call
traditional national economic policy choices into international question:
to argue for amendment of one government's domestic fiscal or monetary
policy, for example, on the ground that it increases interest rates or un-
employment in other countries. And hence a varied but widespread reas-
sertion of distinctive cultural traits and values, from Islamic austerity and
Gallic autarchy to the American dream, as parts of a national or ethnic
defence against the evident menace of 'globalist' interdependence.

In large measure, those stimuli and responses take on a cyclical rhythm,
and the world currently seems to have embarked upon a phase of the cycle
in which reactions against globalism will predominate. It can be argued,
some would even say demonstrated, that the phase began in the 1970s.
Its most obvious effects are the sorts of commercial protectionism and

cultural counter-reformation already noted at the level of individual countries. But nationalism is not the only form of defensive reaction to globalism, nor often the most plausible or tenable one. Regionalism may have at least an equally significant role to play in the coming decade.

THE WORLD BEYOND EUROPE AND THE SUPERPOWERS

Economically, commercially, and at least in principle ideologically, Europe is already a cockpit of regional coalitions, dominated in the West by the European Community (EEC) and in the East by the Council for Mutual Economic Aid (CMEA). Militarily, of course, the pattern repeats itself in the North Atlantic Treaty Organisation (NATO) and the Warsaw Pact. One sort of question for the 1990s is whether the politics of regional association in any of those European systems will be imitated elsewhere in the world and especially around the Western Pacific basin or in the Americas. Another sort of question is whether economic regionalism, already evident outside Europe, will progressively be matched by more narrowly regional approaches to planning and organisation for military security.

There is a fair chance that the answer to both those questions will turn out in the 1990s to be 'yes'. Albeit haltingly, movement is apparent, for instance, towards a renewal of regional bias in Western hemisphere patterns of trade and investment, not least in regard to primary materials and fuels. Similarly, Japan and Korea are emerging as increasingly important industrial pivots for resource development and trade in the region reaching from Australasia to coastal China. Regionalising pressures in those two cases feed, moreover, on each other as instances of economic interpenetration or arrogance in both directions encourage political reactions. It will be no surprise, in fact, if a slowly strengthening hemispheric stress in United States external economic policy is countered during the next decade by efforts to reinforce and extend regional institutions for economic and political collaboration in the Western Pacific as well. Nor will trade be the only focus. Just as the United States banking system is already committed inextricably to Latin American economies, so Japanese banks will steadily assume more responsibility for loans and settlement around the Pacific.

Turning to the second question, regional collaboration in the Pacific area on trade and economic matters can obviously over time lay part of the foundation for cooperating on security as well. Fragments of such cooperation already occur, in the form, for example, of coordinated arms supply or the occasional joint naval exercises. Equally obviously, given twentieth century history, development from those small beginnings will not be at all rapid. Indeed, little is likely actually to have happened by 1995. What is probable, however, is a gradual but considerable shift of perspective leading, for example, to both the Japanese and Australian governments thinking of their provisions for national security a little less in terms of separate bilateral links with a superpower and a little more in terms of relations with each other in a regional context.

Any such adjustment of focus towards a regional security perspective on the part of American allies or clients in Asia and the Pacific is most unlikely to be imitated by associates of the Soviet Union. North Korea's fascinating balancing act between Moscow and Peking will continue and Sino-Soviet rivalries may well cost more lives in Indo-China, where the residuum of Vietnamese independence will never be negligible. But there is no real prospect of a quasi-autonomous security coalition among the Asian centrally planned economies. For while resurgent regionalism does not stem in its contemporary form from any one ideology, it tends to arise in the first instance in areas outside the Soviet Union's 'socialist commonwealth', if only for practical reasons of geography and economic organisation.

Those areas include the bulk of the Third World. In much of it, however, greater regionalism will owe less to indigenous impulses, such as protectionist behaviour in trade, than to the effective reduction or elimination of non-regional options as a result of policy choices on the part of external powers. To some extent, that means choices made in Western Europe, or even in Japan and Australasia. Above all, however, it means choices made in Washington and sometimes, it must be added, in Moscow as well. To be more specific, stronger regional preoccupations are likely to be forced upon some parts of the Third World in the 1990s by explicit or tacit superpower decisions. Some of those decisions to reduce or avoid commitments to the Third World will flow from prudence. Others may reflect political or military inability to sustain particular responsibilities. But some will undoubtedly result from resentful impatience on the part of both superpowers with what appears as ingratitude or obduracy by Third World governments.

A case in point may prove to be Southern Africa, where violent conflict will probably expand in the years ahead but from which both the United States and the Soviet Union, with all their major allies, now seem likely to stand increasingly aloof. And another case, *mirabile dictu*, could yet turn out to be the Middle East. Neither superpower can be indifferent to what happens there. But the interest of each in Middle Eastern security affairs has come to be largely engendered, in the last analysis, by fears about the interest or involvement of the other. It is by no means impossible, therefore, to envisage a Soviet–American concordat, probably tacit, constraining them to hold but not enter the Middle Eastern ring. Ironically, the experiences of Iran and Afghanistan have both enhanced that possibility by demonstrating that even for a superpower, insulation may be at least as effective a policy in the Middle East as intervention and a great deal less costly.

A crucial part of the background to any such judgement about the Middle East must, of course, be the view taken of the importance of Middle Eastern oil. It will never in any foreseeable future be a trivial part of the world's energy supply. During the next ten years, however, Middle Eastern exporters of oil are likely persistently to find themselves faced with a buyer's market. This will enhance the willingness of external powers to let the Middle East region settle its problems regionally, though caution and qualification are still needed. There is an evident danger, for instance, that large and chronic reductions in oil revenue may undermine the social and political order in some of the Middle Eastern countries. Beyond that, there is a significant probability that actual oil demand and potential oil supply will move closer to each other again after 1995, with one result being a strong revival in the relative importance of the Middle Eastern fields. The next decade nevertheless seems likely, on balance, to represent a 'window of opportunity' for addressing the Middle East's several conflicts on a regional basis.

Taking a somewhat broader view, the notes of caution sounded in the case of the Middle East have to be emphasised. Recent, but certainly not ephemeral, changes in the world oil market probably herald a long recession in world prices for oil, and thus in the national income of the countries heavily dependent on its export. In the shorter term, that must have a major impact on the levels and significance of international indebtedness, predominantly by Third World borrowers to lenders who are members of the Organisation for Economic Cooperation and Development. Of equal significance for the 1990s, however, may be the abrupt changes produced by falling prices in the relative economic prospects of Third World exporters and importers of oil. These are bound to find some expression in a readjustment of their political relations and regional rankings.

That process will have special significance in the Middle East. Although too much should not be made of a change which will be slower and less dramatic than many now suppose, it is reasonable to expect that the regional influences of countries such as Syria and Egypt will have grown considerably by the 1990s, at the expense of others like Saudi Arabia or Kuwait whose political as well as economic weight will by then have fallen victim, at least temporarily, to straitened circumstances. But the Middle East is not unique in all respects. Africa and Latin America are other continents where similar political adjustment will be needed as between oil exporters and their neighbours. But Latin America, returning to an earlier theme, will also be an area whose politics and economics in the 1990s will be increasingly affected by regionalist pressures emanating from the United States, as well as by their indigenous counterparts. Indeed, a more sceptical, pragmatic and self-interested attitude to the Third World is already apparent in the visible contrast between the United States' heightened interest in Latin America and growing indifference to Africa or even the Middle East.

EUROPE AND THE SUPERPOWERS

This background of Third World adjustment places in sharp relief questions about politics in the First and Second Worlds during the 1990s. In particular, what will be happening in and to Europe? What will be happening between the European countries and their respective superpower patrons? And what will be happening between those superpowers?

It is precisely in Europe that the initial warning against exaggerating the pace or reach of possible changes becomes most relevant. Any formal alterations in either the East–West division of Europe or the constitution of security alliances on both sides of that divide is highly improbable. As part of the broader inclination to withdraw from globalism into regionalism, there will naturally be voices raised in favour of scrapping the North Atlantic alliance: they already exist, especially in the United States. It is not beyond the bounds of possibility that those voices will prevail, conceivably even by accident. But the greater probability is that NATO, at least in form, will survive beyond 1995, as even more probably will the Warsaw Pact. What is certain, however, is that informal changes in the atmosphere of security relationships and alliances in Europe will be both considerable and asymmetrical.

The dissociative tendency to reassert regionalism during the current phase of the international political cycle will thus have its impact on Europe. One corollary will be a tightening of the intra-regional bonds between Eastern Europe and the Soviet Union, another that inter-regional links between Western Europe and the United States will be stretched and attenuated. Everything already points in those directions. On one side the

Gorbachev administration in Moscow, while hardly overjoyed by Eastern Europe's increasing economic dependence, is evidently ready to exploit it as one means of reasserting a more consistent political discipline. On the other side, the Reagan administration in Washington and any of its plausible successors, while irritated by some of Western Europe's economic demands, will be more inclined to find in them a justification for insisting on greater European self-reliance in matters of security and diplomacy.

Something of Western Europe's reaction to that insistence will depend on which of the West European countries attain the greatest economic and political impetus within their region during the 1990s. It is hard to resist a temptation to speculate on that issue at length and in laboriously specific terms. Suffice it to say here, however, that relative political influence in Western Europe will inevitably reflect relative economic achievement, and that a pre-eminent consideration on the economic front in the 1990s will be the region's poverty in natural resources. In such a case, as Japan has demonstrated elsewhere, the key to economic success can only lie in receptivity and adaptability to technological innovation. To predict how political standing will shift in the 1990s within a more regionally oriented Western Europe it is first necessary to form a view of how quickly and effectively different West European nations and societies are likely to apply evolving technology to the formation of an economic base for political action.

A premise of all that is the expectation of some significant, if informal, loosening of Atlantic ties. Because reciprocal irritation and resentment currently appears to be waxing on the two sides of the ocean, as they do from time to time, some such dissociation has to be expected as a response to genuine divergences of international interest and analysis. But it is not inevitable. Despite rising pressures, many in Western Europe will remember that they value the Atlantic connection not only as an ultimate guarantee of their safety against the East but also as the unique adhesive holding together traditionally antagonistic European states in the West. Meanwhile, the mood in the United States is likely to prove even more complex and the arguments over policy towards Europe even fiercer as 1995 approaches, with their outcome consequently even more difficult to predict.

In that connection, looking towards the 1990s, one striking fact about the United States is that the old isolationism has finally been reborn. During the later 1960s, as the pain of Vietnam increased, it was a familiar mistake to allege an earlier reversion to American isolationism with regard to Europe. In reality, that mood had almost nothing to do with the complacent myopia of the 1930s and almost everything to do with a frustrating struggle to reconcile different foreign commitments. It would be a much greater mistake, however, for Europeans to suppose on that ground that explicit advocacy of isolation in the United States during the later 1980s will again prove misleading or a delusion. This time the wolf is here. But one effect is to reveal also how deep and strong are the roots put down by internationalism in the United States since the Second World War, not least among younger Americans. In that sense, the situation today is quite different from that in the earlier isolationist heyday and the eventual influence of isolationism on formal United States policy towards Europe in the 1990s must remain in some doubt. It has to be said, however, that the odds at present seem to be on the side of an increasingly harsh attitude to alliance and association with Western Europe: an attitude in tune with criticisms of European performance on trade or defence, but in line also with a much more general, less focused, retreat from globalism.

RELATIONS BETWEEN THE SUPERPOWERS

There remains only the overarching questions of relations in the 1990s between the two superpowers. Once more, suggestive generalisation must stand here in place of too detailed a commentary. This is no time, for example, to range too enthusiastically over motives for seeking a strategic defence of the 'star wars' variety or over the effects of that effort. With the overall shape of the international system in mind, it is more appropriate to suggest that the superpower relationship will increasingly appear in the 1990s as the archetypal case of interplay between associative and dissociative pressures in international politics.

There is no reason to suppose that rivalry, suspicion or hostility between the United States and the Soviet Union will abate significantly during the next ten years. Nor are there obvious reasons why the two should not continue to collaborate tactically on appropriate occasions, when a shared interest has been clearly recognised, as they have consistently collaborated throughout the last twenty years on, for instance, non-proliferation policy. At the same time, however, they seem likely to find themselves increasingly segregated, by power and perspective alike, from most of the rest of the world. One reason will be their perennial and perhaps inevitable preoccupation with strategic military competition and armament: a preoccupation increasingly viewed elsewhere as even more irrelevant than dangerous or expensive. Another reason in the security domain will be the extent to which their extraordinary technical sophisti-cation marks them off from either challenge by other countries or true partnership. And that in turn will reflect the widening gap between the material, technical and industrial strengths of the superpowers and those of their respective allies.

The irony is that while the United States and the Soviet Union may well appear in the 1990s as increasingly preponderant within their own eco-nomic and political spheres, as well as in their military alliances, they are unlikely to appear also as increasingly successful, if success is to be measured by the international influence of ideas or policy preferences. In relative as well as absolute terms, superpowers in 1995 will probably be even more powerful than superpowers are today. But power segregates as well as persuades. Moreover, many international actors will still be recoil-ing, if only temporarily, from globalism. As a consequence, the United States and the Soviet Union may find themselves with a smaller routine role to play in the international system of the 1990s than they do today.

The final caution must again be against overestimating the extent of any such change over so short a term as a decade. In as far as there is a leitmotif of political change for the 1990s, it is likely to be the multifarious retreat from economic and political globalism. More of the Third World will be left to resolve more of its own conflicts, sometimes no doubt by violent means. Regional identification will become more influential in Europe, the Western Pacific basin and the Western hemisphere. And one result is likely to be that a number of problems formerly regarded as predominantly global, including not least the problem of nuclear prolifer-ation, instead will have to be understood and addressed as compounded of separable regional and local issues. In South America, South Asia and elsewhere, some inkling of that result and that requirement can already be recognised: in a reviving interest in nuclear-free zones, for example, or in proposals for nuclear verification between regional neighbours. The need will be to fit appropriate local or regional arrangements for handling specific problems into a consistent and demonstrably equitable code of universal standards. And that may well prove to be typical and symptoma-tic of a much wider prescription for coping with the international system of the mid 1990s.

4   Third World perspectives on security and nuclear non-proliferation: an Indian view

Aswini K. Ray

INTRODUCTION

The move away from globalism to greater regionalism identified by Ian Smart in Chapter 3 is a reflection of significant Western perspectives on the current international trends in international politics, economics and military affairs. For scholars in many other countries, however, a major issue for the 1990s is that the structural characteristics of the modern world and the methods of thinking that predominate within it make significant movement away from increased interdependence and globalism difficult, if not impossible. In this chapter an attempt will be made to explore these issues in the context of the linked problems of the widely differing concepts of the Third World and security that currently exist. Finally, some ideas will be presented on the type of context in which nuclear proliferation and non-proliferation decisions will be made in the 1990s.

THE NATURE OF THE THIRD WORLD

Any social scientist attempting to investigate the contemporary and future significance of the concepts of Third World and security has first to accept that they are very imprecise. Moreover, they have been further confused by their recurrent, uncritical overuse in post-war international relations. Since the early Cold War days policy-makers and analysts, particularly in the Western hemisphere, have used these terms for so many different purposes and in so many different senses that they now lack inherent meaning.

These analysts have compressed the wide-ranging variety of states within the global system into a simple taxonomy, whose origins can be found in Western perspectives upon security arising out of the European Cold War and its global ramifications. This taxonomy regards the Third World as the residual conglomerate of state systems outside the First and the Second Worlds. These worlds consist, respectively, of the liberal democratic countries of the Northern and Western hemispheres and the communist countries of Europe. This classification of states was further reinforced by the security perspectives adopted by the Soviet Union after 1952, when that state's global diplomacy was reoriented in a manner which conformed to its structural logic.

The Soviet Union's global view prior to 1952 was based on the Zhdanov thesis that there existed two worlds, the capitalist and the socialist. This provided no scope for a Third World. Newly liberated countries like India and Indonesia, which were pursuing a foreign policy of non-alignment, were dubbed 'lackeys of imperialism', while their foreign policy differences with the West were seen as manifestations of 'intra-imperialist rivalry', a concept rooted in Marxist/Leninist ideology. In 1952, Soviet diplomacy implicitly acknowledged the 'progressive' aspects of these foreign policy differences, though it was not until Khrushchev came to power that the full potential of this reassessment was used in Soviet diplomacy towards the Third World. The Soviet Union then reoriented its foreign policy of aid and punishment to further its global security interests, in parallel with the messianic pursuit by the Western alliance partners of their policy of containment through similar carrot-and-stick diplomacy.

The concept of a Third World thus emerged out of the security compulsions of both the superpowers in the Cold War era. Operationally, the two superpowers pursued divergent policies towards the Third World. The Western alliance partners perceived the newly liberated countries as falling within their historic area of influence and aggressively pursued a policy of entangling them in their global network of alliances against communism. Soviet foreign policy aimed at cutting its potential losses by keeping them non-aligned. Both superpowers, in their own way, thus reinforced the nebulous concept of an amorphous Third World comprising the newly emergent post-colonial countries. Later, the concept was extended to include the countries of South America, thus adding to its conceptual mystification.

The historical roots of this concept suggest a number of conclusions. First, the taxonomy within which the Third World emerged as a generic category did not originate indigenously. Moreover, the sequential location of the Third World as the third and last element in the post-war global system reflects the relative hierarchy of the superpowers' concerns.

Second, the taxonomy is inadequate to describe the composition of the region described as the Third World. States deemed to be within it have accepted different delimitations of this region over time. For example, during the high tide of the Afro-Asia solidarity movement, culminating in the Bandung Conference of 1955, the Third World consisted of all the countries in the geographic region of Asia. This included Pakistan and China, even though both were then militarily aligned to a superpower. By the time of the Belgrade summit in 1961, the Third World had come to consist exclusively of the militarily non-aligned countries of the world, cutting across both the ideological barriers and the geographical divisions of the globe. Subsequently, such close military allies of the superpowers as, for example, Cuba on the one hand and Pakistan on the other have been included within it. Moreover, Cuba has been canvassing for a 'tricontinental movement' of the Third World consisting of all the underdeveloped countries of Asia, Africa and South America. In addition, during the North–South confrontation on the need for a New International Economic Order (NIEO), the so-called Group of 77 was often regarded as a synonym for the Third World. The term has thus frequently been used for different purposes and has encompassed different states. Sometimes, a classification has been based on economic factors, sometimes political, at other times geographical. Sometimes it has been foreign-policy based, occasionally it has been related to historical factors and often it has been issue based. All this has added to its conceptual mystification within contemporary international relations.

While this Third World finds itself in a perennial crisis over its own identity, the taxonomy upon which it rests has often proved to be an inadequate perspective from which to analyse many critical problems of contemporary international relations. On the issue of nuclear proliferation, the global system consists of the 'haves' and the 'have nots' with no Third World. Similarly, during the energy crisis of the 1970s, a Fourth World of the OPEC countries emerged to challenge the Cold War taxonomy.

Countries like China, Japan, Austria, Switzerland, Australia and New Zealand also pose problems for any generic global taxonomy. China, an economically underdeveloped post-colonial country with a Communist regime and many of the pretensions and even some of the attributes of a superpower, continues its global crusade against 'superpower hegemony' and has often preferred to be treated as part of the Third World. Similarly India, a post-colonial country spearheading the non-aligned movement, with a democratic structure and with a strong industrial base including technological nuclear capabilities, is rather dissimilar to other Third World stereotypes. Japan, despite being a part of the Third World geographically, is considered for most purposes to be part of the First World as borne out by its inclusion within the Trilateral Commission.

All attempts at classification of the wide-ranging diversities within the global system thus seem to be structured around the goals sought by their instigators. It is difficult to conceive of a single all-purpose global taxonomy that is equally valid to analyse, explain and assist in the provision of policy options on all the critical problems of contemporary international relations. Moreover any taxonomy possesses latent values and results in an uneven distribution of benefits: in this case it results in a reinforcement of the global hierarchy inherited from the colonial era.

Despite some internal policy differences, the two worlds in the Northern hemisphere appear to be easily distinguishable from one another in terms of their social, economic and political institutions and their history, geography and ideological orientations. The First has stable democratic institutions, free market economies, social roots in Christian ethics and has ideological orientations against communism in different degrees. The Second has corresponding attributes within the context of its Communist ideology. Variations within the structural parameters created by these relatively constant factors have been more in terms of form than content. Since institutions, problems and perceptions have been relatively comparable within each of these areas, the Cold War taxonomy has been valid for Europe and North America, and basing policy upon it for relations between the First and Second Worlds has created relatively few distortions.

The Third World is much less homogeneous by comparison with the other two. It is scattered between three continents, with an internal hierarchy determined by the global importance of specific countries to the strategic interests of the superpowers. It is inhabited by a total population much larger than in the rest of the world and includes political regimes as diverse as clerical despotisms, liberal democracies of a Western type and Communist regimes. If one were to reorganise the Third World in terms of democracy and human rights, the resultant groupings would be different from a classification based on their respective perception of the Soviet Union, the United States and China. Such diversity makes a single factor classification inadequate.

SECURITY IN THE THIRD WORLD

The Western Cold War taxonomy has proved inadequate not only to conceptualise the Third World but also as a basis for any durable structure of global security. Global insecurity has increased in the post-war era almost in direct proportion to the obsessive concern of Western countries to enhance their own security. The re-emergence of the Cold War after the brief interlude of detente, the increasing level of global terrorism and violence, and the proliferation of international espionage are all indicators of the increased general level of global insecurity. Moreover, the Strategic Defence Initiative (SDI) now threatens to include outer space in the global arms race.

Instability and insecurity in the Third World has been proportionately higher than in the first two worlds. Apart from the general increase in the level of social and political violence in the Third World there is other evidence in support of this assertion. Since the advent of the Cold War all armed conflicts have been fought within the Third World. Most of them have been either proxy wars or wars encouraged by one or other of the superpowers. The short-lived era of detente between the superpowers in Europe had no visible effect on this situation.

This inequitable hierarchy of insecurity is the structural corollary of the global system created by the superpowers' security syndrome of the Cold War days. It has been an abiding existential reality within the Third World since the start of the era of their national liberation. An explanation of why this structural development and its practical consequences have occurred is not difficult to find. United States Secretary of State Dulles, one of the principal architects of the global diplomacy of the Western alliance systems, succinctly summed up its philosophical foundations during the Cold War when he said 'those not with us are against us'. Operationally, this implied a global search for states which had shared security concerns and a related desire to reward them while punishing non-allies. The resulting global structure provided no scope for any alternative or parallel system for national security outside the framework laid down by the policies of the superpowers.

Within the geographic region of Europe and North America, such a policy posed relatively few problems and created fewer complexities. The region simply bi-polarised in a relatively stable manner along ideological lines. The Marshall Plan in the West and revolutionary zeal in the East provided the infrastructure and the necessary challenge for relatively stable economic development. Indeed the Cold War was a blessing in disguise for Europe from an economic perspective.

The globalisation of this Cold War to the newly liberated countries of Asia and Africa, imbued as they were with various forms of anti-colonial nationalism, proved far from simple. Except in countries such as China and Indo-China, where the national liberation struggle was under the leadership of a Communist Party, the nationalist elites had reservations about Communist ideology and varying perceptions of the Soviet Union and China. Their relations with the West and perceptions of it were even more complex. The nationalist elites in the bulk of these countries had been created through the colonial process of 'modernisation' and shared many of the sociological traits, political ideas and ideological commitments of the West. Often, the political, economic and social institutions in these countries were initially modelled on those of their respective Western colonial rulers. Yet in almost all of them there was an elite hatred of Western colonialism and its various manifestations like racialism, which generated complex and ambivalent love–hate relationships with the West.

In practice, however, the Third World as a whole never had the option of being a part of either of the two Cold War blocs. Membership of the Communist bloc was only open to the few countries where the liberation movement was led by a Communist Party. The non-Communist parts of the Third World were presented by Western Cold War diplomacy with the apparent choice of either being their military allies or remaining isolated. Yet this was operationally a non-existent option for many states, given their historic, deep-rooted structural linkages with the West. In addition, Western diplomacy 'forced them to be free' in those cases where, as with Pakistan, their territory was seen to be geo-strategically critical.

This policy conflicted with the latent anti-Western pressures within these states. Its implementation involved many forms of intervention in their internal affairs, resulting in subversion of fledgling democratic institutions and the imposition of undemocratic regimes based either upon the military bureaucratic elite of the colonial era or traditional feudal oligarchies. The repression practised by these undemocratic regimes was ignored and their rule was underwritten by economic and military aid and political and diplomatic support.

This Western diplomacy of the Cold War era, subsequently reinforced by Soviet diplomacy, created a range of distortions and complexities from which most of the Third World countries have yet to emerge. Indeed, many of these distortions may be irreversible. Moreover, the Third World that has emerged from the Cold War is more distorted and divided within itself than the structure that existed during the colonial era. It has thereby gained a complex dynamic of its own, whereas the European situation remains relatively dependent upon the ebb and flow of superpower relations. Conflicts and tensions, social and political violence and territorial disputes have been among the most abiding features of the existential reality of the Third World. Some of these have been inherited from the colonial era and have been accentuated by Cold War rivalry. They have also led to a self-perpetuating vicious circle of massive arms transfers by the superpowers, regional tensions and global insecurity.

The non-Communist countries of the Third World thus continue to be plagued by three interrelated tiers of insecurity arising out of:

(1)   the arms race and arms stockpile of the superpowers, particularly in respect of nuclear weapons;
(2)   the territorial, ethnic and other forms of regional conflicts in which the superpowers have some involvement, either directly or indirectly;
(3)   internal political instability caused by either acute economic distress or some externally induced pattern of development within an extremely narrow social base.

Europe and North America share with the rest of the world only the first tier of insecurity; the Third World is plagued by all three layers.

THE IMPACT OF THE SUPERPOWER'S SEARCH FOR SECURITY ON THE THIRD WORLD

The contending security perspectives of the superpowers have had a differential effect upon the regions of the world. The ability of Europe and North America to absorb the shocks of the Cold War has been largely a product of its externalisation and globalisation as its focus has shifted to the endemically unstable Third World. The perceived success of the security perspectives of the superpowers has thus been largely dependent upon continued instability and insecurity outside of Europe and North America. From the viewpoint of the Third World this prevents these perspectives serving as an acceptable or adequate basis for a global security structure.

The ability of the superpowers to impose these perspectives and their consequences upon the world has prevented alternative concepts being given an opportunity to prove themselves. No post-war regional security arrangement in the Third World has been created without one or other of the superpowers being involved in it, either directly or indirectly. Collective security as envisaged by the United Nations, one possible alternative model for global security, has been given no decent chance to prove itself. The superpowers have consistently bypassed the United Nations in their search for security, even when it became more representative of the multistructured plurality of the global elites. In addition, some Western countries are impatient with the potential threat to their interests posed by the principle of global political democracy operating within this nascent collective security system. While any global structure of security without either of the superpowers is unthinkable, it is equally misguided to predicate it on the continuity of insecurity among the overwhelming majority of the world's population.

This dilemma is likely to become increasingly complex as demands for a more democratic global order arise out of the existing trends towards greater international integration. These demands will occur in a situation in which an increasingly large part of the resources of the globe are being utilised by an increasingly smaller proportion of its population. The resultant contradictions will be comparable to those found within both Western democracies in the early phase of their modernisation and some of the post-colonial countries in recent times. Europe resolved them by its colonial expansion and increased domestic democratisation. The post-colonial countries, lacking a similar option, have resolved them by means of repressive political regimes of one variety or another.

This unstable global situation poses a continual potential for crisis, given both the absence of any recognisable sovereign authority at the global level and the continued legitimacy of national sovereignty within the Third World. For although the security problems of that world are largely a product of the security perspectives of the other worlds, the operationalisation of these perspectives prevents the implementation of the global democratic system which would provide equal security for all states.

THE INTERNATIONAL POLITICAL ECONOMY AND THIRD WORLD SECURITY

Under present conditions, any analysis of Third World perspectives on security must also involve exploration of the organic linkage between the sphere of security and that of political economy. This necessitates the exclusion of Communist countries from the generic Cold War category of the Third World. Although their problems and perceptions are comparable with those of non-Communist states, they have been somewhat insulated from both the reinforcement of the colonial structural distortions to the economies of other Third World states that resulted from the Cold War and from the processes that have made these distortions so difficult to reverse. They have also been relatively insulated from external manipulation and the rigours of an inequitable global economic order, leaving them with a wider range of developmental options and a more stable base. Their economic and political changes are rooted in indigenous factors, resulting in the relative absence of the mass poverty and human degradation clustered around enclaves of affluence and modernisation that characterises the bulk of the non-Communist countries of the post-colonial world.

By contrast, the non-Communist countries of the Third World are more closely integrated into the global order. They feel the rigours of its inequitable hierarchy to a much greater extent, while their relatively open systems make them more vulnerable to external influences and restrict their political and economic options. Their enclaves of 'modernisation', which are distorted versions of Western counterparts, are located within vast hinterlands of mass poverty. The resulting societies are complex, conflict-prone and relatively unstable. These economic distortions give rise to a common political perspective, institutionalised within the Group of 77. This group has worked together for the creation of the NIEO and the related democratisation of the United Nations system, as well as presenting a united front on other macro-level global political questions.

Increasingly, the range of options available to liberal Third World states in the economic and political spheres is becoming restricted and skewed because of constraints imposed by the existing global security and political economy systems. The result is the death of democracy and the growth of authoritarianism. Within the First World this appears to have produced a visible conservative political backlash, while within the Third World it has manifested itself in terms of more centralised, repressive regimes operating from an extremely narrow social base. Mass poverty has increased in many of the latter countries, despite an increase in GNP stimulated by external aid. Yet the consequent social conflicts tend to reinforce this political structure of oppression.

This trend accelerated following the economic recession in the First World during the mid-1970s. While some of the countries in the First World seemed to have reached the plateau of the recessionary phase and are about to move to the upswing phase, its inevitable impact within the bulk of the Third World is yet to appear.

Political centralisation and repression have thus created intolerable pressures within the plural societies of the Third World. This will make them vulnerable in the 1990s to processes of Balkanisation along one or other of their multiple divisions. While this may lead to more effective management of repression within the resultant smaller territorial boundaries, it will not necessarily produce greater stability of the global order: indeed if pre-1914 Europe is any guide, the opposite seems more likely.

THE GROWTH OF THIRD WORLD SECURITY ELITES

Another manifestation of the link between economics and security is the positive correlation between the strength and intensity of certain Third World states' political and diplomatic relations with Western alliance partners and the proportion of their national budgets allocated to defence expenditures. This proportion in many cases amounts to more than half the total budget. The cause/effect relationship underlying the apparent insecurity felt by these close political allies of the West is unclear. While in the case of countries like Israel, for example, external threats cause the regime to seek closer relations with the West, in cases such as Pakistan and South Africa domestic insecurity appears to have been the main motive. In yet other cases, it may be competition between regional rivals which stimulates the strengthening of these linkages. Conversely, potential political allies such as India have been driven to seek alternative sources of superpower support by the Western states' overbearing demands for loyalty and fidelity.

Western aid packages to Third World countries tend to be proportionately higher to those with close political diplomatic and/or military ties. Within these packages the component of military aid has generally exceeded developmental aid, especially where the latter is directed towards social security related projects. Thus there is an inverse relationship between a Third World state's level of dependence on the West and attempts to create domestic social security. Western allies also tend to be directly integrated into the global nexus of the world economy. This generates some economic spin-offs, but they are adversely affected by any downturn in its business-cycle, as they lack the political and institutional cushions to absorb the shocks of its adverse impact. The result is often the brutalised repression of social discontent and political dissent, assisted by external aid.

All this has led to a flourishing arms bazaar involving large parts of the Third World and a growing arms production industry in those Third World countries which have the necessary infrastructure. Technology is imported from the West and the arms that are subsequently exported are those that are relatively inexpensive to produce because of the availability of cheap raw materials and labour. Obsolete Western weapons technology is thereby given a longer life-cycle.

It has been calculated that seven Third World countries (Israel, India, Brazil, Taiwan, Argentina, South Africa and South Korea) manufacture some 90% of the total production of armaments in the Third World. Brazil and Israel alone account for 75% of this total. All are allies of the West to some degree. Even India, which during the 1980s has moved closer to the West despite its rhetoric of non-alignment, has spent 1.26 billion dollars on arms manufacture and has the dubious distinction of being the contemporary Third World's second largest producer and ninth biggest exporter of arms.

In parallel to this development, there is a mushrooming chain of 'security establishments', particularly in those Third World countries with close political and diplomatic relations with the West. These are miniature replicas of their Western counterparts and are paralleled by a new generation of Western-style 'national security' elites who think and talk in a similar security language to their Western counterparts. This contrasts with the earlier generation of nationalist elites, who were steeped in the political culture of post-colonial nationalism with its emphasis on nation-building, development and economic and social transformation. Moreover, the political culture produced by the arms bazaar is being reinforced by the insistence by these new national security conscious elites that 'what is good for the West is also good for us'; and 'what the West can do, we can do as well'.

SECURITY ELITES AND NUCLEAR PROLIFERATION

The political and strategic culture and technological expectations of this new breed of Westernised security elites seems likely to provide increasing legitimacy to demands from within Third World states for nuclear weapons and nuclear technology. Such demands may also be reinforced by the many interweaving patterns of regional conflict which have been both created and exacerbated by the Cold War. It is ironic that the nuclear deterrence concepts which have dominated security thinking in the West are in danger of enhancing the global threat of horizontal proliferation through their uncritical acceptance and imitation by these emerging Third World national security elites. Yet as in the rest of the world outside the present nuclear powers, there are two parallel elements to the non-proliferation debate in these countries. One is the ethical debate, which highlights the dangers for mankind of nuclear weapons and their inherent immorality. The other is on the plane of *realpolitik*, where the emphasis is on the right and the obligation of states to seek independent deterrence in an insecure world of nuclear threat.

The new generation of national security conscious elites in the Third World is aware of both these arguments, though any future desire to seek nuclear weapons will be conditioned by factors ranging from the availability of technology and raw materials to the elite's political autonomy within both the global and national contexts. A general acceptance of the Western view that the state has an absolute right to provide for its own security, exemplified by France, explains the relative consensus among Third World countries, along with many others, that the existing global non-proliferation regime is inequitable because it lacks effective provisions for disarming the existing nuclear weapon states. Yet there currently exists no agreement on how to change this situation, the available options being unattractive to most Third World regimes because of the constraints imposed upon them by both the global hierarchy of power and the economic order.

That there should even be a debate about acquiring nuclear weapons within the Third World, given its existential reality of widespread mass poverty and human degradation, highlights the unfortunate contribution and true nature of the superpowers' narrow concern for security rather than enhancing the quality of life around the globe. In parallel, universal commitments to human and social progress are slowly becoming atrophied across the globe as a direct consequence both of the superpowers' concepts of national security and their search for it. In the Third World this has also led to the irretrievable attenuation of the tide of post-independence nationalism which sought to stimulate economic development, social transformation and nation-building. In its place has arisen economic and security dependencies upon the First World which generate a self-perpetuating momentum of their own. These dependencies have created a world which is generally less stable, less secure, more complex and more difficult to manage than if states of the Third World had more autonomy.

Superpower policies have also led to imitative thinking concerning nuclear weapon possession which could yet rebound adversely upon the other two worlds. The argument that nuclear weapons are essential to safeguard the security of the two superpowers and their close associates may yet reap its own, undesired reward in the shape of horizontal nuclear proliferation. But the greatest tragedy of our times and danger to the world emerges from the fact that even this dismal reality has failed to provide the intellectual challenge to stimulate sufficient creative unorthodoxy of ideas and institutions to reverse the process.

5   Nuclear trade relations in the decade to 1995

William Walker

INTRODUCTION

Contrary to most expectations, the 1980s have not so far given rise to serious difficulties where nuclear trade is concerned. The leading nuclear exporters have avoided conflict, North–South disputes have subsided, and nuclear trade policy was a secondary issue at the 1985 NPT Review Conference. This relative calm after the storms of the 1970s has partly resulted from improved understandings among traders and a more realistic assessment of the risks of nuclear proliferation. But it has also resulted from the near-total cessation of nuclear ordering in export markets.

This situation raises a number of questions. Can we rely on recession to keep the lid on conflict over nuclear trade for much longer? How are we to cope with the increasing number of suppliers, some of whom lie on the fringes of the non-proliferation regime, who will be competing for nuclear orders in the 1990s? Can we live with the substantial discrepancies between existing codes of conduct? The answers to these questions will go some way to allowing an evaluation to be made of the possible nature of nuclear trading relations in 1995.

THE COMMERCIAL OUTLOOK

Only the briefest of assessments of the future development of nuclear markets and industries will be attempted here. The discussion will be divided into two parts: the outlooks for power plant and the fuel-cycle.

Power plant markets

The rate of ordering of nuclear power plant in the West has plummeted over the past fifteen years from an average of 33 units per annum around the turn of the 1970s to a mere 4–5 units in the first half of the 1980s, nearly all of the latter being in France. While nuclear power has had its special difficulties, the downturn has hit all types of large power plant. Its roots have lain primarily in mistaken expectations of growth in economic activity and electricity demand.

In advanced industrial nations, the forecast annual rate of growth of electricity demand has fallen from what was typically 7 to 10% in the early 1970s to 2 to 4% today. The result has been substantial spare capacity which, notwithstanding important pockets of scarcity, will allow much of the growth of demand to the end of the century to be met with plant now installed or under construction. Moreover, when additional capacity does appear necessary to meet higher demand, the very large ordering programmes of more expansionist periods will not be required.

Among the OECD countries, substantial nuclear investment to substitute for other fuels is also unlikely, particularly now that fossil fuel prices are falling and there is a large prospective surplus of internationally tradeable coal. Future power plant demand therefore will depend significantly on the need to renew the very large established stock of generating capacity. But what will renewal entail, and when? Before utilities embark on replacement, economic and political considerations are likely to lead them to give priority to extending the lifetimes and improving the performance of existing power stations. But for how long can they be extended? This is unclear, especially in relation to nuclear stations where safety questions loom even larger after the Chernobyl accident. It nevertheless seems a reasonable assumption that the average life-time of nuclear power plant will tend towards forty years rather than the thirty years commonly assumed hitherto and that life-times of other thermal plant will be even longer.

This leads to three conclusions about OECD markets. First, substantial industrial effort to refurbish nuclear power plant will be made in the 1990s, causing the postponement of large-scale ordering for replacement until the first and second decades of the twenty-first century, or roughly forty years after the large wave of ordering between 1965 and 1975. Second, the rate of nuclear plant ordering in the 1990s will be low by the standards of the 1960s and 1970s, and could even approach zero if safety fears arising from the Chernobyl disaster are not allayed. If ordering does occur, it will be limited to countries and regions with relatively high electricity demand growth, such as Japan, or an unusually old stock of power plant, such as the United Kingdom, or a particular need to substitute for fossil fuels, such as the Netherlands. The recession in power plant markets will be most prolonged in France due to the size and youth of its installed nuclear generating capacity. Third, the improvement of thermal reactor designs, especially as regards safety, will be the main technological objectives. Except in the unexpected event of severe and prolonged uranium shortages, fast reactors will have little commercial role in the next two to three decades.

Turning to developing countries, electricity demand is expected to grow more rapidly. Yet the scale of Third World nuclear investment is still small. In 1985, only 12 gigawatts (GW)[1] had been installed in these countries, compared to 200 GW in the OECD region, and a significant upturn in demand may again have to await the twenty-first century. Given the financial and technical problems encountered with nuclear power, and the availability of alternative energy sources, especially natural gas, coal and hydro power in several regions, it is unlikely to receive priority in the Third World taken as a whole. In the larger industrialising countries where nuclear power has already put down roots, notably Argentina, Brazil, India, South Korea, Pakistan and Taiwan, or where there is a strong commitment to its development, as in China, further investment can be envisaged, although it is bound to be modest and hesitant. An expectation that nuclear power will have to assume a larger role post-2000 in the production of bulk electricity could, however, lead in the 1990s to broader Third World interest in building up civil nuclear capabilities.

Power plant ordering rates in the Third World are therefore highly uncertain and will probably be more responsive to conditions in the world economy, particularly to the availability and cost of capital, than OECD ordering rates. They will also depend on safety records. While we must not overestimate demand, it seems unlikely that the almost total recession that has gripped Third World export markets since 1979 will persist far into the 1990s. This said, ordering is more probable in the second half of the decade than in the first, and the remaining years of the 1980s could be barren.[2]

Finally, mention should be made of the CMEA markets in Eastern Europe and the Soviet Union. Given the desire to lessen dependence on oil and coal and meet expectations of electricity demand, a steady stream of power plant ordering was anticipated before the Chernobyl disaster. It remains to be seen how extensively this accident will affect construction plans. Capital scarcity and industrial inefficiency may also keep nuclear investment well below the ambitious targets that have been set.

Power plant industries

Partly arising from the above, four aspects of the power plant industry's evolution in the remaining years of this century seem particularly relevant to the discussion of trade relations.[3]

First, the maintenance, modernisation and refurbishment of the large stocks of operating reactors will provide both the most consistent and possibly the largest market for the power plant producers up to the end of the century, with utilities also playing an important role. While protection of national markets must be expected, this could lead to a degree of market interpenetration that has not been seen hitherto. The United States will be the single largest market and is already being regarded as an important target by Japanese and European, especially French, firms. As it is also the most open, the question of reciprocity may become a significant issue in bilateral relations.

Second, substantial reactor manufacturing capacities which the maintenance and modernisation market cannot fully support, especially with regard to hardware manufacture, now exist in a broad range of countries. The main bidders for power plant contracts will be technology holders such as the United States, France, West Germany, Japan and the Soviet Union, but there are design and manufacturing capabilities in a number of OECD countries including Belgium, Italy, Spain and the United Kingdom and in Third World countries such as Argentina, Brazil, India, South Korea and Taiwan. All these countries will be seeking entry to world markets. With the exception of the Soviet Union, all will suffer from more or less persistent surplus capacity, since protectionism will impede rationalisation within and across national frontiers. The 1990s, like 1980s, will be a buyer's market with an even wider choice of suppliers.[4]

These 'peripheral capacities' will, however, only gain entry to export markets for large power plant in joint ventures with the technology holders, which will themselves be forced to form and maintain alliances to optimise competitiveness and share development costs in a limited market. Strong competitive pressures will therefore be accompanied by searches for viable forms of cooperation. At the same time several of the peripheral suppliers, including Argentina, Brazil and India, will have an indigenous capability to supply complete research reactors.

Third, the gradual shift in prestige and technological competence among the main technology holders that has occurred over the past two decades seems likely to continue, with the United States ceding industrial authority to France, West Germany and Japan. While the cooperation between Westinghouse and Mitsubishi to develop a new generation of pressurised water reactors (PWRs) will help the former to defend its position in technology, the principal beneficiary in the 1990s will be Mitsubishi, especially since the reference plant will be built in Japan. If it appears successful, this cooperation could well lead to new defensive alliances between the other leading suppliers in Japan, Europe and the United States, with France possibly in the vanguard now that she can no longer rely on the cushion of a large domestic market.

Fourth, the priority given to fast breeder and fusion reactors in research and development (R&D) programmes will probably continue to decline. Beyond efforts to improve existing thermal designs, the search for 'inherently safe' thermal reactor technologies may acquire greater momentum in the wake of the Chernobyl disaster. To succeed, the development of such reactor types will inevitably involve broad international collaboration among the leading Western industrial nations and, possibly, between East and West if Gorbachev's recent proposal is followed up.

In summary, competitive pressures within the power plant market will be considerable in the remaining years of the century, although they will be mainly channelled towards maximising shares of OECD markets. A consensus on trade policies will have to be sought among a wider and more diverse congregation of suppliers, but the market for new power plant may not re-emerge on any significant scale until the twenty-first century.

The fuel-cycle

The outlook for nuclear fuel supplies to the end of the century is more straightforward. As the plant ordered over the past fifteen years is commissioned, the demand for uranium and enrichment services in the West will rise to a plateau where it will stay until the next large tranche of power reactors enters service. Outside the CMEA region, demand will thus be determined until well into the twenty-first century by the needs of an installed capacity of around 300 GW.

The uranium and enrichment industries should have no difficulty in meeting demand from known reserves and existing facilities.[5] The expansion of nuclear electricity production in countries without indigenous capacities will, however, lead to an increase in the share of demand that is met by internationally traded fuels. But providing secure supplies are maintained at reasonable prices, which is probable in the competitive conditions which are likely to apply, there will be little incentive to invest in significant new uranium or enrichment capacity. Having the largest enrichment capacities, the United States and France will remain the principal suppliers of enrichment services, with URENCO and the Soviet Union providing alternative sources of supply on the margin. Laser enrichment cannot materially affect the market until the late 1990s at the earliest.

The back-end of the fuel-cycle presents greater uncertainties. The deferral of fast reactors has weakened the economic case for reprocessing. However, the legacy of past contracts makes it probable that commercial reprocessing will proceed on a substantial scale in France and the United Kingdom, although failure to improve safety at Sellafield could impede British reprocessing. Legal and political problems in dealing with growing stocks of spent fuel may increase the pressures to reprocess, leading to calls for investment in reprocessing facilities beyond those now under construction in West Germany and Japan, or alternatively for participation in those already in existence or currently being established.

Whatever the outcome of these reprocessing activities, the amounts of separated plutonium in storage and circulation and the commitment to its recycling in thermal reactors are bound to increase. These activities will largely be limited to Western Europe and Japan, and may therefore be judged 'safe' with regard to proliferation, as conventionally defined. But they raise important questions about physical security, particularly where transport between Europe and Japan is concerned. How will movements of plutonium be made immune to terrorism and accident, and at what political and economic cost?

There remains the question of the enrichment and reprocessing capacities under development in the Third World threshold countries and China. With the possible if improbable exceptions of enrichment in China and heavy water production in Argentina, it is unlikely that they will serve power reactors outside domestic markets for reasons of cost, capacity and reliability.[6] These countries are, however, potentially important sources of training, technology and equipment for those wishing to develop indigenous capabilities; enrichment capacities in these states and heavy water facilities in Argentina and India may be sufficient to provide adequate supplies of fuel and moderator for research reactors.

In the West, the bulk of the trade in the fuel-cycle will thus be conducted among OECD parties to the NPT. The exception to this last rule is, of course, France, which has acquired a pivotal position in both the front- and back-ends of the international fuel-cycle while remaining outside the NPT. This is the single greatest anomaly in the nuclear trading system, whose management will increasingly depend on the achievement of cooperation between France and the United States, despite their very different historical stances on non-proliferation and rivalry in nuclear export markets.

NUCLEAR TRADE POLICIES

The historical legacy

Let us briefly recall the evolution of nuclear trade policies. Prior to the NPT negotiations, there was no concerted effort to achieve a comprehensive agreement on nuclear trade. It is true that the IAEA safeguards system was gaining broader international support in the 1960s, that the EURA-TOM Treaty governed nuclear trade among the original six member countries of the European Communities and that regular discussions were held among uranium producers. But at that time nuclear trade policy was primarily a national affair and specifically a United States concern, since her industries dominated nuclear trade and technology.

The NPT, and specifically Articles I to IV, therefore provided the first broad political framework for the conduct of nuclear trade. Articles I and II contained the main pledges not to transfer, seek access to or in any way assist the spread of nuclear weapons. Article III outlined the IAEA safeguards that would be applied under the Treaty, with Articles III.1 and III.2 covering safeguards on trade with countries inside and outside the Treaty respectively. Article IV enunciated non-nuclear weapon state parties' rights of access to nuclear technologies, materials and equipment for peaceful purposes. Article III was further underpinned by both the IAEA's introduction in 1971 of INFCIRC/153, a document which outlined the Full Scope Safeguards (FSS) which non-nuclear weapon state parties must accept, and by the Zangger Committee's publication of a trigger list of materials, equipment and components to which safeguards would be applied. The Zangger Committee also endorsed the interpretation of Article III.2 which did not require NPT exporters to insist on FSS when trading with countries outside the Treaty. They merely had to insist that INFCIR-C/66/Rev.2 safeguards would apply to the materials and facilities directly linked to any trading activities.[7]

Support for the NPT was by no means universal, and its trade rules no longer seemed adequate in the wake of the turmoil caused in the mid-1970s by the Indian nuclear explosion, the expansion of trade with countries outside the NPT and the grandiose plans for nuclear expansion that resulted from the first oil crisis. A Nuclear Suppliers Group, known as the 'London

Club', therefore met to seek agreement among the leading exporters in East and West on a new and more detailed code of conduct.[8] The guidelines which emerged from these meetings made no reference to the NPT, nor did they discriminate between NPT and non-NPT countries in their recommendations. Adherents would henceforth exercise 'restraint' in transferring sensitive materials and technologies, making access to them no longer a general right. They retained the right to veto the reprocessing or further enrichment of fuels or the retransfer of exported items, their products and derivatives supplied by them. This was known as the 'prior consent' clauses. Suppliers would consult one another also about future transactions. The guidelines only required exported items to be safeguarded: FSS, either *de facto* or *de jure*, were not to be conditions of trade.[9]

Hence the guidelines added fresh conditions to the honouring of Article IV of the NPT, but it is important to recognise that they were supplementary to the NPT rules and did not supercede them. Implicitly, Articles I and III stood unamended in the eyes of the suppliers.[10] Indeed the guidelines could *not* be free-standing since they had so little to say on safeguards and nothing on the transfer of nuclear weaponry. France's statement that she would behave 'as if' she were an NPT party was a necessary adjunct to her support of the guidelines, since it gave an assurance that Articles I and III would be honoured.

The guidelines were published in 1977. Along with Articles I and III of the NPT, they have since been adopted by Japan and most European countries as the foundations of their trade policies. But they were regarded as insufficient by other leading suppliers who subscribed to them. Canada had already announced that no further trade would be conducted without FSS and Australia went further by refusing to sell uranium to non-NPT countries. The Soviet Union continued with her idiosyncratic but effective policy of not insisting on FSS yet requiring the return of spent fuel from exported reactors. And most significantly, the Nuclear Non-Proliferation Act (NNPA) which the United States Congress passed in 1978 committed the country to a policy of denial in trade and opposition to civil nuclear expansion. Among other things, it stipulated that all future United States trade must be covered by FSS. Exports of enrichment and reprocessing technology and other sensitive items were henceforth prohibited and the reprocessing of fuels of United States origin would only be approved on a case-by-case, or even batch-by-batch, basis. While the Reagan administration has since jettisoned the anti-nuclear rhetoric that surrounded the NNPA and has generally become less confrontational in its handling of nuclear trade relations, United States policy remains anchored to this Act.

However uncoordinated their actions, the 1970s therefore saw the assertion of authority over nuclear trade policy by the supplier countries, with only fleeting regard for the interests or feelings of importers. The universalist approach to nuclear trade was effectively abandoned for the time being. Following the outcry that greeted the publication of the guidelines, the Carter administration convened the International Nuclear Fuel Cycle Evaluation (INFCE) which all states were invited to attend. But this was essentially an exercise in pacification. No real agreements emerged, except that no 'proliferation-proof' fuel-cycle existed. Nor have INFCE's offspring, the discussions on International Plutonium Storage (IPS) or within the Committee on Assurances of Supply (CAS), brought suppliers and recipients much closer to a consensus. It is not expected either that great progress will be made at the United Nations Conference on the Peaceful Uses of Nuclear Energy (UNCPICPUNE) when it is eventually convened.

Mention might also be made here of the Convention on the Physical Protection of Nuclear Material which was negotiated between 1977 and 1979 under the auspices of the IAEA and opened for signature in March 1980. This will only enter into force once the required twenty-one instruments of ratification have been deposited in Vienna.[11]

By the end of the 1970s, nuclear trade policy was thus in a state of considerable disarray. The NPT rules had come to be regarded as insufficient, the guidelines appeared to contravene the spirit of cooperation in trade and development between suppliers and recipients and the leading suppliers could not agree among themselves on what constituted the proper conduct of trade. This position has not fundamentally changed since 1980.

Why is it therefore widely perceived that nuclear trade relations have substantially improved in the 1980s? No doubt better understandings and the wiser handling of policy, notably by the United States, have played an important part. But the primary explanation lies in the collapse both of nuclear markets and the vision of a great expansion of nuclear power in response to energy scarcity and in the appreciation that nuclear proliferation is a problem relating to particular countries and regions, rather than the generality of nations. The recession has virtually killed the export market for nuclear plant so that there has been little for the suppliers to fight over. Surplus capacity in the fuel-cycle has reduced concern over supply security and weakened the case for developing indigenous fuel-cycles while the priority accorded to nuclear power as an energy source has been much reduced. As a consequence, nuclear trade has become a

Table 2. *Official nuclear trade policies (1986): a rough guide*

	Safeguards on exported items	Full-scope safeguards		Transfer of sensitive technology		Prior consent to reprocess & retransfer	Return of spent fuels
		de facto	de jure	NPT	non-NPT		
NPT	Y		NPT NNWS*	Y	Y		
Guidelines	Y			Restraints		Y	
United States	Y	Y		Denial		Y	
Soviet Union	Y			Denial			Y
Australia, Canada, Nordic Countries	Y	Y**		Denial		Y	
European Comm. suppliers	Y			Denial of reprocessing, restraint otherwise	Y		
Argentina, Brazil, India, Israel, Pakistan***	Y (?)			?	?	?	

y = yes * NNWS = non-nuclear weapon states ** Australia will only trade with NPT member states *** South Africa declared her support for the guidelines in 1984

more peripheral concern for many developing countries and some of the sting has gone out of the North–South dispute. In parallel, the 'problem countries' have now been firmly identified, at least in the eyes of the Northern suppliers, shifting the emphasis in non-proliferation policy towards a case-by-case assessment and a more rounded political approach.

This period of comparative quiet has also allowed progress to be made in disposing of irritants and loose ends in trade relations. The United States has extricated herself, with European assistance, from embarrassing arguments over supplies of enriched uranium fuel to Brazil, India and South Africa. The Zangger trigger lists have been refined and extended. The guidelines have been rendered compatible with the EURATOM Treaty and the Treaty of Rome. Australia, Canada and the United States have gradually moved towards giving blanket approvals for reprocessing to individual countries.

These adjustments should not, however, blind us to the unsatisfactory state of trade policy (see Table 2). What we have to consider is whether the present mishmash of national and international codes of conduct and an essentially pragmatic approach to trade will suffice in the 1990s, especially if some revival in nuclear investment should occur. And how can the Third World threshold countries be integrated safely as exporters into the nuclear trading system?

The transatlantic accord

We have seen that the Northern suppliers other than the Soviet Union fall roughly into two camps where trade policy is concerned. The divisions are clearest on the issue of FSS where the United States, Canada, Australia and the Nordic countries require that they be applied to all exports and most other European suppliers and Japan do not. Can and should these positions be reconciled in future?

The key countries within these two camps are the United States and France. They will ultimately determine the scope for convergence. The United States policy on safeguards is clear: under the NNPA, *de facto* FSS must be applied to all exports. It is doubtful whether Congress would in future sanction exports to a non-nuclear weapon state without NPT-equivalent safeguards. It is improbable that this policy will change in the foreseeable future.

France's position is more deceptive. Her continued opposition to FSS is paralleled by an increasing and possibly lasting unwillingness to trade with non-NPT parties. The French government is thus behaving as if it required the application of FSS. The only exception is China, which as a nuclear weapon state constitutes a special case. There are four principal reasons for this unwillingness. First, France does not wish to risk the opprobrium that would follow a nuclear weapon test by any recipient of French nuclear assistance. Hence the decision not to respond to Pakistan's call for tenders for the Chashma power station, despite the belief that a light water reactor would contribute nothing towards a Pakistani military capability. Second, it now recognises that the commercial opportunities outside the NPT will remain slight, at least for the next few years. Argentina and Brazil are economically constrained, have cheaper alternative energy supplies and are firmly tied to German technology and capital, Pakistan could not pay for another nuclear power plant, while India is committed to its policy of autarky in nuclear technology. Third, foreign policy interests largely unconnected with nuclear proliferation, in particular the desire not to offend Arab and Black African opinion, effectively rule out further nuclear trade with Israel and South Africa.

74

The fourth reason is arguably the most conclusive. France has increasingly strong interests in good nuclear trade relations with the United States. There exist concerns that a dispute over nuclear trade could inflict political damage on a relationship that has become increasingly central to French security policy, but in addition the balance of commercial interests in the nuclear field now points emphatically in the direction of taking no political risks with the United States. Any dispute between them could cost the French industry dearly through the loss of a potentially large market in the United States, while United States industry might exploit any infringement of Congress's export policies to pull up the protectionist barriers around its home market. The 10 to 15% share of the United States enrichment market that COGEMA seeks would bring it business far in excess of that deriving from reactor exports to the Third World, while the reprocessing of foreign spent fuels at Cap de la Hague still depends substantially on prior consent from the United States. American goodwill is thus essential for the expansion of France's foreign trade in nuclear fuel services.[12]

India is perhaps the one country with unsafeguarded facilities to which France would be strongly tempted to sell power reactors, but there are no signs that the Indian government will reverse its policy of independence in reactor design, although such a step cannot entirely be ruled out. Hence it seems unlikely that France will depart from what is equivalent in practice to a policy of FSS. While resisting their adoption as a common standard, the French government may regard with displeasure trade by other European countries that requires anything less than FSS. For, in any consequent dispute with the United States, France could not avoid siding with her European partners in the Nuclear Suppliers Group and hence jeopardising her political and commercial interests in good relations with the United States.

France is by no means alone among European suppliers in her reluctance to trade with countries which do not accept FSS. West Germany is probably committed politically to a policy of at least *de facto* FSS. Moreover, one frequently hears it argued that the lesser European suppliers, including the United Kingdom, would willingly change their policies if they could be sure that their neighbours would follow suit.

The inevitable question then arises: why not formalise the position and make FSS a condition of trade for all Northern suppliers by means of a series of unilateral declarations or amendments to the guidelines? With so few trading opportunities outside the NPT, the next few years might be the best time to seek a consensus. Such a step would bring greater solidarity among the leading suppliers and redress the imbalance in safeguards applied to trade inside and outside the NPT.

There are three main arguments against taking this initiative in the near term. The first is that there can be little confidence that it would succeed, in which case it should not be attempted for fear of opening up greater rifts. If the initiative came from the United States it would be treated with suspicion, for memories of gas pipelines and other efforts to restrict trade are still fresh in European minds. And within Europe, the bureaucratic commitment to the guidelines as they stand is too strong, for historical reasons if for no other. Moreover, if Paris changed its mind it could not be sure that Bonn would follow suit, particularly in view of Bonn's desires to maintain trade links with Argentina and Brazil.

Second, it is maintained that any tightening of the guidelines would compromise efforts to increase the number of countries adhering to them. Although the Suppliers Group has not met since 1977, its membership has steadily expanded. Since aspiring exporters like Spain and South Korea have yet to declare their support for the guidelines, their contents should be left unchanged for fear of scaring off possible newcomers.

The third argument deserves to be looked at in more detail. It is that the adoption of a policy of FSS would be unwise in the context of relations with the threshold states, who would regard it as confrontational. It would have little effect on their attitudes towards the safeguarding of indigenous facilities, and if anything it might cause them to become even more intransigent and more strident in their attacks on Northern suppliers within the Group of 77. Perhaps most importantly, in view of their ambitions to become nuclear exporters, it would hamper the task of bringing them safely into the trading system.

The export policies of emerging suppliers

The problem posed by the emerging nuclear suppliers should not be exaggerated. Indeed their need to formulate export policies may lead them to a rather different view of the rights and wrongs in nuclear trade. Their actions to date are also encouraging. China has joined the IAEA and is now displaying considerable caution in her foreign dealings, whilst South Africa has announced her support for the Suppliers guidelines. All the emerging suppliers seem to be exercising restraint with regard to the transfer of sensitive materials and technologies and there is no known recent instance of any export of unsafeguarded items.

There are nevertheless obvious dangers. The slowdown in civil nuclear investment, together with the constraints on exploiting the military options available to emerging suppliers, create strong pressures to export. These pressures are reinforced by the emerging suppliers' grievous lack of foreign exchange. There are also signs of growing strategic and commercial competition in nuclear trade and exchange between them, such as the contest between Argentina and Brazil to sign cooperation agreements inside and outside Latin America. In these circumstances, there is inevitably some risk that the offer of sensitive nuclear materials or technology, with or without safeguards, could be used to gain entry to international markets or to promote foreign policy interests. The issue of physical security also should not be overlooked. Some emerging suppliers could appear the easiest sources of weapons-usable material to the aspiring terrorist.

Looking towards the 1990s, the trading behaviour of the threshold countries among the emerging suppliers, principally Argentina, Brazil, India and Pakistan, is arguably the most important issue in nuclear trade policy.[13] The resort to political and economic arm-twisting to ensure restraint by them is an insufficient remedy. Anxieties are compounded by their lack of allegiance to, indeed their historic rejection of, any of the established sets of trade rules. While they must abide by Article III when trading with non-nuclear weapon parties to the NPT, in other respects they cannot embrace the Treaty's provisions. Nor can they follow France's example and declare that they will behave 'as if' they were Treaty members, since they are not nuclear weapon states and would thereby lay themselves open to the charge that they should accept NPT-equivalent safeguards on their own nuclear activities.

It is conceivable that China and Israel will join South Africa in declaring their support for the guidelines. It is difficult, however, for the other four threshold countries to embrace the guidelines in view of the bitter criticisms they have levelled against them over the past decade. Indeed, they have driven themselves into a corner where it is exceedingly difficult for them to declare openly that they will impose any restrictions on trade beyond the safeguarding of exported items.

This brings us back to the argument that any further tightening of trade policy by the Northern suppliers could only hinder the resolution of this problem. This contends, first, that the threshold countries cannot be forced or embargoed into applying trade rules similar to those accepted by the established suppliers. The only viable tactic is to establish a dialogue with individual governments and gradually to draw them towards acceptance of 'sensible' trading practices. Confrontation should be reserved for occasions when they clearly depart from accepted standards of behaviour, and should not be resorted to in the conduct of bilateral relations. Second, it would be counterproductive to try freezing the threshold countries out of the trading system. Instead, an effort should be made to engage their industries in cooperative ventures in international markets, though in practice this policy can only be applied by West Germany in relation to Argentina and Brazil, since there are few remaining industrial ties with India and Pakistan. Third, the guidelines should be advertised as the model for their export policies, even if they cannot openly declare allegiance to them. Any attempt to make the guidelines more restrictive would render them even less acceptable.

It is, however, in relation to the transfer of sensitive materials and technologies, especially where the prospective customer is an NPT country and thus bound to accept FSS, that the greatest problem may lie in future. The guidelines demand no more than 'restraint'. This is interpreted by most Northern suppliers as prohibition. The only exceptions are highly 'reliable' NPT countries with large nuclear power programmes, such as Japan and West Germany, which can justify an indigenous fuel-cycle on economic grounds. With the threshold countries emerging as alternative suppliers of enrichment and especially reprocessing technology, it may no longer be possible for the Northern suppliers to keep such a tight grip on sensitive parts of the fuel-cycle. Furthermore, by trading more liberally the threshold countries may lay claim to the moral high ground in view of the commitments made in Article IV. How then is the term 'restraint' to be defined, and by whom? Can an unwritten agreement be reached with the threshold countries over 'no-go' areas, particularly in the Middle East? Can fresh initiatives be taken to establish multinational fuel-cycle facilities in order to pre-empt the spread of indigenous capacities? One suspects that the need to begin providing answers to these questions will become more urgent in the 1990s.

Taken together, the arguments against a further 'tightening' of the policies of the Northern suppliers and in particular against the general adoption of FSS as a condition of trade make convincing reading. For the time being the guidelines, together with Articles I to III of the NPT and the IAEA safeguards system, form the basic framework for nuclear trade relations. While the United States remains justifiably unhappy about the guidelines, its administration seems increasingly to share the view that the acceptance of this framework by a wider community of nations is the most important diplomatic task in the years leading up to 1995. It may be tempting to strive for more significant innovations, but a policy of incrementalism seems likely to bring the greatest reward. Whether this view would be endorsed by the United States Congress and its advisers, or by the Australian and Canadian governments, is more questionable. Gaining agreement on the broad approach to be adopted in nuclear diplomacy will arguably prove a more important undertaking for the nuclear countries than ironing out the many discrepancies in preferred trade rules.

NPT RENEWAL AND TRADE POLICY

Four points stand out concerning nuclear trade policy and the renewal of the NPT in 1995. First, no one should be in any doubt that the collapse of the Treaty and its associated safeguards would be a disaster for the nuclear trading system. The great majority of civil nuclear trade is conducted under the umbrella of the NPT and, as Charles N. van Doren argues in Chapter 13, there is no substitute that could give an equivalent level of confidence. In particular the guidelines would have limited value without the NPT.

Second, it seems unlikely that the renewal of the NPT will hinge on the evolution of nuclear trade policy. Ultimately, it will depend on the observance of Articles I, II and VI, and on the security benefits that are perceived as deriving from NPT membership. It should not, however, be concluded that trade policy will be an irrelevance in 1995. Great care will be required to ensure that serious trade disputes are avoided in the meantime and that Treaty members are provided with no new grounds for complaint that their trading rights are being eroded.

Third, the question arises whether special efforts should be made to bring export policies closer to the spirit and letter of the NPT. It would be prudent to restrict efforts to gain wider adoption of FSS as a condition of trade to circumstances where there is both a good chance of success and confidence that other non-proliferation objectives will not be compromised. And so long as there are 'unreliable' countries within the NPT, it would not be prudent to venture towards a strict observance of Article IV. However, there are obvious dangers in 'restraint' becoming a general policy of denial of sensitive materials and technologies to NPT members.

Finally, any attempt to renegotiate the NPT's provisions on nuclear trade and development would almost certainly end in tears and should thus be avoided. With opinions still so sharply divided, it is hard to see how a more robust consensus could be fashioned. The message for the future thus appears to be that the international trading regime should be consolidated by patient diplomacy and incremental changes; that no attempt should be made to amend the NPT itself and that the most delicate issue will remain the need perceived by the main suppliers to deny or restructure the transfer of certain technologies to 'unreliable' NPT and non-NPT parties alike, despite the right of access to all nuclear technology that appears to be incorporated in Article IV of the Treaty.

NOTES

1. A gigawatt (GW) is one thousand million watts.
2. The most thorough recent analysis of prospects in power plant markets is contained in *Nuclear Fuel and Power: Capacity, Demand and Trade Prospects*, prepared and published by Ian Smart, 3 Grosvenor Avenue, Richmond, Surrey, UK, March 1984. In his 'most probable' scenario, the OECD would account for 50% of generating capacity added between 1985 and the 'late century', CMEA (Europe) for 36% and the Third World for only 14%.
3. Evolving industrial structures are discussed in detail in W. Walker and M. Lönnroth, *Nuclear Power Struggles: Industrial Competition and Proliferation Control* (George Allen & Unwin, London, 1983).
4. This encompasses also the 'netherworld' of small materials and components suppliers that Leonard Spector discusses in *The New Nuclear Nations* (Vintage Books, New York, 1985).
5. Present enrichment capacities (in million separative work units [SWU]) are: USA = 27.3 (of which roughly 3–7% serve military requirements); Eurodif = 10.8; Techsnabexport (Soviet Union) = 3.0; URENCO = 1.4. Combined civilian capacity is thus a little over 40m SWU. To this should be added today's 29m SWU of surplus inventory. Civil demand in 1985 was 22m SWU, and is projected to rise to 33m SWU in 1995. In 1985, market shares were as follows: USA = 47%; Eurodif = 22%; Techsnabexport = 9%; URENCO = 5%. The remaining 17% was provided from utilities' surplus stocks.
6. Visitors from China tell of a long history of technical breakdown in enrichment plants. There is also reluctance to commit more electricity generating capacity to enrichment in view of severe regional shortages of electricity.
7. For a recent analysis of the safeguard system see *Safeguarding the Atom: a Critical Appraisal* by David Fischer and Paul Szasz (SIPRI, Stockholm, 1985).
8. The seven original participants in these negotiations were Canada, West Germany, France, Japan, United Kingdom, United States and Soviet Union. In January 1978, Belgium, Czechoslovakia, German Democratic Republic, Italy, the Netherlands, Poland, Sweden and Switzerland also declared their allegiance. Subsequently, Australia, Finland, Denmark, Greece, Luxembourg, Eire, Bulgaria and South Africa have announced their support for the code of conduct, making a total of 23 nations.
9. Fischer makes the following distinction: 'The term *'de facto* full-scope safeguards' is used if all nuclear plant and material in the country concerned happens to be under IAEA safeguards because a complete mosaic of individual agreements exist. *'De jure* full-scope safeguards' are applied if the country has concluded a single comprehensive safeguards agreement covering all present and future nuclear activities (e.g. an NPT or Tlatelolco safeguard agreement)', Fischer and Szasz, 107, note 7.
10. Since Article II contains the potential importer's pledge on non-proliferation, it is not strictly relevant to an agreement among exporters. However, the guidelines require exporters to seek assurances from recipients 'explicitly excluding uses [of exported items] which would result in any nuclear explosive devices'. This is a much weaker undertaking than in Article II.
11. This Convention entered into force in early 1987 following its ratification by the requisite 21 states.
12. During discussions in early 1986 with senior representatives of the French nuclear industry, considerable enthusiasm was expressed for France to take steps to join the NPT. For a discussion of France and the NPT, see William Walker, 'La France et la Traité de Non-Prolifération', *Economie et Humanisme*, no. 28B (March–April 1986).

13. The reason for excluding Israel is that she seems unlikely to engage in nuclear exporting, except possibly of a highly clandestine nature. South Africa is excluded because she has recently declared her support for the Suppliers guidelines. In addition, neither country plays a part in the Group of 77's deliberations on nuclear trade, except as objects of condemnation.

6   New technologies and the nuclear non-proliferation regime

Dennis Fakley and Ronald Mason

INTRODUCTION

In the opening chapter, Mohamed Shaker implied that one of the key reasons for the 1985 NPT Review Conference agreeing a Final Document was that many states and statesmen now perceived that the contribution made by that Treaty to their national security was more important to them than their frustrations over the non-fulfilment of arms control or civil nuclear energy promises made by the nuclear weapon states. Concerns over national security, particularly in its regional context, and the role played in it by the NPT thus seem likely to be major variables in the future support given by states to the non-proliferation regime. Yet continuing restraints on horizontal nuclear proliferation will also depend on the sensitivity of this regime to significant developments in weapons technologies; to changes in military strategy; to the prospects for reductions in nuclear arms inventories, particularly those of the superpowers and to events in the international political environment. These technological trends, the changes in military strategy they may generate and the implications of both of these developments for the non-proliferation of nuclear weapons form the subject-matter for this chapter.

Relevant technological trends can be distinguished for the purpose of analysis by their impact upon broad categories of military capabilities and doctrines. On the one hand there are those which directly affect the offence–defence relationship between possessors of strategic nuclear weapons. These trends include the evolving ability of states to acquire nuclear warheads and tailor them to specific military tasks, as well as those developments in non-nuclear technology which threaten the military credibility of certain nuclear delivery systems and are seen by some to hold out the promise of rendering nuclear weapons impotent and obsolete.

On the other hand, there are those developments which enhance the military capabilities of conventional weapons to the point where they become viable substitutes for nuclear weapons in tactical and battlefield war-fighting roles and thus are believed capable of raising the nuclear threshold. Changes in both of these areas are likely to influence calculations by likely nuclear proliferators of the military and political utility of nuclear weapons.

This distinction masks the degree to which the same technological development may have an impact on more than one area. There is, for example, considerable overlap between the generic technologies of the United States SDI and the conventional defence initiatives being sponsored by NATO states in a Western European context. Advanced sensor systems for detecting and monitoring militarily significant activities, based either in space or in tactical deployments, coupled to secure communications and new techniques for processing and analysing information will provide the means both to constantly monitor potential targets with no time-lag and to provide commanders with Command and Control Capabilities that are able to survive under severe attack. Similar types of sensors are also, of course, at the heart of improvements in the guidance and control of weapons and have made possible the development of precision-guided munitions.

This ubiquity is limited to specific areas, however. There is only a limited overlap between the ability to apply new kinetic energy and directed energy weapon[1] technologies to both strategic and tactical contexts. Of perhaps greater significance is the lack of commonality between the structural design or architecture of SDI systems designed to defend the continental United States against strategic nuclear attack and those needed to defend Western Europe against a similar threat or a land invasion.

NEW CONVENTIONAL TECHNOLOGIES AND EUROPEAN DEFENCE

The technological and doctrinal challenges created by those conventional defence innovations which are applicable to Western European security problems are considerable, even if they appear dwarfed by those necessary to create an effective strategic defence. The almost instantaneous detection, identification and localisation of those key military capabilities of a potential enemy that are either in fixed sites or have very low mobility, coupled with the ability to destroy them with great reliability, is a requirement that can now be met in a number of well-defined ways. Less confidence exists at present, however, in being able to develop cheap but effective systems capable of reliably destroying mobile targets using stand-off[2] conventional munitions.

The political context for these technological developments is a policy decision to reduce the need for NATO forces to use battlefield/theatre nuclear weapons in a high-intensity conflict in Western Europe. As a consequence, a strategy has been adopted of developing and deploying these new conventional systems and increasing the quality and quantity of reserve formations and their equipment. The aim is to enhance NATO's ability to engage in more protracted conventional hostilities in Europe. Whether this will have an impact on national assessments by non-nuclear weapon states, especially those outside Europe, of the balance of incentives and disincentives for developing and hence proliferating nuclear weapons is a difficult judgement to make. It is finely balanced for at least three reasons. Conventional defences are, for most scenarios, more demanding on resources than those with a strong nuclear element. Full utilisation of the capabilities of advanced conventional weapon systems demand maintenance skills and levels of training which are not often found in the majority of nuclear weapon threshold countries. Finally, the requirements for regional deterrence in areas other than Europe are much more varied and ill-quantified.

In these circumstances first-generation nuclear weapons and relatively simple delivery systems will inevitably be seen as a possible option by a state with a national security problem. Moreover, the relative importance of this option may change if non-nuclear weapon states start to acquire and to use either other weapons of mass destruction or very accurate and lethal conventional weapons for strategic purposes. The use of chemical weapons in the Gulf War is an illustration of the possibilities in this area. On balance, however, it seems unlikely that the changes in force structures and doctrines being implemented in NATO will have a direct effect on future nuclear proliferation or non-proliferation decisions by Middle Eastern, South American and South Asian countries. Yet the broader psychological and political impact of advanced industrial countries seeking enhanced security through less reliance on nuclear weapons, although very difficult to quantify, cannot be overemphasised.

SDI AND ITS CONSEQUENCES

If the impact of these NATO conventional defence initiatives upon political calculations and perceptions in the threshold countries is somewhat uncertain, even more difficulty exists in making a judgement on the effects of strategic defences, if and when deployed, on nuclear non-proliferation. Arguments concerning the SDI abound and are distinguished largely by their multiplicity. The aim of the SDI has been a fluid one. It appears to have moved slowly from the creation of a comprehensive defence system, which would render nuclear weapons obsolete, to one increasingly preoccupied with devising a ballistic missile defence to protect land-based and immobile strategic offensive and defensive systems at acceptable cost. It can at least be hoped that one result of the development of these extended point defences as part of the SDI will be the achievement over the next decade of a greater qualitative and quantitative symmetry between the strategic forces of the United States and the Soviet Union, an evolution which could simplify the calculus of strategic arms control.

If the aims of the SDI are fluid, so too are interpretations of its current and future impact upon strategic concepts and doctrines. Although the United Kingdom and United States governments publicly agree that the object of the SDI is to enhance deterrence, problems remain because there exist a number of different notions of the nature and the most desirable basis for deterrence. There are those who attach most importance in this context to an ability to threaten massive damage to an opponent's population and property, a countervalue policy; others believe in an ability to threaten the destruction of an opponent's strategic offensive systems, a counterforce policy; and yet others assign first priority to measures for protecting their own military and/or civilian assets from destruction by an opponent's attack, a defence-orientated policy. Conflicting Western perspectives on the SDI may thus be as much related to differences over the desirable conceptual basis for deterrence as to disagreements over the limitations inherent in the technologies involved.

This debate over the most effective way of deterring aggression and, particularly, surprise nuclear attack is viewed with incomprehension and intense suspicion in the Third World. The various bases for deterrence are rarely evaluated in any rational manner against alternative policies for achieving national and international security and the emphasis placed on nuclear deterrence by the United States and NATO is, therefore, widely regarded as an addiction. The coolest analysis one may expect from the non-aligned countries is that the SDI represents another attempt to find security through technology. In the latter context, the 23 March 1983 speech of President Reagan could be interpreted as a bid to alter the balance between the search for technical and for political solutions.

Whether such a hidden agenda was a significant motivation for the SDI is uncertain: what is clear is that the President's speech set in train a series of developments which have left the SDI meshed in many issues involving both security and technology. Widespread interest and concern has been generated by the existence of the SDI over, *inter alia*, the current and projected uses of space, anti-satellite weapons, assessments of the relative evolution of measures and countermeasures in offensive and defensive technologies and its ability to act as a stimulus to innovation for the advanced industries of certain Western countries.

The impact of the SDI upon the technological capabilities of these countries is linked to perceptions in the Third World that the technology gap between the leading four or five countries and the rest is widening. This in turn is bringing confusion to the international security scene over issues such as whether these countries have an increasing or decreasing ability to intervene or threaten to intervene with military force in Third World states and regions. Thus, indirectly, the SDI may have a significant effect upon perceptions of security and insecurity in neutral and non-aligned states and consequently on their attitudes towards the nuclear non-proliferation regime.

The impact of the SDI upon the prospects for nuclear arms control agreements between the superpowers is also rather problematic. On the one hand, SDI can be regarded as a high-technology flight of fancy and little or no real prospect exists of eventually deploying an operationally effective defence system: it is thus an irresponsible and irrelevant use of scarce resources. Moreover, because the technical failure of SDI cannot be predicted with complete confidence, it could provoke an expansion of strategic nuclear capabilities which would later be found not to have been necessary, resulting in the destabilisation of the strategic nuclear balance, the creation of increased distrust between the superpowers and the discouragement of further arms control negotiations. On the other hand, there are those who believe that the SDI will be a major lever to enable those future arms control negotiations to achieve broadly based security at lower levels of armament. This reflects an almost total uncertainty over the mechanisms and processes which could bring about significant reductions in strategic weapons. Views on this vary between assertions that technical obsolescence will cause both superpowers to move in this direction to the belief that declaratory statements committing states politically to the abolition of nuclear weapons are more important in this process than well-thought-out schemes for its practical achievement.

While accepting that arguments about the commitments contained in Article VI of the NPT will continue to be rehearsed by the neutral and non-aligned states *a fortiori*, it seems likely that most of the currently non-nuclear weapon states will continue to make their judgements on the incentives and disincentives of proliferation in a relatively parochial context rather than on the basis of the state of superpower nuclear relations. Only the uncertain predictions of nuclear winter hold out the prospects of an enhanced awareness of the global implications of nuclear exchanges and thus some erosion of such an exclusively regional preoccupation with the effects of nuclear armaments.

THE IMPACT OF NEW TECHNOLOGIES UPON THE NON-PROLIFERATION REGIME

While the SDI and innovations in conventional defence technologies will indirectly affect the non-proliferation regime by their impact on the security and political environment of states, there are some technological developments which will have a much more direct impact on that regime by appearing to make it easier for non-nuclear weapon states to gain access to the capabilities necessary to construct relatively simple fission weapons. These changes are largely in two areas. First, the pervasive knowledge of micro-electronics and the availability of certain electronic devices make it likely that more states will be able to acquire the basic capability to precisely control the implosion of conventional explosives. This combination of ordnance, fusing and detonator expertise would facilitate the design and production of the non-nuclear components of simple fission weapons. Second, the opportunities for covert production of highly enriched uranium and plutonium provided by laser isotope separation techniques[3] are considerable. These two developments taken together suggest that more states could in the 1990s rapidly convert their basic knowledge and capabilities into a stockpile of reasonably reliable weapons.

To move beyond this to the construction of the more complex second generation thermonuclear or hydrogen weapons[4] would be very difficult and it is highly unlikely that it could be accomplished without recourse to extensive nuclear testing. The development of such weapons might be assisted by information gained from civil programmes investigating the generation of electricity by inertial confinement fusion (ICF) systems.[5] Published ICF information should, therefore, be monitored and if it promised to be applicable to nuclear weapon development, the publishing authority should be warned to exercise restraint in the interests of non-proliferation. It is, however, not likely that ICF information could substitute for that currently obtainable only from nuclear testing.

The technological environment of nuclear energy developments in the

1990s will thus demand a continued reliance on international nuclear safeguards and national export controls. Some of the developments cited earlier mean that safeguarding will face additional challenges. Continued work on more efficient isotope separation techniques will call for a continuing review of experiences gained in applying the Nuclear Suppliers Group guidelines. Extending the list of items triggering the application of IAEA safeguards to include those new technologies and equipments which also have applications in civil research and development programmes will be far from straightforward. The problem is that these technologies and equipments are unlikely to have unique properties allowing them to be distinguished from other technologies and equipments for which there would be a legitimate civil requirement.

It can be expected that the proliferation sensitivity of technologies and equipments will vary with time. For example, research facilities and light water power reactors producing low-grade plutonium may be regarded as increasingly sensitive if reprocessing and isotope separation technology demanding less expertise from the recipient becomes available. Such a development could lead to supplier controls to prevent misuse of exports taking on a more overtly subjective character. Increasing restraints will have to be applied to potential recipients whose commitment to international law is in doubt, despite their formal non-proliferation undertakings.

It also seems likely that there will be increasing pressure on some of the nuclear weapon states to accept the principle recognised by the Final Declaration of the 1985 NPT Review Conference that a nuclear weapon state's civil nuclear industry should be completely separated from any military use it makes of nuclear energy. The EURATOM distinction between safeguarded material and facilities for civil use and unsafeguarded ones for military use is probably more acceptable in the long term to the international community than the NPT's distinction between unsafeguarded nuclear weapon states and safeguarded non-nuclear ones. A change in the basis of NPT safeguards to conform to EURATOM principles might therefore be a valuable contribution to strengthening the international safeguards system.

NON-PROLIFERATION AND A COMPREHENSIVE NUCLEAR TESTING BAN

Although the vast majority of delegations which attended the 1985 NPT Review Conference were emphatic on the importance of negotiating a

CTBT in order to strengthen the non-proliferation regime, such a treaty seems increasingly unlikely to be negotiated despite the apparent support for it from the Soviet Union. Is, therefore, a CTBT likely to be an essential determinant of proliferation over the next few years?

A CTBT is more or less neutral to any national ambition to develop a primitive nuclear capability: this could be done without testing. Moreover, it would be counterproductive to any 'build down' as against a freeze of strategic nuclear offensive forces, for this would inevitably allow for some modernisation of delivery vehicles and a related evolution of warhead design. For there is no doubt that, at present, the complex processes found in the explosion of a multi-stage nuclear warhead cannot be simulated adequately on a computer or in laboratory experiments. In addition, there is no question that the confidence in the reliability of weapon design obtained by underground testing programmes is important to those given the task of advising political leaders in nuclear weapon states on the viability of stockpiles. Indeed the lack of such reassurances could enhance arguments for 'insurance through many', a familiar refrain in the context of the lack of any perfect solutions to other strategic defence requirements. A CTBT would certainly prevent the development of radically new strategic weapon designs, but that result could also be achieved by a treaty banning tests above a low yield, say 10 or 20 kilotons. Such a low-threshold treaty, if associated with on-site verification arrangements for measuring the yields of tests to an adequate accuracy, could be more acceptable and realisable than a CTBT.

CONCLUSIONS

It is not easy to draw any clear-cut conclusion on the implications of new technologies for the non-proliferation regime. On the one hand, the development of simpler methods for producing the special nuclear materials required for nuclear weapons and the diffusion of information on the design of weapons tend to make it easier for a non-nuclear weapon state to acquire an initial nuclear capability. On the other hand, developments in conventional defence equipment and the interest being shown by the nuclear weapon states in altering the balance between their nuclear and non-nuclear defence capabilities could discourage proliferation. Whatever the impact of new technology proves to be, it will be essential to continue to seek policies which will inhibit proliferation through national action and international cooperation and which will make it plain to would-be proliferators that proliferation would entail major costs.

NOTES

1. Directed energy weapons are designed to achieve their effect by projecting energy, normally generated by a laser or a particle beam system, onto their targets. Kinetic energy weapons intercept their targets with some form of missile or projectile, accelerated to high speed within the weapon system; a rail-gun, in which a projectile is accelerated to high speed within the weapon by an electromagnetic generator, is an example of a new type of these kinetic energy weapons.
2. These would include air-launched cruise missiles and ground launched cruise and ballistic missiles offering very high accuracies and a limited ability for an opponent to destroy them in flight.
3. Uranium, enriched in the isotope uranium-235, and/or plutonium with a high concentration of the isotope plutonium-239, are essential, for all practical purposes, for the manufacture of nuclear weapons. These materials do not occur in nature, although suitable plutonium can be made, at considerable expense, in specially operated nuclear reactors. They can also be produced by isotope separation processes using, as feed material, either uranium or plutonium in which the required isotope is found in inadequate concentration. Uranium and plutonium isotope separation has hitherto been difficult and costly, but the development of a laser separation process now promises a more attractive route. In this process, highly tuned laser radiation is used to excite preferentially a chosen uranium or plutonium isotope so that, thereafter, it can be distinguished from the other isotopes that are present and can be separated from them. Laser separation promises to be cheaper than the methods that have been used previously, such as gaseous diffusion and ultra high speed centrifuges, primarily because it demands only a relatively small electricity supply. It is also significant in the non-proliferation context because a laser plant could be built to any scale. To meet the relatively small demands of a would-be proliferating state it could be so compact that it would be relatively easily hidden.
4. These are also known as fission-fusion weapons because, in them, a fission device is used to initiate fusion reactions. The yield from the fusion reactions can, in turn, cause further fissions, in which case the weapon can be classed as a fission-fusion-fission device.
5. In an inertial confinement fusion system, targets containing fusion materials, such as deuterium and tritium, are compressed and heated by laser radiation or by particle beams to the point where fusion reactions are initiated. It is an alternative to the magnetic confinement route for generating energy from fusion reactions.

7 Strategic arsenals, arms control and nuclear disarmament in the 1990s

Steve Smith

INTRODUCTION

In the previous chapter, Dennis Fakely and Ronald Mason discussed the indirect nature of the links between the actions of the superpowers and nuclear proliferation. It seems obvious that what happens at the superpower level of international society will affect, as well as be affected by, events within and between other states in the international system. Unfortunately, it is very difficult to conceptualise this linkage. In the nuclear non-proliferation area this poses particularly acute problems because diplomats and politicians argue that there is a self-evident relationship between superpower behaviour, particularly their nuclear disarmament activities, and horizontal proliferation. They reinforce this assertion by the existence of references to both such activities in certain parts of the preamble of the NPT and in its Article VI.

Many factors will determine trends in superpower relations and yet it is impossible to say anything concrete about how these will interact. Among these factors are the outcome of the 1988 presidential election in the United States, the size of that country's federal budget deficit, the performance of the Soviet economy and the domestic security of the Gorbachev regime. For the future of United States–Soviet Union political relations will depend more on developments within these two countries than on events between them. Furthermore, the nature of the United States–Soviet Union political relationship is likely to be a determining factor in developments in weapons system deployment and arms control, rather than being determined by them. With these thoughts in mind, this chapter attempts to outline some parameters of the superpower strategic relationship in the 1990s and analyse their likely impact on the 1995 NPT Extension Conference. It will do this by concentrating on two main areas of United States–

Soviet Union strategic relations: developments in their strategic arsenals and the possibilities of nuclear arms control agreements between them. The starting-point for this analysis will be the identification of both the dominant trends of the nuclear age and the direction in which they are evolving.

TRENDS IN THE DEVELOPMENT OF SUPERPOWER STRATEGIC ARSENALS

Historically, a number of major trends can be identified in United States–Soviet Union weapons development. The two superpowers have been engaged in essentially the same set of developments in weapons systems since the 1950s, resulting in two associated phenomena. The first has been a built-in dampener on any possibility of one side achieving a breakthrough. The two sides' research programmes have been extensive and intensive enough to keep them broadly in step with one another. Not only has each side been working along similar lines, but each has also been working on the whole range of strategic systems. The end result has been an inter-relationship between their research, development and deployment activities that has effectively ruled out any sudden tactical, strategic and political breakthrough.

The second phenomenon has been that with the exceptions of the first test of an ICBM, the development of heavy ICBMs, and the deployment of the Galosh ABM system, the Soviet Union has followed rather than led United States weapons development. Within the United States there was a noticeable tendency to let technology drive procurement decisions, leading to a proliferation of weapons systems. The United States has thus basically dictated the direction of the development of superpower strategic weaponry.

There has also been a continued division of the two superpowers' strategic nuclear forces between land-based, sea-based and air-based platforms. This feature has often been portrayed as problematic, with each leg of this triad being threatened by imminent technological advances. Penetrability of bombers has been a constant issue in United States defence circles, and yet the use of bombers as platforms for Air Launched Cruise Missiles (ALCMs) has assured a continued role for this leg of the triad. Similarly, there have been periodic concerns over the vulnerability of ICBMs. In the late 1970s this led to a search for new basing modes for the United States MX ICBM, but eventually no alternative to placing them in existing, if superhardened, silos was found to be acceptable.[1] Finally, there has been

92

much talk about both the possibility of a breakthrough in anti-submarine warfare (ASW) technology and the inherent limitations of Submarine Launched Ballistic Missiles (SLBMs) for certain missions. Yet despite fears for the fragility of each of its legs, the triad has persisted as a central feature of both superpowers' arsenals.

One reason for this is that although the nuclear age has witnessed a constant tension between offensive and defensive systems, the dialectical dynamic between them has resulted from the pursuit of offensive counter-measures to overcome defensive innovations. The SDI is the single most important strategic issue in the mid-1980s precisely because it threatens to reverse this trend.

In many ways, the different force structures of the superpowers have been the most crucial feature influencing perceptions of vulnerability and weakness.[2] Whereas the United States has about 30% of its missile war-heads on land, and 70% at sea, the Soviet Union has about 73% on land and 27% at sea. This has led to very different ideas of what is stabilising and destabilising. The United States has some 1,020 land-based laun-chers, threatened by some 7,340 Soviet ICBM warheads, and this 6 to 1 ratio makes the American missiles appear very vulnerable to a first strike. Conversely, the relative invulnerability and accuracy of United States SLBMs poses a similar threat to the 1,398 Soviet ICBMs carrying 73% of their missile warheads. Given the natural tendency of each side to assume that the adversary's equipment will work perfectly and with great accu-racy, each side perceives the other's force structure as capable of inflicting enormous damage on their retaliatory forces and thus possessing pre-emptive capabilities, if not pre-emptive intentions.

These differences in force structure have caused considerable problems for nuclear arms limitation negotiations. This has been reinforced by the absence of agreement between the two superpowers on which strategic nuclear systems are most useful. These differences reflect their diverse conceptions of nuclear strategy. Much has been made of the convergence of the two sides' strategies in the early 1980s, though this perceived shift in United States thinking from a single massive countervalue response in the 1960s to a series of counterforce responses or pre-emptions in the mid-1980s may be misleading. The Soviet Union, despite its public statements renouncing the option of the first use of nuclear weapons, appears com-mitted to a strategy of pre-emption that has significant effects on the types of system it deploys. United States SLBMs, usually considered appropriate only for second strike countervalue purposes, have also begun to acquire a counterforce capability.[3] Whilst neither superpower is likely to base a pre-emptive counterforce attack upon the use of SLBMs, an overlap is developing between the legs of the triad in terms of their technical capabilities. This makes it dangerous to try to deduce strategic objectives from studies of force posture. Despite this development, however, a broad difference persists between the strategies of the superpowers, with the United States relying on deterrence by punishment and the Soviet Union deterrence by denial.

One technical trend in strategic weaponry that is nearing its theoretical limits is the steady increase in the accuracy of warheads. A circular error probable (CEP) of around 600 feet is now claimed for United States ICBM warheads compared with 5 miles in the early 1960s.[4] Estimates of the CEP of the MX and the Midgetman ICBMs are around 300 and 400 feet respectively. A similar, if lagged, trend can be observed from Soviet tests. This makes it possible for both states to consider targeting hardened silos and command facilities. Improvements of a similar magnitude have occurred with SLBM warheads, though these do not possess the same targeting flexibility as ICBM warheads.

Another major technical development has been the miniaturisation of nuclear warheads. This has been combined with the development of Multiple Independently Targeted Re-entry Vehicles (MIRVs) to produce systems mounting several warheads on a single missile. Soviet fractionation plus improvements in accuracy and the deployment by them of a large land-based missile force has created perceptions in the United States of ICBM vulnerability and has fuelled concern about pre-emption. The Soviet SS18 missile has been seen as particularly threatening as it could potentially carry up to thirty MIRVs, instead of the ten it was limited to under SALT II. This led in the late 1970s to proposals for making future ICBMs mobile and limiting them to a single warhead.

Despite the varying impact of technical developments on the two superpowers' nuclear arsenals, however, a continuing feature of their relationship has been the existence of strategic stability. In particular, overall assessments that it is in neither side's interests rationally to initiate nuclear hostilities have sustained crisis stability. Yet in the last decade there have been worrying signs that this evaluation might be subject to change, as improvements in accuracy and MIRVing have created perceptions of vulnerability and as the future extension of the arms race to space places increased reliance on fragile Command, Communication, Control and Intelligence (C^3I) systems. It is not difficult to imagine future scenarios where perceptions of C^3I vulnerability might lead to advice being given to leaders in a crisis that it would be better to go first than to go second. Moreover, any period of transition from an offence-dominated world to a defence-dominated one would probably be a most worrying time for crisis stability.

TRENDS IN ARMS CONTROL NEGOTIATIONS

Superpower arms control negotiations during the nuclear age appear to have been influenced by several main features.[5] The strategic arsenals of the two sides possess diverse technical attributes. Not only are they at different technological levels, although this is increasingly less so in certain areas, but they have changed at varying paces. This poses very obvious difficulties in placing any static controls, such as political agreements, on dynamic technological processes. The iron law of arms control seems to be to seek both to ban testing of anything you lead in and to stop the deployment of anything in which the other side is superior. Even with genuine intentions to reduce armament levels, negotiation would still be very difficult.

Each superpower has chosen to deploy its systems in unique ways and this has created very different notions of what is stabilising and destabilising and thus of priorities for reductions. These dissimilarities in force structure result from differences over politico-military objectives and strategies and together make agreements between the two superpowers complex and inherently difficult to achieve. If, of course, each state accepted a similar view of strategy this would make nuclear arms control much easier. The evidence is, however, that they do not, even though they might agree that nuclear war would involve mutual destruction. Accepting this as an outcome does not necessarily mean accepting Mutual Assured Destruction (MAD) as a policy. United States support for MAD is axiomatically related to its abilities to operate an SLBM force, whereas public Soviet reticence to accept MAD reflects their belief that a much broader military capability is the best deterrent.

Each side's differing force structure is reflected in the bureaucratic composition of their military organisations and arms control negotiating teams. The result is that different mind-sets emerge on what is the most pressing problem to be addressed and on which kinds of systems are most threatening. What to one side may appear unnecessary systems may to the other seem essential; what to one may appear strategically destabilising may to the other seem to reinforce stability.

A radically different feature of arms control negotiations has been domestic disagreements over objectives and tactics. Published studies of the negotiating history of SALT/START show that the most serious problems were within the United States national security community rather than between the two governments.[6] Similar information on the Soviet side is not available, although Garthoff's penetrating analysis of the Soviet military and SALT indicates precisely the same types of tension.[7] Each country contains military and political leaders whose bureaucratic position leads them to support certain kinds of force structures and specific weapons systems. This results in attempts to try and satisfy all the major parties in the domestic debate and explains why the SALT process was relatively conservative in terms of banning or limiting certain technologies and imposing force ceilings.

Additional problems are posed by differences in political perspectives. Within each superpower there exists differing perceptions of the intentions of the other state and how to deal with them. These internal differences may be equally as important in understanding the slow pace of SALT/ START as differences in the superpowers force structures and strategy.

Arms control agreements thus arise through a process of compromise between various national and intra-national preferences. In actual negotiations, it is common to see side A giving way on issue X in return for side B giving way over issue Y. The SALT I and II agreements were the results of complex bargaining within and between national delegations. Attacking the SALT/START process for failing to produce any purposive movement towards disarmament is thus to fundamentally misunderstand the negotiating process and its possibilities.

The different geopolitical settings of the two superpowers have also influenced nuclear arms control negotiations, in particular those concerning United States Forward-based Nuclear Systems (FBS). The critical geopolitical feature is the fact that the Soviet Union is part of Europe as a result of its geographic position whilst in the United States case it is through political choice. Thus United States FBS serve entirely different purposes to Soviet systems with similar capabilities; the former can hit the territory of the other superpower, the latter cannot. This has had a massive impact on the ability of these states to negotiate nuclear arms control agreements.

A further feature of the arms control environment is that whilst it was fashionable in the late 1960s and early 1970s to believe that arms control was the best way of enhancing security, this view was clearly less popular in the United States by the late 1970s. The major alternative, security through unrestrained modernisation of weapons systems, seems to have been preferred by President Reagan and has always been a very powerful strand in Soviet thinking.

Strategic nuclear arms control negotiations between the United States and the Soviet Union have thus been overwhelmingly political in character, and this has determined their outcomes. When United States–Soviet Union relations were cordial, then the types of compromises needed to deal with their different force structures, rates of modernisation and strategy could be achieved. The issues that held up SALT I and SALT II were not resolved by technical or philosophical discussion of stability or of disarmament strategies, but by old-fashioned political compromise. If political will is lacking, then arms control is very unlikely to be successful.

This review of the major features of the weapons strategy and arms control dimensions of United States–Soviet Union relations leads to two questions about the strategic and arms control setting of the mid-1990s: what will the two superpowers' strategic arsenals look like by that date and what are the possible arms control regimes for that period? For ease of analysis, these questions will be discussed separately.

THE NATURE OF THE UNITES STATES AND SOVIET STRATEGIC ARSENALS IN THE MID-1990S

Both quantitative and qualitative assessments can be made of the likely nature of United States and Soviet strategic arsenals in the mid-1990s. Both are heavily dependent on whether existing arms control agreements are sustained and negotiating proposals implemented. Four alternative visions of future force numbers can be envisaged.[8]

The first assumes continued compliance with SALT II. If both sides continued to abide by the main provisions of this Treaty, it would leave them in the mid-1990s with the forces listed in Table 3.[9]

Extension of SALT II would constrain the Soviet Union more than the United States, although both sides would have to reduce existing systems to stay within its limits. Additionally, each side would only be allowed one new ICBM system: the MX and the SS24. Deployment of the SS25 by the Soviet Union would not be permitted unless the United States accepted it as an allowed modification of the SS13. For this and other reasons the absence of qualitative controls on modernisation in SALT II probably works to United States advantage. In the early 1990s, however, a problem would arise over the Midgetman ICBM as the Treaty does not permit both it and the MX to be tested and deployed.

A second possibility assumes the termination of the United States–Soviet Union political commitment to continue to abide by the terms of SALT II. This could lead to the strategic forces listed in Table 4 being deployed by the mid-1990s.[10]

Table 3. *Superpower strategic forces in 1995 given continued compliance with the SALT II agreement*

System	United States	Soviet Union
ICBMs	914	1,394
ICBM warheads	2,542	7,146
SLBMs	736	714
SLBM warheads	7,760	3,530
Bombers without ALCMs	221	92
Bombers with ALCMs	120	50
Total bombers	341	142
Total bombers warheads	4,568	1,184
Total warheads	14,870	11,860

Table 4. *Superpower strategic forces in 1995 given no arms control constraints*

System	Unites States	Soviet Union
ICBMs	2,000	1,648
ICBM warheads	3,800	8,920
SLBMs	736	1,150
SLBM warheads	7,760	4,286
Bombers without ALCMs	120	143
Bombers with ALCMs	180	50
Total bombers	300	193
Total bomber warheads	4,560	1,286
Total warheads	16,120	14,492

These are very conservative estimates, since they assume that the pace of modernisation of United States–Soviet Union strategic forces continues at its current rate.

Alternatively, the arsenals could be based on a third possibility, an agreement based on Soviet ideals for a superpower arms control regime for the late 1980s. Mikhail Gorbachev outlined these on 3 October 1985. They included:

(1)   A 50% reduction in strategic launchers;
(2)   A maximum of 6,000 strategic warheads;
(3)   No more than 60% of these warheads to be on any one leg of the strategic triad;
(4)   A ban on long-range cruise missiles;
(5)   A ban on new types of missiles;
(6)   The termination of the United States SDI programme.

Two points are noteworthy about this proposal: first, it is, by Soviet standards, a very radical one, especially since it requires the Soviet Union to cut back its land-based ICBM warheads from 6,400 to 3,600. The second point is that it contains many features that make it unattractive to the United States. The most obvious is that it requires the halting of the SDI programme. There was also no commitment to reduce SS18 missile numbers, and thus the proposal did not address a major concern of the United States, that of strategic stability. In addition, given the Soviet definition of strategic warheads, the 6,000 figure would include those on short-range attack missiles and in gravity bombs based in Europe.

The United States responded with a proposal tabled on 1 November 1985 which constitutes the fourth possibility. This was based on four principles: deep cuts, no first-strike advantage, defensive research, and no cheating. Its main elements were:

(1) A maximum of 4,500 strategic warheads;
(2) A maximum of 3,000 warheads on ICBMs;
(3) A maximum throw-weight for each side of 50% of the existing Soviet figure;
(4) A maximum of 1,500 long-range ALCMs;
(5) Limitation of ICBMs to 1,250–1,450;
(6) A ban on the modernisation of existing heavy missiles and on the building of new ones;
(7) A ban on all mobile ICBMs;
(8) A limit on INF of the number deployed by the United States in Europe on 31 December 1985;
(9) The continuation of SDI research in 'open laboratories';
(10) A halt to Soviet actions impeding United States verification of arms control agreements and compliance with other aspects of existing agreements.

This proposal contained many features likely to make it unattractive to the other superpower, the most obvious being that it allowed the SDI to continue. It also involved a massive cut-back in Soviet missile throw-weight and a freeze in its heavy missile numbers. Although the two sides seemed close on the target figures for strategic warheads (6,000 v 4,500)[11] and ICBMs (3,600 v 3,000), they differed radically on the systems allowed within these limits.

Superpower nuclear arsenals in the mid-1990s could therefore range between the 6,000 warheads envisaged by the 1985 proposals and the 16,000 resulting from the abandonment of arms control agreements. How the figures at either end of this range might affect either the pace or the strategic consequences of horizontal proliferation is unclear. The only detailed exception is that if adoption of the Soviet proposals led to the withdrawal of most, if not all, United States warheads from West European territory, this could increase pressures for the strengthening of national nuclear forces in Europe and even for a West Germany nuclear capability.

Numbers, however, will be only one dimension of superpower strategic relations in the 1990s: another will be the attributes of the systems involved. It seems likely that in the mid-1990s the arsenals of the two superpowers will still contain systems covering all three areas of the triad. Whether the two sides have 6,000 or 16,000 warheads in their arsenals at that point, they will continue to place the bulk of their forces in different legs of the triad, with the United States relying most heavily on SLBMs and the Soviet Union on ICBMs. The only area of uncertainty is in the percentage of United States warheads on ALCMs: if a 6,000 warhead limit was accepted, the percentage of ALCMs in the American strategic arsenal would be larger than with a 16,000 warhead total.

Threats will, however, continue to exist to each of the legs of the triad. The main ones are improvements in air defences, which could lead to a degradation of the ability of the bomber forces of the two sides to penetrate to their targets; more effective ASW capabilities, which could undermine the role of SLBM forces as a second-strike guarantor of MAD and increased offensive missile accuracy, which could threaten to increase the vulnerability of silo-based ICBMs to attack.

Of these threats to the triad, the third is of greatest significance. Neither side plans to use its bombers in a way that will make them vulnerable to improvements in air defence, and an ASW breakthrough sufficient to make all SLBMs vulnerable seems unlikely by the mid-1990s. The threat to land-based missiles, however, was taken sufficiently seriously in the last years of the Carter administration for much effort to be expended on trying to find a less vulnerable basing mode for MX. The four trends comprising that threat were and are improvements in accuracy, increased MIRVing, the continued Soviet reliance on 'heavy' ICBMs, and the development of Manoeuvering Re-entry Vehicles (MARVs). The combination of developments in these four areas seems likely to result in *both* sides' land-based systems being much more vulnerable in the mid-1990s than is the case today. Of these trends the critical one is that of accuracy improvements. Perceptions of ICBM vulnerability do matter to politicians, however theoretical the calculations upon which they are based, and this can therefore be expected to affect strategic planning and crisis behaviour. Unfortunately, ICBMs have targeting capabilities that make it unthinkable that their vulnerability would lead to their removal from the superpower arsenals. It is this combination of vulnerability and military value of ICBMs that might cause serious problems for crisis stability.

This issue is linked to another relationship, that between offence and defence. The nuclear age has seen a constant struggle between offensive and defensive systems. The reaction to the possibility of a successful threat to the triad has been one of finding ways to defeat such challenges. Improved air defences have led already to the development of ALCMs, which do not require bombers to penetrate air defences. Enhancement of ASW capability has been countered by attempts to reduce submarine noise; perceptions of the increasing threat to ICBMs has resulted in increased silo hardening, development of mobile ICBMs, movement to single-warhead ICBMs and an increased counterforce capability for SLBMs.

Although little change can be expected in the relationship between offence and defence, it does seem likely that the next ten years will see a change in the nature of strategic stability, due to qualitative developments in weaponry posing serious problems for crisis stability. This arises from the threat to C^3I facilities and silos posed by the increasing accuracy of ICBMs. It is often thought that the destructive power of nuclear weapons prevents their use. But scenarios can be envisaged in which, just as in 1914, each side wrongly imputed an intention to pre-empt to the other and a leader might then think it was better to pre-empt than to be pre-empted. The MAD world of the 1960s and 1970s, with its absence of defensive systems and a low level of accuracy giving no incentive for pre-emption, may have been the safest of all nuclear worlds. All this might change in the 1990s, when each superpower seems certain to rely more and more on technological facilities to provide both military options and targeting information to leaders in a crisis.

When missiles were primarily targeted on cities, little updating of targeting information was needed: if the targets of the 1990s include mobile missiles, this capability is of critical importance. Moreover, the increasing sophistication of surveillance and warning systems creates a strategic environment in which non-human systems become more and more important in decision-making. The result is a situation in which each side's C^3I facilities are prime targets in any conflict. A curious circular process is then created in which the need for information to target such facilities leads to intelligence systems being deployed in several mediums that themselves become prime targets. This clearly has implications for crisis stability and the practice of imputing intentions to the behaviour of each side.

At the qualitative level the United States seems likely to continue to dominate strategic developments over the next decade. In most fields of technical development the United States is ahead of the Soviet Union by several years. Qualitative changes will thus reflect American views of the desired direction of weapons systems developments. The most obvious area for future technological development and competition is that associated with the SDI. The militarisation of space is probably going to be the linchpin of the whole question of strategic developments in the next decade. Space is militarised already through reliance on communications satellites and surveillance systems, but the next decade could witness a massive growth in these types of system.

By the mid-1990s, the fate of the United States SDI programme will have been determined: if it continues it threatens not only to produce a collapse of strategic arms control efforts and agreements but also to lead to a massive proliferation of offensive systems, given the strategic attractiveness of negating the SDI systems by saturation attacks. Yet even if the SDI is halted, space still seems set to become the arena for a superpower arms race because of increased reliance on space-based communications systems, which are vulnerable to anti-satellite (ASAT) technologies. At best, by the 1990s there may be a controlled proliferation of weapons systems into space; at worst it will host an unconstrained expansion of both offensive and defensive systems. The superpower arsenals look likely, therefore, to include an ASAT capability by the mid-1990s. They may also see deployments of the initial elements of the SDI and countervailing increases in offensive systems.

ARMS CONTROL REGIMES IN THE 1990S

Negotiation of a strategic arms control agreement along the lines of the superpowers' 1985 proposals would have a massive impact on the number of warheads deployed by either side by the mid-1990s. Unfortunately such an agreement seems very unlikely to be achieved. The most commonly cited reason for this is the SDI, yet there are other factors which also limit the chances of agreement. These factors, among others, contributed to the breakdown of the START negotiations and United States non-ratification of SALT II.

The major concern of the United States has always been to cut back or ideally eliminate Soviet 'heavy' missiles and reduce that state's ICBM force. The Soviets for their part have been concerned to limit United States FBS, such as Cruise and Pershing II, and to halt the deployment of long-range cruise missiles. It remains unclear how far the SDI is negotiable, what the Soviet Union would give up to halt it and when the SDI becomes unstoppable. Even if the SDI was not on the agenda, it would still be difficult for the two sides to reach agreement on an arms control regime.

The critical period for the future of the SDI and arms control looks like being 1987–90. The crucial determinant appears to be the outcome of the 1988 United States presidential election. If, despite the Gramm–Rudman amendment, the United States budget deficit really does get out of control or if a Democrat candidate reaches the White House, then the prospects for United States–Soviet Union strategic arms control will improve. If not, it may be impossible to prevent the development and deployment of the SDI systems and a potentially destabilising period of strategic transition seems likely to occur. In such a situation it will be very difficult to reach agreements on reducing nuclear stockpiles, as the systems under negotiation will be those that are of most use in overwhelming any defensive system, be it area-defence or point-defence.

CONCLUSIONS

In this chapter the changes that are most probable over the next decade in the areas of strategic weapons and arms control have been surveyed. The factors discussed above are the most likely variables in the strategic relationship between the two superpowers. The parameters of their relationship over the next decade are the dominance of nuclear weapons; the maintenance of the triad in the basing of these weapons; the drift towards more accurate systems and the militarisation of space. At the arms control level it looks unlikely that there will be any agreement to limit strategic systems unless the SDI is negotiable, and this in turn seems unlikely. Without such an agreement the number of warheads in the strategic arsenals seem likely to be some 50% larger in quantitative terms in the mid-1990s than in 1985 and crisis stability will decrease.

It must be reiterated, however, that the single biggest imponderable is the nature of United States–Soviet Union political relations. Arms control is the key determinant of the size of the superpowers' nuclear arsenals of the mid-1990s, but is itself dependent on the willingness of the superpowers to make concessions to obtain compromise agreements. Unless United States–Soviet Union relations improve it is difficult to imagine this occurring. The most likely source of such improvement may be changes in the United States domestic political environment. The perception of the Soviet Union held by the winners of the 1988 and 1992 presidential elections will be crucial in this process. The paradox, of course, is that this may largely be an unintended result of elections fought over mainly domestic, primarily economic, issues. Thus arms control, and hence the size of the strategic arsenals of the superpowers in the mid-1990s, may be crucially dependent on the success or failure of Reaganite economics. The qualitative evolution of the arsenals, however, will be largely independent of those factors.

These complex linkages between arms control, weapons systems and domestic politics at the superpower level are paralleled by similar ones in the area of nuclear proliferation. Challenges to the conventional wisdom that proliferation is 'bad'[12] are mirrored by the need to reflect on whether superpower proliferation actually impacts significantly on horizontal proliferation. Although William Epstein has argued persuasively that continued superpower vertical proliferation undermines the non-proliferation regime,[13] this may not be the major determinant impelling states to acquire nuclear weapons at some future date. To assess the effect of superpower weapons development on nuclear proliferation, conventional arsenals rather than nuclear ones ought perhaps to be examined, since these affect regional balances of power and influence perceptions of the value of going nuclear. What is clear, however, is that the superpower weapons development and arms control environments influence the *context* of proliferation. It is more difficult to maintain a strict nuclear non-proliferation regime if the superpowers continue to act as if the development of additional, and more sophisticated, weapons systems increases their security. The linkage is, therefore, not obvious, nor is it direct.

NOTES

1. For a discussion of the window of vulnerability issue, see S. Smith, 'MX and the Vulnerability of American Missiles' *ADIU Report* 4 (1982), 1–5.
2. For details see John Collins, *US/Soviet Military Balance: Statistical Trends, 1975–1984* (Washington, Congressional Research Service, report no 85–83F, 1985).
3. Although much is made of this in the literature [see, for example, John Aldridge *First Strike* (Boston, South End Press, 1983) Ch.3] it is by no means clear that SLBM warheads are suitable for counterforce targeting.
4. Strictly speaking, CEP is not a measure of accuracy, but a measure of precision. Accuracy is composed of two separate measures, CEP and bias. The former measures the radius of the circle of impact points, the latter the relationship between the centre of this circle and the target. See S. Smith, 'Problems of Assessing Missile Accuracy' *RUSI Journal* 130 (1985), 35–40.
5. The section that follows is based on part of S. Smith, 'US–Soviet Strategic Nuclear Arms Control: from SALT to START to Stop', *Arms Control* 5 (1984), 50–74.
6. John Newhouse, *Cold Dawn: The Story of SALT* (New York, Holt, Rinehart and Winston, 1973); Strobe Talbott, *Endgame – the Inside Story of SALT II* (New York, Harper & Row, 1980); Strobe Talbott, *Deadly Gambits* (New York, Knopf, 1984).
7. Raymond Garthoff, 'The Soviet Military and SALT', in J. Valenta and W. Potter (eds.) *Soviet Decision-Making for National Security* (London, Allen & Unwin, 1984), pp. 135–61.
8. Such options are discussed in Harold Brown and Lynn Davis *Nuclear Arms Control*

Choices (Boulder, Colo., Westview Press, 1984); Congressional Budget Office *Modernizing U.S. Strategic Offensive Forces: The Administration's Program and Alternatives* (Washington, Government Printer Office, 1985); Gil Klinger 'Strategic Nuclear Weapons and Superpower Arms Control', in W. Goldstein (ed.) *Fighting Allies* (London, Pergamon-Brassey's, 1986): see also *Aviation Week and Space Technology* 122 (18 March 1985), 27–9.

9. These figures are derived from the tables presented in Brown and Davis, *Nuclear Arms Control Choices*, pp. 8–15.

10. Figures based on Brown and Davis, *Nuclear Arms Control Choices* and Congressional Budget Office projections in *Modernizing U.S. Strategic Offensive Forces*.

11. In fact the warhead totals are identical, since the US offer calls for a maximum of 4,500 on missiles plus 1,500 on ALCMs; the Soviet offer has a single total of 6,000 for missiles, with long-range ALCMs banned.

12. See, most infamously, Kenneth Waltz, *The Spread of Nuclear Weapons: More May Be Better* (London, IISS, 1981); also see the discussions in Dagobert Brito, Michael Intriligator and Adele Wick (eds.), *Strategies for Managing Nuclear Proliferation* (Lexington, Mass., Lexington Books, 1983).

13. William Epstein, 'A Critical Time for Nuclear Non-Proliferation' *Scientific American*, vol. 253 (August 1985), 3–9.

Part 3: Options for strengthening the non-proliferation regime

Overview

In the period through to 1995, much thought will be given to policies and initiatives aimed at supplementing and enhancing the existing nuclear non-proliferation regime. Such policies will have a number of objectives including smoothing the path to a prolonged extension of the NPT by increasing the commitment of existing parties to the Treaty; attracting new parties to it, particularly states with unsafeguarded nuclear facilities; deterring non-nuclear weapon states from publicly declaring their nuclear weapon status and making it as difficult as possible for such states to acquire unsafeguarded materials and facilities. During the 1970s policies were largely aimed at creating a regime whose rules both had universalist application and could be implemented unilaterally by the main supplier states: in the 1990s the requirement seems to be to devise means of supplementing those rules with particularist, regionally based policies while yet sustaining a universalist framework for the regime.

The three chapters in Part 3 approach these issues from different directions. In Chapter 8, Lewis Dunn argues a case for strengthening existing policies, rather than embarking on radically new ones. He sees a need to expand existing efforts at export control to include key components necessary for nuclear weapon manufacture and nuclear delivery systems, particularly ballistic missiles. He also envisages a major effort to devise procedures to handle the use of plutonium as a fuel. But it is in the area of regional arrangements that he sees most potential, while at the same time recognising that although some potential proliferators can be dealt with by this method, it is not applicable to others. Dunn sees little value in politically symbolic gestures such as instituting a comprehensive safeguards regime for civil facilities in nuclear weapon states, but argues for advance planning to coordinate international responses to non-proliferation events.

In Chapter 9, Harald Müller examines in considerable depth the argument that amending the NPT would strengthen the regime, but concludes that in all cases except inspection on challenge the necessary changes can be made without changing the Treaty. Indeed, the core of the complaints about the Treaty concern its implementation rather than its content. He examines means of preventing defections from the Treaty and bringing new parties into it, concluding that only a limited number of states are potential defectors from the Treaty, and that their motivation would mainly arise out of local or regional conflicts. He agrees with Dunn that the central policy challenge for the future is how to construct a regime in which a universalist core is integrated with mechanisms of a more limited and regional nature, aimed at dealing in a tailored way with specific, often local, motivations to proliferate.

Chapter 10 sees Philip Gummett examining the delicate question of whether policies could be devised to influence directly and indirectly both the motivations of states to proliferate and their decision-taking systems. He suggests that subtle influence may be acquired if externally orientated technical elites are in existence or can be created, but acknowledges that one of the major problems in this area is both understanding the nature of state decision-making processes and gaining access to the relevant decision-takers. He echoes Aswini Ray in Chapter 4 in discussing the role of Western-educated military and technical elites in this process, and also raises the disturbing question of how the international system of the 1990s could cope with the acquisition of military nuclear propulsion systems by non-nuclear weapon states. Gummett's overall conclusion is very similar to that of Dunn and Müller: that the need is for policies involving a judicious mixture of universal rules and judging each case on its merits. This appears to apply particularly to attempts to influence internal debates within states which are potential nuclear proliferators, for whether active intervention is likely to be effective or counter-productive will be heavily dependent upon the circumstances of the specific case and time. Overall, the judgement of all three authors is that although there is scope for some innovation at the margin prior to 1995, the main requirement is to sustain existing structures rather than engage in a wholesale rebuilding exercise.

8 Non-proliferation policies in 1995, or plus ça change...

Lewis Dunn

INTRODUCTION

By the mid-1990s, more than a half-century will have passed since the initial development and only use of nuclear weapons. Many of the central institutions designed to prevent the global spread of these weapons, and to facilitate the use of the atom for peaceful purposes, such as the International Atomic Energy Agency (IAEA), the Nuclear Suppliers guidelines, a strong set of Western alliances and the Nuclear Non-Proliferation Treaty (NPT) will be mature. What types of problems will confront these non-proliferation institutions? Can they meet those challenges, or will adaptations to them, if not completely new approaches, be needed? What surprises could occur, and how would non-proliferation policy be affected?

A 'SURPRISE-FREE' PROJECTION OF 1995

Any attempt to 'predict' the political and technical environment which will confront policy-makers ten years hence is fraught with dangers. Recent history is littered with predictions that went awry, whether of an 'invincible OPEC cartel'; of Soviet unwillingness to resume arms control talks while the United States was deploying its intermediate range missiles in Europe; of the unassailable power of the Shah of Iran; or of Egyptian unwillingness to make a separate peace with Israel. Nonetheless, there are certain political and technical developments whose occurrence would not be surprising between now and the mid-1990s. An understanding of these is the backdrop to any discussion of broader policy matters.

Despite periods of relative calm, conflict and tension is likely to continue to dominate the political climate of many regions. The prospect of large-scale warfare will remain close to the surface in the Middle East and the

Persian Gulf, and may erupt into limited military action on occasions. Terrorism can be expected to remain an instrument both of states and of radical groups throughout this region. Elsewhere, the long-standing clash between India and Pakistan may be tempered somewhat, and recent steps by Argentina and Brazil to mute their traditional political competition probably will continue. But in both cases, past suspicions, if not old disputes, may sour moves to better relations.

At the same time, there is little reason to expect an erosion of United States alliances with Europe, Japan, and South Korea, which will continue to provide needed stability and security in these regions. In parallel, European countries and Japan will probably play an increasingly active and independent global political role.

The basic pattern of United States-Soviet Union relations is likely to remain one of competition more than cooperation. But both superpowers will continue to stress their commitment to reduce the role of nuclear weapons in that relationship and some limited but significant arms control agreements may have been reached to advance that goal. By contrast, there is unlikely to be agreement on a comprehensive ban on the testing of nuclear weapons, a measure called for by many countries over the years.

Considerable continuity is likely to be found in the politics of non-proliferation in the mid-1990s. The overall number of NPT parties will continue to rise in the decade ahead, as evidenced by the decisions of North Korea, Spain and Malawi to adhere to the Treaty since the 1985 Review Conference. But with isolated exceptions, the chances are not good that today's hard-core holdouts will change their posture between now and 1995.

The well-known set of so-called problem countries is unlikely to change much, if at all, in the years to come. This group will continue to include six to eight countries that are thought to be weighing the pros and cons of acquiring nuclear weapons and/or that already have, or are moving rapidly towards operation of, significant unsafeguarded nuclear facilities. But new candidates to add to these 'usual suspects' are hard to identify. More important, there is a very good chance that in the decade ahead no additional country will detonate a nuclear explosive device and openly become the next nuclear weapon state. It may prove very difficult, however, to prevent one or more countries from covertly coming increasingly close to that threshold.

Turning to the technical dimension, there is every reason to expect that by the mid-1990s the number of countries with a capability to design and build the facilities needed for a nuclear explosives programme, once a decision has been made to devote scarce resources to that objective, will have grown further. This will inexorably result from the processes of industrial development and global technological change, which will make it increasingly difficult to contain what by then will be a very old technology.

By the mid-1990s, the capabilities in chemical processing, metallurgy, materials handling, engineering, machining and theoretical and practical physics that were at the forefront of scientific discovery in 1943 will be within reach of dozens of countries. Already Pakistan claims to have the technology for centrifugal enrichment of uranium, Argentina to have mastered the process of enriching uranium by gaseous diffusion and India is operating a plutonium reprocessing plant. Thus technical constraints will continue to be a declining obstacle and new technological breakthroughs in the enrichment area could speed up this process.

As a result of these on-going processes of industrialisation and economic change, the problem countries generating most concern could alter. With the passage of another decade, one or more countries which now are relatively underdeveloped technically and industrially could effectively implement plans or aspirations to develop nuclear weapons.

On the supply front, cohesion among major nuclear suppliers, as measured by adherence to the existing guidelines and resistance to pressures to use less rigorous safeguards conditions or transfers of sensitive technology as commercial sweeteners, probably will remain the rule. Some 'grey market' purchases will possibly slip through the international export control network, however, despite conscious efforts by nuclear suppliers to control exports to countries of proliferation concern. In particular, controlling dual-use items that have both legitimate civilian and military nuclear uses will pose continued problems. And the readiness of the emerging nuclear suppliers such as Argentina, Brazil, India, Yugoslavia and others to hold off cooperation in sensitive areas could be tested.

Finally, judging by current plans, there may be more extensive use by the mid-1990s of plutonium as a civilian nuclear fuel for breeders or for recycle in light water reactors in Europe and Japan. One or two developing countries, including some of proliferation concern such as India, are currently moving in that direction also. Other developing countries, with advanced nuclear power programmes, such as South Korea, may also seek to use plutonium for these purposes. Such use of plutonium will place added burdens on physical protection procedures for its international shipment and provide new challenges for IAEA safeguards on facilities that process and use it.

OLD WINE IN OLD BOTTLES

Within this basic political and technical environment, non-proliferation policy in the mid-1990s will still concentrate on three major lines of activity: measures to make it technically harder for a country to acquire nuclear explosives; steps to reduce incentives to try to do so; and institution-building. As a result, no 'great leaps forward' should be envisaged and the basic core of policy will remain relatively unchanged.

Despite the decreasing impact of technical measures, they will still be important in making it as hard as possible for a country to acquire nuclear weapons. It will be essential to sustain frequent consultations among nuclear suppliers in order to maintain support for their cooperation and to ensure that existing guidelines and norms are followed; to coordinate supplier efforts to head off specific exports to countries of proliferation concern; and to take multilateral steps to upgrade export control procedures to keep pace both with changing technology and with new ways of evading the system. Such measures can buy time for more political efforts to take effect or for other changes, such as the emergence of new leaders, to occur.

Politically, efforts to preserve and strengthen Western and United States alliances and security ties will remain vital to check motivations for acquiring nuclear explosives in Western Europe and Asia. There also will be demand for an active diplomacy to lessen regional tensions and reduce other motivations to acquire nuclear explosives.

Institution-building in all of its facets, however, will be perhaps the most essential part of the basic policy approach, especially in the light of the weakened impact of technical constraints. Support for a strong and effective International Atomic Energy Agency (IAEA) will continue to be a buttress of non-proliferation. The IAEA's safeguards system can provide confidence that a country is committed only to the peaceful uses of nuclear energy, whereas the presence of unsafeguarded activities will continue, as now, to sow suspicion and discord. The risk that misuse of peaceful nuclear assistance will be detected also can help to tip the balance against a weapons option.

To ensure the continued effectiveness of IAEA safeguards, however, still more stress will have to be placed on the political benefits they provide to all states and on the need of all states to cooperate to facilitate the job of the Agency. Without strong political support, the Agency cannot do its job. In addition, continuous informal discussions among key technology holders and between them and the Agency's experts on the safeguards requirements for future facilities using plutonium will need to be brought to a successful conclusion. More broadly, the credibility of safeguards will depend, as now, on their vigilant application by the Agency and on the steady improvement of safeguards technology.

An equally important element of the basic non-proliferation strategy will continue to be support for the NPT. With over 130 parties, it provides the confidence that countries will not seek nuclear explosives, helping thereby to check the political pressures and suspicions that can lead countries in that direction. The NPT also supports the safeguards system, which is vital to international confidence, and is a key legal underpinning to nuclear supplier undertakings. Most important, the Treaty symbolises the norm of non-proliferation, creating a perception around the world that it is no longer legitimate to acquire nuclear weapons and that a world of dozens of nuclear weapons states is not only undesirable but avoidable. As such, it helps to increase the political costs of decisions to acquire nuclear weapons, and affects the thinking of countries weighing that option.

Focusing attention on the Treaty's security benefits not only to its parties but to all countries will still be essential in support of NPT. It can be strengthened by continuing to give preference in peaceful nuclear cooperation to parties to the Treaty and by achieving greater success in pursuing the NPT's aim of movement towards a world without nuclear weapons. Although it will become increasingly difficult to convince additional countries to adhere to it as the number of holdouts steadily shrinks, efforts to make the Treaty universal a decade hence must continue. In this sense, as well, much of non-proliferation policy in all probability will comprise old wine in old bottles.

ADAPTATION AND INNOVATION

Within this basic pattern of continuity, however, there is likely to be some adaptation of existing approaches and possibly some innovations to deal with the political and technical environment of the mid-1990s. The adaptations are beginning to take shape now, with several of them entailing 'political' measures to compensate for the longer-term reduction in impact of technical constraints.

By the mid-1990s, so-called emerging nuclear suppliers such as Argentina, Brazil, China, India, South Korea, and Yugoslavia are likely to play an increasing role in the nuclear export market. This will make it important to intensify the dialogue with them in order both to justify the existing nuclear supply norms and to urge these countries not to undercut them. This can partly take place through bilateral discussions between old and new suppliers, but it also may be desirable to explore multilateral methods of facilitating exchanges on these issues among all suppliers.

Some adaptation of major suppliers' efforts to prevent proliferation also is likely to be needed by the 1990s, in response to the increasing difficulties of keeping pace with the spread of technical knowledge and capability to make nuclear weapons. Currently, these efforts have focused on preventing a country acquiring the nuclear weapons material needed for a bomb by stressing, for example, restraint in the export of sensitive reprocessing or enrichment facilities. But as this hurdle of access to nuclear weapons material becomes easier to cross for more countries, supplier controls on key components and items needed for a weapons programme will grow in importance. This will require identification of these items, and international co-operation to control exports of them. In that regard, it will remain important to encourage all suppliers to adopt uniform interpretations of the overall international understandings and to put in place the domestic laws and procedures necessary to implement them. Since many of these components have dual uses, it will be especially important to pay careful attention to the types of end-users involved.

Closely related to this is the need for an international regime to govern exports of space and missile technology. Already, many problem countries have access to advanced high-performance aircraft that can be used to deliver nuclear weapons. Access to missiles would increase significantly the military threat posed by a nuclear force. Steps toward such a control regime would include agreement on the key expert items to be controlled and on procedures governing trade in them.

Another task for the years ahead will be to put in place a set of bilateral and multilateral procedures and norms to govern the use of plutonium as a civilian nuclear fuel. In part, this will require the design and effective implementation by the IAEA of safeguards approaches for fuel fabrication and reprocessing facilities that handle plutonium in bulk. Physical protection and security measures will also need to keep pace with growing numbers of intra-state and international shipments of plutonium and mixed oxide fuels. Norms of behaviour for the use of plutonium fuels outside of Europe and Japan are likely to be difficult to evolve, particularly if their potential sale to countries with advanced peaceful nuclear programmes but in sensitive regions is at issue. Should such use of plutonium prove economic, which is highly uncertain, it may be desirable to arrange for the latter countries to exchange their spent fuel and its plutonium content for new low-enriched uranium fuel from Europe or Japan. This would permit any benefits to be reaped from such use but would check proliferation risk. International mechanisms for storage of separated plutonium could play a role in the latter also, including possible establishment of international plutonium storage on a regional or sub-regional basis.

Turning to more political and institutional adaptations, in recent years India and Pakistan on the one hand and Argentina and Brazil on the other have begun to explore steps towards mutually agreed arrangements for nuclear restraint. In both cases what is under discussion is not the grafting onto a region or relationship of a global or even an overall regional approach, such as adherence to the NPT or to the Treaty of Tlatelolco in Latin America, but an effort to tailor the bilateral arrangements to the specific situation. Underlying that effort is the belief of the countries themselves that mutual nuclear restraint would serve their own security interests. It also entails a recognition that a key to restraint is greater confidence that neither side will obtain a unilateral preponderance in this area.

In the coming years, more thought should be given to the details of such regional or sub-regional arrangements and their implementation. This will entail addressing questions such as:

what types of safeguards or reciprocal inspections of nuclear facilities could provide and enhance needed confidence?
Could unilateral national pledges play a role even without precise verification?
What should be restrained in such arrangements?
Are there ways, ranging from diplomatic support to providing technical input on verification, for outsiders to support steps towards regional nuclear restraint, recognising that the influence of outsiders is, at best, limited and, at worst, might backfire?
How can we ensure that such sub-regional or regional approaches reinforce rather than undermine the more global measures?

Although it should be possible to head off additional overt nuclear proliferation, it may be impossible to prevent some additional countries from acquiring all the technical elements needed to make nuclear weapons in the 1990s. Both the weakening of technical constraints and the prospect of continued regional political tensions point in that direction. If this occurs, diplomatic and political pressures to raise the costs of open nuclear weapons activities will be especially important, as will steps to strengthen the norm of non-proliferation.

To compensate for this spread of technical capabilities, still more attention will have to be paid in the 1990s to ways of strengthening internal restraints and domestic opposition to acquisition of nuclear explosives. Past experience indicates that diplomatic approaches, though important, have the greatest impact when they reinforce serious internal disagreement about the nuclear weapons option. At the same time, too activist an attempt to support domestic opponents, leading to charges of outside meddling, could prove counterproductive.

Balancing these considerations, public diplomacy could emphasise the risks of acquisition of nuclear weapons and the problems that this step would raise for their new possessors. In some cases, building up a commercial sector interested in peaceful uses of nuclear energy might help to create an 'in-house' institutional counterweight to a nuclear weapons programme, particularly if it were made clear that peaceful nuclear cooperation with others required effectively renouncing nuclear weapons. Significant progress towards the goal of reductions of superpower nuclear weapons, while not affecting more basic regional security calculations, also could change the climate for decisions to acquire the bomb. Each of these elements would serve to raise the threshold of motivation needed to outweigh the greater costs of such a decision.

An extended and enhanced United States–Soviet Union non-proliferation dialogue also might buttress future non-proliferation efforts. The two sides have met for several years on average once every six months to review the overall non-proliferation situation, including export controls, safeguards, NPT and problem country issues. These discussions have provided an opportunity to identify problems and issues on which the two sides could work in parallel for solutions consistent with their shared non-proliferation objectives. In the next decade, these discussions could begin, as needed, to think about ways to ensure that any proliferation crises could be resolved without leading to a United States–Soviet Union confrontation. To that end, simply exchanging views on such potential situations would be an initial helpful step that could lessen chances of later miscalculation. Though more desirable, discussions of parallel action to defuse potential proliferation crises are likely to be limited by the divergent interest of the two sides in many regions.

Continued steps also will be in order to convince other countries to take a more active political role in preventing the spread of nuclear weapons. Here, too, the purpose would be to compensate politically for the changed technical environment. Specifically, the European countries and Japan already strongly support the varied multilateral supplier initiatives designed to make it harder for a country to acquire a nuclear weapons capability. Some, such as the United Kingdom, now use their political and diplomatic weight to encourage nuclear restraint through efforts to increase the political costs of decisions to acquire nuclear weapons or to contain moves in that direction. Others could more actively take a similar role. This might take the form of bilateral exchanges with key problem countries or through statements at periodic gatherings of Western political leaders.

'RED HERRINGS' OR NEW INITIATIVES TO AVOID

Some new initiatives that have been proposed would not help to prevent the spread of nuclear weapons. These range from calls to amend the NPT to proposals that the IAEA become more actively involved in international nuclear disarmament efforts. These suggestions are 'red herrings' and should not divert attention and energies from real non-proliferation measures.

Suggestions made to amend the NPT risk damaging if not destroying the Treaty with little chance of gaining the positive pay-off promised. The NPT is a careful balance of articles and obligations. Once one set of proposed changes is made, more amendments will be sought to 'balance' those already made or to fix new 'problems'. The resultant reopening of key compromises in the Treaty would replace strong support for the existing document with divisive bickering over changes acceptable to some but not to others. Moreover, seeking to change the NPT to make it more attractive to the hard-core holdouts would undermine its most basic elements. These countries oppose the NPT's emphasis on preventing the spread of nuclear explosives, not simply nuclear weapons, and refuse to accept FSS on their peaceful nuclear activities. Finally, these countries propose that there be no limits whatsoever on the transfer of sensitive enrichment and reprocessing technologies. Thus the key to the extension of the NPT in 1995 is not to try to amend it, but to work to ensure both greater progress towards all of its goals and a greater understanding that, despite its limitations, the Treaty is vital for all countries' security.

Another idea which has received attention recently is that the IAEA should be required to safeguard all peaceful nuclear activities in nuclear weapons states. Each of the nuclear weapons states already has accepted safeguards on a voluntary basis, even though the terms of their respective voluntary offers differ. The United States and the United Kingdom have placed all of their peaceful nuclear facilities on a 'list' from which the IAEA itself selects a limited number to safeguard. The Soviet Union and the

IAEA have agreed on specific types of facilities that the IAEA may select to safeguard, while France has specified facilities for safeguards. China has also made a voluntary offer. The nuclear weapons states have shown their readiness to accept some safeguards by these offers and have also provided useful experience for the IAEA.

However, to require the IAEA to apply safeguards at the more than 250 peaceful nuclear facilities in these states would increase significantly the safeguards budget, probably doubling it. Moreover, because there is an attempt to maintain some equivalency between the safeguards budget and that for technical assistance, safeguarding all peaceful nuclear facilities in nuclear weapons states would also require significant increases in technical assistance. More fundamentally, since these countries already possess nuclear weapons, to require safeguards in these nuclear states facilities would not have a decisive non-proliferation pay-off.

Another notion that risks damaging the IAEA's non-proliferation and peaceful uses mission is for the IAEA to become more actively involved in international nuclear disarmament efforts. This is not to say that the significant experience that the Agency has had in verifying national commitments concerning the use of nuclear facilities through its safeguards system does not offer valuable guidelines for the future. But one of these is that the effectiveness of IAEA safeguards is increased greatly when there is strong political cooperation from the inspected state, a condition that cannot be assumed in the disarmament area. Moreover, for the IAEA actually to take a more active role within this field would absorb scarce managerial resources which could be more effectively used to contribute to global peace in their current safeguards role. Not least, such involvement would risk politicising the Agency and bringing it for the first time into the middle of potentially damaging East–West controversy over compliance with arms control agreements. As a result, support for the Agency would drop and its effectiveness would be greatly reduced.

SURPRISES – AND POSSIBLE CONSEQUENCES

In thinking about non-proliferation policy in the mid-1990s, events that are unpredictable but might occur should not be overlooked. These could significantly affect the scope and character of any future policy initiatives.

A nuclear test by a current non-nuclear weapon state, overt deployment of nuclear weapons by such a country, or even use of nuclear weapons by a new nuclear power all would be profound shocks to the existing regime. In their aftermath, there most certainly would be a period of intense concern about non-proliferation, similar to that after India's 1974 nuclear test. Such an environment could enable agreement to be reached on some long-standing but contentious non-proliferation initiatives, such as FSS as a condition of supply, and increasing diplomatic pressures to defuse still other non-proliferation problems. Depending on the surprise, it also might give impetus to efforts in other regions to achieve mutual nuclear restraint. If the international response to such a shock was weak, however, that could undermine the norm of non-proliferation and lead countries to reassess the costs of acquiring a nuclear arsenal. Thus, it is important to give some thought in advance as to how best to use such a shock to strengthen non-proliferation efforts; it also will be absolutely essential not to become disillusioned after such a shock about the chances of preventing still more proliferation.

Still another surprise would be the loss of a national non-proliferation commitment, such as violation or abrogation of safeguards or of the NPT. Here, too, the shock could generate pressures for specific non-proliferation initiatives. If it involved violation of an agreement, such a development could provide the impetus for setting up some sort of international non-proliferation sanctions system. If the violation was of a safeguards commitment, the system's credibility would be either enhanced or undermined depending on how well it had worked in detecting it.

On the energy front, unexpected events could include the complete collapse in the price of oil or its take-off once again, a major loss of life in a nuclear accident involving plutonium, or a change of public attitude in the United States and other democracies towards the return of spent nuclear fuel. By influencing the context of decisions on the nuclear fuel-cycle, these events could have different but significant non-proliferation implications. Increases in the price of oil could revive prospects for nuclear power exports, but without producing excessive competition. A major accident involving the use of plutonium could produce so much opposition to that fuel that the once-through fuel-cycle could come to be seen as the only safe and politically acceptable approach to nuclear power generation. And greater readiness to take back spent fuel could help long-standing proposals for international spent fuel storage, and thus reduce demands in certain countries for reprocessing.

Important, but unlikely, political changes also should not be overlooked. A Middle East peace breakthrough, comparable to the Israel–Egypt peace treaty, would help to reduce the risks of proliferation in that region. Conversely, another India–Pakistan war would have the opposite impact. A major terrorist incident involving seizure of a shipment of plutonium would, at the very least, force a major shake-up of physical protection and transportation procedures for that material. It might even lead to a reassessment of the risks of using plutonium for civilian purposes, and to a discussion of whether the United States should give additional consents to reprocessing of material it controlled.

It would be foolhardy to try to assess the relative chances that one or another specific surprising event might occur or to specify its consequences. What can be said with some confidence, however, is that some such surprise will occur, and that it will significantly affect global non-proliferation efforts. Past history shows that only too well.

CONCLUSIONS

In the mid-1990s, the basic thrust of international non-proliferation policy is likely to remain much as it is now. Though that policy will have to adapt to changing circumstances and assimilate some new initiatives, its overall contours will probably look quite familiar. Similarly, the fundamental commitment to preventing any additional countries from acquiring nuclear explosives will remain the guiding objective. But it also is likely that one or another surprising event will occur. What these events are, and how nations will respond to them, has the potential greatly to affect the specifics of non-proliferation policy a decade hence.

9 Smoothing the path to 1995: amending the Nuclear Non-Proliferation Treaty and enhancing the regime

Harald Müller

INTRODUCTION

It is not hard to find reasons for seeking a new and better Non-Proliferation Treaty. Almost every serious analysis of non-proliferation over the last decade or so has found some fault with it. The staunchest United States supporters of non-proliferation policies, particularly those in Congress, criticise the Treaty for not really preventing or impeding proliferation in the physical sense, for not being universal, and for not addressing the issue of clandestine facilities.[1] By contrast, those from, or sympathetic to, the developing world complain about its inherently discriminatory character. Widespread and diverse pressures thus support the idea of improving the Treaty by amending it if an opportunity to do this can be created in the context of the Extension Conference in 1995.

There is, however, one powerful argument for leaving the NPT in its current form: it exists, and it has survived for some fifteen years despite its shortcomings. The 'power of fact' argues for caution in attempting to change it without the certainty of getting a substitute, or of only attempting to change it by deleting existing elements and not replacing them. Such a philosophy may be an unconvincing excuse for a lack of creativity and foresight on the part of this author. Yet any consideration of changing a regime should seek to build up the existing structure rather than risk destroying it.

The following pages will therefore discuss some possible changes to the NPT and some deletions from it which might be thought to improve the present situation. In addition, one implicit proposition put forward by some of the most zealous supporters of non-proliferation policies is explicitly dismissed, namely that the goal of any regime should be to prevent, in all possible cases, the emergence of new nuclear powers. Such a policing regime could exist only in a world with universal government: the current world is one of nation states. In this world, regimes exist and are robust only to the degree that sovereign nations decide it is in their best interests to accede and to stick to them. This must be borne in mind if regime changes and ways to achieve them are being discussed.

What, then, should be the main goals to be sought in any attempt to improve the non-proliferation regime and thus strengthen the Treaty? Three such goals are conceivable: to make the Treaty meet its objectives more efficiently; to prevent defections; and to attract new parties. By and large, the last two goals rely on the same measures; concerns which might cause defections are much the same as those motivating abstentions, and incentives to stay within the Treaty should be equally powerful attractions to accede. For this reason, these two goals will be dealt with together.

The following sections will analyse, step by step, the major possibilities for achieving all these goals by changes in the regime supporting the NPT. The probability of defections and accessions will then be examined, and the efficiency of the proposed changes assessed. The final paragraph will then try to explore the nature of the non-proliferation regime and to suggest ways of improving it other than through amending the NPT.

ENHANCING EFFICIENCY

The existing safeguards structure, while highly valuable, is deficient in several respects. Correcting these deficiencies would greatly strengthen the non-proliferation regime. Delays in the introduction of state of the art monitoring equipment due to resistance from the host country or operator, the right of the host country to refuse inspectors and limitations on access have all been quoted as areas in need of change. This kind of improvement is, however, far too technical to be addressed at the Treaty level. Indeed, David Fischer has even warned against implementing them by amending the IAEA's INFCIRC 153[2] because any attempt to change this would have similar unpredictable results to attempting to change the NPT.[3] Sustained pressure for incremental improvements in the practice of safeguards thus appears to be the best hope of eliminating these shortcomings.

Currently, the IAEA is permitted to start inspection activities only when it is told by an NPT party that fissile materials have been introduced into a facility. There thus exists no legal basis for the Agency to approach a country suspected of constructing or having constructed a clandestine nuclear facility designed to produce weapons grade fissile materials. The introduction of inspections on challenge could alleviate this problem. Under such an arrangement, an IAEA inspection team would, if authorised by a qualified majority of the IAEA Board of Governors, be permitted to go to a specified site in a member country and to check that no illegitimate activities were going on there. Obviously, an agreement of this kind would greatly reduce the risk of parties to the Treaty using it as a cover for illegal activities.

Regrettably, such arrangements and the related procedures to implement inspections on challenge would be extraordinarily difficult to negotiate at present, as no precedent exists. The Tlatelolco Treaty and the Antarctica Treaty, which both provide for such inspections, are not comparable with the NPT. The parties to these Treaties are equals so far as the Treaties' purposes are concerned; in the NPT, the central problem is the inequality of the participants. Moreover, if inspectors can, in theory, be sent anywhere in a country, understandable concern is likely to arise over industrial espionage. Moreover, non-nuclear weapon states will resist any further increase in their non-proliferation obligations unless the burden on the nuclear weapon states grows in kind.

The possibility of introducing inspections on challenge thus depends on precedents set in other forums and the explicit participation of the nuclear weapon states. The successful conclusion of a treaty banning chemical weapons, a CTBT or a treaty cutting off the production of fissile materials for military purposes would all rely on the acceptance and implementation of on-site inspections following challenges. If one or several arms control agreements of this kind were to be concluded, then inspections following challenge would become a possibility in the non-proliferation area. Unfortunately, such developments will probably be independent of the requirement to strengthen the non-proliferation regime before 1995.

Recent evidence has shown that some ostensibly innocent exports regularly end up in unsafeguarded nuclear facilities despite the efforts of the Zangger Committee, the Nuclear Suppliers Group and individual governments to prevent this. The closing of this 'grey market' loophole is thus a pivotal task in enhancing the regime.[4] In the same vein, it has been suggested that it would also be strengthened by stopping all trade in, and even use of, nuclear weapons grade material such as plutonium or highly enriched uranium, and changing the present constraint on the export of sensitive facilities to a fully fledged legal proscription. Indeed, some critics have suggested that the free access to nuclear technology implied by Article IV is in strong contrast to the very purpose of the NPT.

These prohibitions could be implemented by rewriting Article III and, in the case of the second one, Article IV. Alternatively, they could be incorporated in an independent supplier/recipient agreement or undertaking. Such suggestions, however, are likely to be opposed by many non-nuclear weapon states, notably several in the Third World who have little or no current interest in nuclear technology, yet who feel that the unconstrained right of access to such technology is an essential part of the NPT bargain. An attempt to formalise export restrictions would thus be very bad regime politics. It seems far more sensible to attempt to close the 'grey market' and constrain sensitive materials and technologies through formal and informal understandings among suppliers. Little change can be anticipated in this judgement over the next decade.

Article V of the NPT, concerning peaceful nuclear explosions (PNEs), is occasionally criticised as legitimising the claims of non-parties to have a right to engage in programmes for the development of nuclear explosives. If Article V were deleted, or an independent peaceful explosions prohibition negotiated, potential nuclear powers would be deprived of the possibility of justifying their military ambitions by cloaking them in PNE arguments.

In practice, Article V can be viewed as obsolete, given the worldwide scepticism about the benefits of PNEs. Yet it does legally constrain all NPT non-nuclear weapon states parties from suddenly claiming they are embarking on a national PNE programme. By proscribing an agreed procedure for utilising PNEs, in the unlikely situation where there existed an economic or technical case for doing so, it also closes rather than opens a loophole. Further, it makes it impossible for outsiders to legitimise their abstention from the Treaty by claiming that it prevents them from reaping the benefits of the use of PNEs, rather than mastering nuclear explosive technology *per se*. Finally, it gives the Review Conferences the chance to refute the alleged utility of PNEs. Article V thus does little harm and may even prevent possible ambiguous interpretation of the Treaty. It certainly does not justify engaging in difficult negotiations just to tidy up its obsolete aspects.

It has been argued that the strength of the NPT is seriously reduced by both the complicated processes which of necessity precede any official acknowledgement of a breach of the Treaty and the very vague consequences stipulated in it for such a breach. Specifying a range of mandatory sanctions to be applied in the event of a breach would, in this view, greatly add to the deterrent value of the Treaty.

This argument is not, however, supported by insights from deterrence theory. While the certain prospect of vigorous retaliation is undoubtedly a good deterrent, so too is uncertainty about the response to breaches of the Treaty. The deterrent power of uncertainty is the main argument upon which present French deterrence strategy is based, and it also permeates NATO's 'flexible response' strategy, which relies on giving the potential enemy something to guess about.[5] Uncertainty would only lose its deterrent effectiveness if the range of possible outcomes was very narrow. This is not the case with an act of nuclear proliferation. Since many countries, and particularly the major powers, place a high value on non-proliferation, breaching the NPT could result in consequences as diverse as weak public statements or military invasion. Mandatory sanctions, if they could ever be agreed on, would probably never go as far as military action. It can thus be concluded that the present uncertainty over responses to proliferation does not necessarily reduce the deterrent value of the Treaty.

Article XI of the NPT allows a party to withdraw from the Treaty after giving three months' notice. This is certainly a 'loophole' but the question is, how serious is it, and how negotiable would be the deletion of this Article? First, it can be assumed that a state considering 'going nuclear' under the cover of Treaty membership would not be impeded too much by an obligation to stay in indefinitely. Second, it is doubtful that states which feel seriously threatened by a country which withdraws from the Treaty in order to produce nuclear weapons would feel inhibited from retaliating against it just because it previously had been a party. In such highly dramatic 'life and death' situations, nation states would regard legal questions as decidedly secondary issues, though not as entirely negligible.

There must also be doubts if the deletion of Article XI is easily negotiable. In a world where nuclear powers exist, where some countries stay out of the NPT framework and are quite likely to do so for some time, and where threats of conventional attack abound, it is hard enough for sovereign states to renounce the most powerful weapon in the first place. To waive, in addition, the principle of *rebus sic stantibus*, which is incorporated explicitly in the Treaty through Article XI.I, would be too much for several parties to accept. In addition it is questionable whether an implicit *rebus sic stantibus* clause would not exist in any case, even if it were excluded from the language of the Treaty. As an accepted principle of international law, it is a loophole in any treaty, even one of indefinite duration.

Enhancing regime efficiency thus does not necessarily demand any amendments to the NPT. Such amendments could be counterproductive by challenging the existing consensus without creating a new one. The objectives sought by amendments could in practice be obtained through more vigorous efforts to implement what is already in the letter of the Treaty, and by supplementing the NPT through the functioning of the Convention for the Physical Protection of Nuclear Material, the Committee on Assurances of Supply or the Zangger Committee. The one exception is inspections by challenge: they, however, seem non-negotiable given the current unwillingness of the nuclear weapon states to set a convincing example.

THE PREVENTION OF DEFECTIONS AND THE ATTRACTION OF NEW PARTIES

There are two ways of preventing parties from renouncing the Treaty: to improve the advantages accruing to them and to reduce their concerns about non-proliferation. The same measures are appropriate to enhance the NPT's attraction to outsiders.

Measures to improve advantages

The most unambiguous measure to improve the advantages accruing to Treaty members would be to make all nuclear exports contingent upon the recipient's acceptance of FSS. This creates a strong discrimination in favour of parties or party equivalents and it reduces the danger that nuclear exports will be abused. A valid counter-argument against such a move, however, is that cutting off all nuclear trade with Treaty holdouts unless they accept FSS may repel rather than attract them. This would be especially important if the objective were to obtain from the holdouts agreements that fell short of Treaty signature.

Given the increasing role of the holdouts as emerging suppliers, there is a strong imperative to persuade them to operate a sensible and responsible export policy in the 1990s. A more flexible approach to nuclear cooperation with non-parties would possibly stand a greater chance of achieving this important goal. The FSS strategy could risk the creation of a second, uncontrolled market giving access to unsafeguarded materials for would-be wrongdoers. The argument is admittedly contested, some contending that self interest would compel new suppliers to behave responsibly, even if denied the benefits of nuclear trade with NPT parties. Still, one cannot be sure that a policy of defiance will not be seen as a serious alternative by those who have always been somewhat at odds with the non-proliferation regime.

Non-proliferation policy therefore poses a dilemma to NPT supplier states. What would enhance the incentive to accede and stick to the Treaty may reinforce the stance of determined outsiders. A possible, though not fully satisfactory, compromise is a partial bias in favour of those countries accepting FSS. This would mean a presumption of cooperation with them and unconstrained exports to them, with the exception of special cases like Libya. In contrast, there would be a very careful assessment of exports towards non-FSS countries, with the strong possibility that they would be the target of denial policies.

In practice, if not in theory, this is the policy followed by suppliers at the moment. It is reflected in the formula used in the Final Document of the 1985 NPT Review Conference, namely that suppliers should make efforts to achieve acceptance of FSS by all non-nuclear weapon states.[6] This does not entirely close the door for limited nuclear cooperation with non-parties in those selected cases where flexibility seems a more appropriate policy than denial.

It should not be impossible to devise methods of obliging supplier countries which are parties to the NPT to give preferential nuclear assistance to other parties. There are two problems to be overcome, however, if this approach is to become a significant incentive. First, developing countries have some natural limits to their ability to absorb technical assistance. Second, it would be rather difficult to channel such aid through the IAEA, which by its statute has to be neutral towards NPT parties and non-parties. A method of overcoming this objection would be to give extra-budgetary 'Footnote (a)' money[7] exclusively to parties. Unfortunately, this accords only a limited advantage to them, and offers little incentive to those outsiders who already possess a fully developed nuclear programme.

Methods of financing reactor purchases and the acquisition of other costly items of nuclear equipment have long been on the NPT agenda. The first condition for the creation of such a scheme would be, of course, the existence of a market. At present and into the foreseeable future, this seems likely to limit severely the number of potential candidates for assistance. Moreover, it is against standard banking practice to offer general financial guarantees to underwrite the purchase of equipment when the client is unknown. What could be explored is a slight change in the OECD guidelines for nuclear export financing,[8] which would allow the reduced 'proliferation risk' associated with NPT membership to be reflected in lower interest rates. This could, moreover, be done without revising the Treaty.

A major complaint of parties as well as non-parties about the NPT has been the discrimination inherent in it. Three aspects have been identified both within the Treaty and in its implementation:
(1) The way the Treaty appears to legitimise the fundamental difference between nuclear weapon and non-nuclear weapon states;
(2) The unequal distribution of burdens among the parties to the Treaty;

(3) The defects in the detailed implementation of the Treaty which alleg-
edly hamper access to civilian technology by non-nuclear weapon
states.

The implicit recognition within the NPT that there existed a fundamental
division of the world between nuclear weapon 'haves' and 'have nots' was
only acceptable to those non-nuclear weapon states that negotiated it if a
vision of future equality was included within it. This took the form of a
promise to engage in nuclear disarmament negotiations. The nuclear
weapon states, however, succeeded in keeping the language of this promise so vague as to evade any binding obligation. Any strengthening of this
obligation would probably require amendments to the wording of Article
VI, or, at the very least, the addition of protocols to the Treaty. These
would probably take the form of linking-in specified arms control and
disarmament measures, such as a CTBT or a deep cut in the numbers of
nuclear warheads and/or delivery vehicles, to a target date for completing
such steps.

These types of proposal are, however, beset by practical difficulties.
Negotiating an arms control framework which leaves only the technicali-
ties to be agreed through bilateral negotiations between the superpowers
is not easy, and must be done with the superpowers' consent. Yet a
political climate conducive to such consent is by definition one of detente
and successful arms control. In that case, the worries about Article VI
would disappear and the need for action would be removed.

An alternative scenario would be one where proposals for change were
in existence in an international climate of tension. It is inconceivable in
the circumstances that the United States and the Soviet Union could be
persuaded to forego their perceived security interests for the sake of fulfilling Article VI. Moreover, while their refusal would signal an overt breach
of this NPT obligation, it would not devalue the other benefits that can be
derived from the Treaty. In this context, it seems unlikely that non-fulfilment of Article VI would be used as a pretext for withdrawal, except in the
case of parties which already had a sinister attitude towards the Treaty.
Important as Article VI is as an instrument to press the superpowers to
engage in arms control, and dangerous as their malign neglect of this
activity is to the robustness of the regime, the ability of the Treaty to
change the realities of the East–West conflict should not be overrated. One
is thus led to conclude that in the best case attempting to alter Article VI
would be superfluous; in the worst case it would weaken rather than
stabilise the regime, and above all it is extremely unlikely to be negotiable.

The discriminatory obligation placed on the non-nuclear weapon states, but not the nuclear weapon ones, to accept safeguards over their civil activities has been a source of continual complaint about the Treaty. The complete separation of civilian and military nuclear fuel-cycles in nuclear weapon states, and the acceptance of legal obligations to extend safeguards coverage to their entire civilian fuel-cycle would ameliorate these problems. The costs of this proposal would increase safeguards expenditure considerably, but it has several advantages. It abolishes completely any real or perceived commercial benefits that the nuclear weapon states might derive from their current position. Once separation is implemented, verified material balances could be established for the military facilities and a limitation, and later a cut-off, of the production of fissile material for weapons purposes could be initiated. Separation could open up a new path to fulfilling Article VI, simultaneously with eliminating the discrimination inherent in Article IV.

Separation appears likely to be costly, and acceptable only to the United States and the United Kingdom. Much resistance is to be expected from the Soviet Union. It took them many years to make their voluntary offer to place some of their nuclear facilities under safeguards and the list of such facilities is still very limited. Moreover, military plutonium and civil electricity production are interlinked in the Soviet nuclear system. Even if the aftermath of the Chernobyl explosion produces a more open Soviet attitude towards releasing information on its nuclear power activities, they are far more likely to acquiesce to a slow, incremental and voluntary process of expanding safeguards coverage on their facilities than a precipitate, sudden expansion as a consequence of being forced to accept a legal obligation. Moreover, if one important task for the next decade and beyond is to draw France and China closer to the NPT, making separation a condition of entry could be highly counterproductive. Both countries have objected to the Treaty on the grounds that it permits other states to intrude into their sovereign internal affairs. Such objections would be much more difficult to overcome if these additional obligations were added to the Treaty. France in particular, with its mixture of civilian and military nuclear activities, would find it a strong deterrent to becoming a party.

The issue of the right of unrestricted access to nuclear technology revolves around the question of whether Article IV of the NPT suspends the quasi-natural right of suppliers to decide on whether to engage in trade in an item and who to trade with. Discussions in the CAS[9] have revealed that such a suspension is unacceptable to exporters. What is accepted is that Article IV creates a positive bias in favour of a transfer to an NPT party unless strong counter-arguments exist, as in the case of Iraq, Iran and Libya. Although in the CAS exporters have moved towards automatically granting supplies to customers which have made credible non-proliferation commitments, they will never accept an obligation to agree to the transfer of reprocessing technology to a Ghaddafi. Indeed, to change Article IV in the direction of greater permissiveness would run counter to the goal of regime efficiency.

HOW LIKELY ARE DEFECTION?

In the last few years, the fear has been voiced occasionally that, because of dissatisfaction with the implementation of the NPT and the operations of the regime, a few withdrawals from the Treaty would be followed by a stampede. After the 1985 Review Conference, different expectations, which cannot be regarded as complacent, are in order. The overwhelming evidence from this conference is that grudgingly the Third World parties to the Treaty have come to view the NPT as a genuine and indispensable contribution to their own national security. While dissatisfaction with the superpowers' arms control record will persist, and heavy pressure on the nuclear weapon states to fulfil their Article VI pledge will continue, there exists now an even greater trend to sustain and uphold the security benefits of the Treaty.[10] Withdrawal under these circumstances would mean shooting oneself in the foot. Only extraordinary circumstances, such as visible and reprehensible acts of bad faith on the part of the nuclear weapon states, or a nuclear attack against a non-nuclear weapon state, now seem likely to induce the average NPT party to consider withdrawal.

Two categories of parties, however, still persist as defection risks. Some states, such as Libya and possibly Iraq and Iran, are suspected of using the NPT to cover the creation of skills and facilities needed for a future weapon programme. Their probable motive in defecting would be security concerns or a very fundamental dissatisfaction with the world order in general, combined with missionary expansionism and political fanaticism. In these cases, regime improvements including amendments to the NPT are irrelevant to their motives for defection.

The second group consists of states threatened by the real or supposed capabilities of holdouts, in particular Black African and Arab states. A spectacular 'proliferation event' in South Africa or Israel might well stimulate defections among such states. Since their priority is security, removing concerns over the regime are not likely to be sufficient to prevent this type of defection.

Improvements in the regime are thus not very relevant to the issue of withdrawal. Their main positive effect is to demonstrate consensus building. This helps to project an unambiguous message to outsiders that non-proliferation is a goal shared by the overwhelming majority in the world and pursuing policies counter to this goal means risking relations with many states.

HOW LIKELY ARE NEW ACCESSIONS?

In order to assess the likelihood that additional states would sign the Treaty if the existing regime could be strengthened, one has briefly to go through the motivations behind their present abstention. For Pakistan and Israel, the issue is security. No regime change is likely to affect directly their main concern. For South Africa and Cuba, keeping the option open is seen as a valuable bargaining chip. It has little to do with the discriminatory nature of the regime. For India, Brazil and Argentina discrimination does play a major role, though their abstention is also motivated by regional rivalries. For them as well as some smaller outsiders, such as Tanzania, changes in the Treaty related to discrimination could help to overcome their reluctance to join it. Unfortunately, any disappearance of the privileges currently enjoyed by the nuclear weapon states could add to the reluctance of two other important absentees, France and China, to sign. In general, all countries which have for many years publicly proclaimed their opposition to the NPT might be persuaded to join it if symbolic changes were made to its language. The same effect could be achieved by incrementally reducing discrimination in the way the Treaty was implemented. 'Changed circumstances' can always be used by a government to justify a change in policy. Significantly, the conditions set by India in the 1970s for signing the NPT, which included negotiation of a CTBT, deep cuts in nuclear arsenals, and the application of safeguards to nuclear weapon states, can be implemented without changing a single word in the Treaty. Thus a new or amended Treaty is both incapable of satisfying those interests of the holdouts which cause them to stay aside and is unnecessary, provided their current arguments for staying out are genuine and Treaty implementation improves.

TOWARDS A REALISTIC UNDERSTANDING OF THE REGIME

What, therefore, are the merits of the NPT? It provides mutual assurances for the parties and it confines concerns about the possibility of nuclear war to conflicts among the nuclear weapon states and to those regional conflicts which involve the major holdout states. The geographic scope of the Treaty covers such traditional trouble spots as Central Europe, where the number of potential nuclear troublemakers is now narrowly circumscribed; the Balkans; a significant part of the Middle East and most of Latin America, South-East Asia and East Asia, including the two Koreas. Moreover, the Treaty contains some countries whose 'natural ambitions' for regional leadership might have led them to seek nuclear grandeur, such as Egypt, Nigeria, Indonesia, Australia, Japan and Mexico. Diplomatic efforts to prevent nuclear war have consequently become focused upon arms control between the superpowers and the four regions in which the more intractable proliferation cases are located. Thus even though it fails to be truly universalist, the NPT serves world order well.

In parallel, it has to be acknowledged that the quasi-universalist approach of the NPT is not the appropriate instrument for resolving these problems of global and regional conflict. The nuclear arms race between the United States and the Soviet Union and its freeze or even its end, is contingent on the state of conflict between those giants. The NPT can only play a marginal role here: its main effect is that even in times of high tension, it still provides an area of common interest and a subject for genuine interchanges. Likewise, regional security concerns cannot be resolved by the NPT. They originate independently of nuclear concerns, which may, however, aggravate them. Moreover, diplomatic action is, like any other good, a limited resource which should be spent in the most efficient way possible. To renegotiate the NPT in order to attract the most hard-nosed Treaty opponents will waste resources which could be better spent on incremental regime improvements and in tackling the difficult regional cases at source.

The recent nuclear rapproachment between Argentina and Brazil is an example of what is possible through such action. It merits being given unqualified support even though it occurred independently of the NPT framework. An agreed scheme of nuclear cooperation and mutual inspection would reduce mutual suspicions among the South American rivals. It could also serve as an example for South Asia, and encourage the leaders of Pakistan and India to tackle the core issues of their conflict, as they promised in December 1985. The agreement not to attack each others' nuclear facilities can be seen as a modest first step to building mutual confidence in a highly volatile situation. This step might then enable them to follow the South American example. The exclusion of such bilateral solutions from the NPT framework makes them more attractive and acceptable to long-time opponents of the Treaty. Moreover, once South America and South Asia are covered by regional non-proliferation networks, the chances of applying heavy pressure on South Africa to put its pilot and commercial uranium enrichment plants under safeguards will be enhanced. This leaves Israel as the last and most intractable regional case for which no handy solution is in sight as long as tension in the Middle East remains high.

This optimistic scenario illustrates that a fundamental misconception of the problem underlies the view of staunch NPT supporters that nothing short of signature and ratification of the Treaty will serve to reinforce the non-proliferation regime. Ironically, some of these supporters may well be willing to risk the whole Treaty to pursue the weak possibility of attracting outsiders into it through renegotiation. It seems far more safe, fruitful and promising to view the non-proliferation regime as a complex order, composed of various substructures which all serve the common fundamental purpose of preventing nuclear war. If regional security and non-aggression arrangements serve this purpose, they should have top priority in non-proliferation policy, even if they lack the legal and symbolic universalism of the Treaty. What is needed is to make the core of the regime, the NPT, flexible enough to relate to these more limited parts of it. Article VII on regional treaties already serves this 'coupling' function. May be the time will come to accept bilateral agreements, including confidence-building ones, as NPT-compatible, and for suppliers to adapt their export policies accordingly.

Amendments to the NPT could serve either to enhance the efficiency of the regime, to prevent defections, or to attract new parties. They might also facilitate a smooth passage for proposals to extend the Treaty in 1995. However, improved efficiency and the reduction of the discrimination inherent in the regime, which is the main cause of potential defections and a major justification for abstentions, can both be achieved through more effective implementation of the existing Treaty. Attempting to amend it will open up a Pandora's box of difficult negotiations, whose prospects are dubious and which run the risk of disaster. Rather than taking this risk and exhausting precious diplomatic capital on a futile exercise, it is time to accept a dual track in non-proliferation policy, strengthening the NPT through incremental steps on the one hand and addressing the regional causes for abstention on the other. Through this method, an atmosphere could be created in which extension of the existing NPT beyond 1995 would become acceptable to all its parties.

NOTES

1. Representative of this view is Edward J. Markey, *Nuclear Peril. The Politics of Nuclear Proliferations* (Cambridge, Mass., Ballinger, 1982).
2. This is the IAEA information circular which contains the standardised wording for use between the IAEA and NPT non-nuclear weapon parties in negotiating a safeguards agreement.
3. David Fischer and Paul Szasz, *Safeguarding the Atom. A Critical Appraisal* (London and Philadelphia, Taylor & Francis, 1985), pp. 84–5.
4. See Leonard S. Spector, *The New Nuclear Nations* (New York, Vintage Books 1985), Chapter II.
5. See the perceptive discussion of Robert Powell, 'The Theoretical Foundations of Strategic Nuclear Deterrence', *Political Science Quarterly*, 1 (1985), 75–96.
6. NPT/CONF.III 64/I Annex I, p. 3, para 4.
7. 'Footnote (a)' refers to an IAEA budgeting procedure. This lists projects which are deemed to be worth pursuing by the Agency, although no funds can be made available for them in the regular budget. Donor countries may then voluntarily select such projects for special financial assistance.
8. *Nucleonics Week*, 31 (1984), 2–3.
9. On CAS, see IAEA GOV/2212, 21.5.1985 and IAEA/GOV. OR 636, 2.7. 1985.
10. David Fischer and Harald Müller, *Non-Proliferation Beyond the 1985 Review*, CEPS Papers (Brussels, Centre for European Policy Studies, 1985).

10 Enhancing internal restraints on nuclear proliferation

Philip Gummett

INTRODUCTION

As in detective stories, so in analyses of the problem of nuclear weapons proliferation: it is necessary to establish that the suspect has both the means to commit the crime and a motive. It is generally agreed that the means are now widespread around the world and are likely to become more so as the number of suppliers grows and as new technologies, such as laser separation of uranium and, possibly, plutonium, become available. While controls over access to the means to proliferate through, for example, the safeguards arrangements of the Non-Proliferation Treaty and the Nuclear Suppliers Group guidelines will remain important, it is now clear that attention must increasingly be focused upon the motives of near-nuclear states.

The question of motives is usually analysed in terms of lists of incentives and disincentives. Incentives for acquiring the bomb or, more subtly, the option of acquiring the bomb, include the following:

To boost domestic support; to postpone unsettled policy debates between pro- and anti-bomb factions in the government; to elicit diplomatic support for the country in return for not detonating a nuclear device; to receive advanced conventional weapons in return for the same promise; to act as a deterrent to nuclear weapons acquisition by regional rivals; to induce caution among other actors by presenting the threat of nuclear escalation; and to bolster the country's other diplomatic objectives.[1]

Disincentives focus on questions of military utility/inutility; direct economic cost (usually not a major factor); both domestic and international political costs (the latter including various sanctions such as loss of financial aid, loss of technical support for the nuclear programme or other programmes, loss of supply of materials for the nuclear programme, and denial of such items as conventional military equipment) and sometimes also anticipated moral responses, as in Japan. To summarise, most analyses of motives for either the acquisition of nuclear weapons or of the option to acquiring them refer to security, economic, technological and domestic and international political incentives and disincentives. Moreover, the boundaries between these categories are inevitably drawn somewhat arbitrarily.

Another way of classifying motivational influences is to distinguish roughly between forces which operate externally to the country in question and forces which operate internally. Clearly this too is an arbitrary division in the sense that the intention behind the external forces is to influence internal decision-making. Nevertheless, one can suggest that the centre of gravity of such influences as the operation of the London guidelines for the supply of sensitive technologies and materials and that of other elements of the non-proliferation regime, such as the threat of trade sanctions and the general balance of international power, depends upon forces external to the near-nuclear state. This is in contrast to other factors, such as the broad type of political system possessed by the country; the state and political influence of public opinion, pressure groups and opposition politicians; and the nature and operation of institutions and professional groups whose centre of gravity lies inside national boundaries. These may include the bureaucracy, including the atomic energy authorities; other relevant government departments; the military and its, often distinct, sub-elements and the scientific and technological community.

The object of this chapter is to explore further the implications for non-proliferation policies of these internal factors. Before doing so, some caveats are in order. First, the discussion will be essentially abstract. The point is to suggest a way of viewing the problem rather than to offer detailed country-by-country studies. In so doing, heavy reliance will be placed upon work by Ashok Kapur.[2] Second, it is important to repeat the point already made about the lack of a clear analytical distinction between external and internal causal influences. Although the focus of this chapter is upon internal factors, one must never lose sight of the fact that these are susceptible to external influence. Indeed, it is precisely this susceptibility that leads to the emphasis within the chapter upon the interface between the external and internal factors. Linked to this is a third caveat that some of the discussion here may seem to infringe upon the traditional conception of national sovereignty and all that goes with it, including the convention of non-interference in the affairs of another state. For where the line should be drawn between legitimate and illegitimate behaviour in the attempt to apply external pressure is unclear. Lastly, much play is made in this chapter of a theoretical approach which draws more or less directly upon the analysis of bureaucratic politics. Objections may be voiced that in many potential nuclear states, the predominance of a small group of political leaders may be greater than in those advanced Western societies which fostered the bureaucratic politics model, and thus its applicability to them may be debatable. One can concede this point while still maintaining that even the most narrowly drawn political elite has to take some account of the climate of opinion in other parts of the governmental system, if only to reject it, and that this will be true in respect of both the implementation of decisions and the initial decision-taking. The proposition that nuclear-weapon decisions are taken by only a handful of people does not necessarily undermine arguments for seeking to influence the advice that those few people will be given.

PREVIOUS WORK

There is nothing novel in suggesting that studies of nuclear proliferation and non-proliferation should include an analysis of factors internal to the country under examination. On the contrary, this is an essential tenet of a large body of the literature, as can be seen from a brief survey of a number of recent books. For example, a recent volume edited by Rodney W. Jones on *Small Nuclear Forces and US Security Policy* explores numerous threats and potential conflicts in the Middle East and South Asia and draws out lessons for United States policy. It refers in particular to the importance of improved intelligence assessments of proliferation, noting the vital importance of high quality political intelligence about decision-makers' motivations, intentions and incentives.[3] It also notes that there may be scope for diplomatic innovation,[4] because rival states with small nuclear forces may become more receptive to outside assistance in forming new diplomatic or arms control arrangements in their locality once they become aware of the range of new risks their nuclear capabilities impose. But the book stops short of exploring the mechanisms necessary to promote these developments.

The volume edited by Joseph A. Yager on *Non-Proliferation and US Foreign Policy* comes closer to the focus of this chapter. Its country studies are replete with references to internal political debates. For example, the discussion of India and Pakistan by Betts notes the relatively high degree of domestic debate on nuclear matters in India and the paucity of domestic opposition in each country to its national defence programmes.[5] While this does not automatically imply popular support for nuclear weapons, there is little opposition to this variant of military preparedness either. However, as Betts also observes, the professional military establishments in these two countries have not acted as united pro-bomb lobbies, and this disunity has been the feature of nuclear politics in other countries too.

Yager's volume ends with a chapter on influencing incentives and capabilities. This focuses on government-to-government relations and it does not penetrate far into the structure of national politics in the countries concerned. In the specific context of the United States goal of seeking to eliminate or weaken the underlying cause of another country's interest in nuclear weapons, this approach is justified if the incentive for acquiring nuclear weapons was concern about national security. Dealing with a desire for international prestige or domestic approbation would, says Yager, be much more difficult, as would frustrating or diverting the aspirations of a technological or military elite.[6] He concludes that it is, therefore, fortunate that national security is by far the most important existing and potential motivation for acquiring nuclear weapons. At the same time, there may also be advantages in considering how to deal with the other incentives Yager identifies.

Lewis A. Dunn, in his comprehensive discussion of the problems in *Controlling the Bomb*, clearly recognises the importance of domestic political considerations in countries' efforts to go nuclear. He notes how the government of General Zia's Pakistan has ignored outside pressures to discontinue its nuclear weapons activities, in part because 'that would have caused popular, elite and even military protests and disaffection', and adds that in the absence of other policy successes, acquisition of a nuclear explosive capability may be the only way for Zia to prop up his domestic position.[7] He also observes that several other motivating factors had been important. These include the fear that an Indian nuclear force could coerce Pakistan into political surrender in a crisis; the belief that nuclear weapons could help compensate for Pakistan's weakness in conventional military forces; national pride and a quest for greater international status; and an aspiration to be the first Moslem country to acquire nuclear weapons. There is no evident concern in Pakistan about India's response either to a nuclear test or to the fully-fledged military deployment of nuclear weapons, nor is there much fear of the impact of a costly nuclear weapons programme on Pakistan's already weak conventional defences.

Dunn also regards domestic factors as being important in India's case too. He mentions the importance of distracting attention at home from economic difficulties and domestic unrest. He also notes that by the mid- to late-1980s, all the components needed for a militarily significant nuclear weapons programme would be in place and that in those circumstances, scientific momentum might tip the balance in favour of a fully-fledged programme.[8] The solutions which Dunn proposes are cast in terms of security guarantees, the fostering of diplomatic solutions to regional confrontations, and the encouragement of international cooperation to impose multilateral sanctions on countries that violate their nuclear obligations. The question of how, short of those measures, to reach out and influence domestic debate in the near nuclear states is not, however, a central part of his analysis.

Dunn's point about the significance of the scientific–technological elite in India is reinforced by Harald Müller's discussion of institutional dynamics and nuclear incrementalism in his chapter in the volume on *Nuclear Proliferation in the 1980's*, edited by Kincade and Bertram. Müller suggests that:

In the nuclear weapon states, the nuclear community is a social sub-system of its own, with its own interests, belief systems, thinking style, communication links, and sources of influence. Every large organizational network develops an institutional pattern of economic and bureaucratic interests, shared images, and decisional momentum; strives to enhance the scope and amount of its power; and defends itself against any threat. Structures comparable to the military–industrial complex exist in the nuclear field and include research centres, the nuclear industry and its labour force, nuclear-oriented parts of the bureaucracy, and the military. Of special importance is the strong identity of civil and military interests. A review of the Indian case reveals that civil scientists and military personnel joined in a successful attempt to enlarge nuclear programmes. This coalition produced such pressure that top politicians had little choice but to confirm step-by-step decisions already prepared in advance by the civil–military nuclear coalition. Similar developments are reported in Argentina and Brazil.[9]

Müller argues that the danger created by this kind of nuclear complex does not lie in its direct influence on political decisions, but in the dynamic combination of subtle civil and military pressures that it produces. In particular, it dissolves the big step to a nuclear weapon into a series of little steps, each of which narrows the distance to the weapons threshold.

The point of this brief survey of recent literature is not to criticise the authors for failing to focus upon the primary concern of this chapter. Rather, it is to show that while there is widespread recognition of the importance of factors internal to the country in any decision about nuclear weapons acquisition, analysts have refrained from probing into the detailed connections between their macro-level analyses and the micro-level domestic decision-making processes. The latter remain as a largely unexamined black box.

INSIDE THE BLACK BOX

A way of proceeding at the micro-level has been suggested by Ashok Kapur. It is important to emphasise, however, that his primary concern was with *negotiations* about nuclear proliferation, and his analysis needs adapting if it is to be extended to national *decision-making* about weapons acquisition.

Although he does not use the expression, Kapur's approach can be seen broadly as falling within the bureaucratic politics tradition of political analysis. The essence of his thesis, which focuses on negotiations between the two superpowers, is illustrated by the following quotation:

The presence of only two parties means that each side views the other as the primary audience and the primary adversary. However, this situation does not necessarily mean that the state is the primary actor. If the hypothesis is sound that international negotiations are less about securing desired outcomes and more about the location of the issue in the bureaucratic debate, *bureaucratic power play* is the real level of analysis. This power play can operate in two different directions. On the one hand, the liberals or hawks in one society may exert an influence on their counterparts in the other society. On the other hand, the power play may influence the location of the issue within a particular society. Therefore, 'two-party' means that two states are involved, but, obviously, many bureaucratic players are involved.[10]

In the same vein, he argues:

the real danger of proliferation lies not so much in the growth of nuclear arms and nuclear wars initiated by irresponsible states as in hysteria caused by unfamiliarity with the decision apparatus and decision psychology of states who possess nuclear options and nuclear arms.[11]

Developing this line of argument, Kapur observes that in certain key Third World states, an attentive community in favour of disarmament has existed since the 1950s. He suggests that this community has spawned a plethora of bureaucratic groupings dealing with most aspects of nuclear energy, including, *inter alia*, civil uses, potential military uses, arms control implications, activities of international organisations, environmental aspects, safety aspects and foreign policy implications. The point, he says, is that:

the debates are becoming public, bureaucratic constituencies are emerging and growing strong, and Western-trained intellectuals are entering the policy ladders.[12]

Moreover, these elites may compete and conflict with other elements of the bureaucratic system, and this may explain the apparently contradictory positions which governments take on occasions. Thus while Pakistan did not follow India in signing the Partial Test Ban Treaty in 1963, neither did it engage in nuclear weapons testing. And although Pakistan warned against the dangers of Indian nuclear proliferation, it did not itself proceed directly to acquire a nuclear weapon. Kapur suggests that in this case competing sub-national elites produced two sets of opposite decisions. The diplomatic elite drafted the anti-India speeches; the elites favouring economic and military modernisation were responsible for decisions to support economic and military modernisation rather than atomic energy developments.[13]

An important development of Kapur's thinking comes with his introduction of the concept of the 'foreign-linked faction'. The term is taken from Dowty and is used in a slightly adapted form by Kapur to mean:

the presence within a state of a competing faction that seeks or accepts aid from other states (or from groups in that state in international organisations) in order to seize and wield power by means that are not publicly defensible.[14]

The assumptions that lie behind this model include the following. First the elite functions secretly. Second, the system is small and closed. Third, political parties, parliamentarians, media managers, scholars and other individuals are sometimes informed, but are not consulted, about decision-making. Fourth, the flow of information between the domestic faction and its foreign collaborator is greater than the flow of information among the competing sub-national elites. Thus, there are differences between this model and that implicit in the more conventional bureaucratic politics model. Not least of these is the assumption that intra-elite competition, motivated by a concern with careerism, is particularly acute in the situations of social immobility that are common in developing Third World societies.[15]

The model which Kapur is advancing is one in which elements of the bureaucratic elite seek support for their position from foreign sources, which may be intergovernmental agencies, companies, governments, or elements within national governments. This model can be applied to the Indian case, where it suggests the existence of a strategy of consciously creating a dependency relationship upon a foreign country.[16] First, the foreign country offers high technology under certain contractual conditions. This is followed by its unilateral decision to alter those conditions after the contract has been implemented. There then follows the cultivation of a foreign-linked domestic faction which is willing and able both to play the foreign game and to sell the revised rules of the game to their political masters. It is, says Kapur, the continuous offer of foreign imports that keeps the bureaucratic base of the foreign-linked domestic faction alive. Discontinue the foreign imports and one would also have to dissolve or reduce the bureaucratic base of the foreign-linked domestic faction.

From the point of view of, say, Indian scientists, there are attractions in collaborating with the foreign supplier. Not to do so would result in a decrease in domestic technological innovation as a consequence of the lack of a full fuel-cycle. As Kapur puts it:

Third World scientists are given the option of demonstrating their failures in their indigenous scientific programs or staying in power and keeping their interests (as well as their jobs) alive by cooperating with external agencies that can promote their interests.[17]

Kapur is himself convinced that such a process has been operating in India and that a foreign-linked domestic faction, consisting of both officials and atomic scientists, has been able to increase India's dependency on external agencies since 1966, even though the declared national position has been against the NPT and against the acceptance of Full-Scope Safeguards on the Indian nuclear industry.[18] As he observes, with the exception of the unsafeguarded CIRUS research reactor and two other facilities (a new research reactor and the Trombay reprocessing plant), the rest of the operational Indian nuclear industry is now under safeguards. One does not need to accept the detail of this specific case study in order to appreciate the general analytical approach which Kapur is proposing.

It is important, however, not to exaggerate the potential value of this mode of analysis. Daniel Poneman, in one recent book which does discuss in detail the decision-making processes in a number of near-nuclear states, argues that any attempts to apply the bureaucratic decision-making model to developing country nuclear policy-making will encounter difficulties. He argues that bureaucratic arrangements heavily influence nuclear policy, but contends that they do not 'relentlessly bend it out of all semblance to national objectives'.[19] He reinforces this argument by suggesting that the direct link which often exists between head of state and the Atomic Energy Commission results in rough equivalence between the priority given to nuclear activities and the interest of the political leadership. Bureaucratic organisation, he says, is an important, but not independent determinant of the success of a nuclear power programme.

The strength of a program reflects the active choice of autocratic executives. The influence of organizational structure wanes for fundamentally important decisions, such as whether or not to build nuclear power stations. Bureaucracies can shape the choice faced by the leadership, but organizational advantages can be overridden.[20]

APPLICATIONS

With Poneman's warnings in mind, how could the relatively theoretical analysis advanced by Kapur be applied in practice? From the point of view of fostering nuclear non-proliferation, a number of possibilities arise. First, there is the straightforward extension of Kapur's own analysis of developments in India. If it is the case that elements of the Indian bureaucratic and scientific elite have been prepared to promote 'Western' arguments in order to ensure a continuous supply of nuclear technology and materials, perhaps the same behaviour might occur elsewhere. Related to this is the possibility of introducing other elements found in recent Western debates about nuclear programmes into the political processes of near-nuclear states.

For example, there has been much discussion in recent years of radioactive waste management. Material from these arguments could be used to foster sub-national elites that opposed all nuclear developments, civil as well as military. Alternatively, if presented in the form of offers to assist with the radioactive waste management problems of developing countries, this issue could be used to support the position of those elements within the nuclear elite that the Western countries wished to encourage. Similarly, one could envisage recent debates over hazards arising from the nuclear fuel-cycle and over the place of nuclear power within national energy policy being taken up by other sub-national elites in developing countries.

One might also envisage injecting a different set of issues into debates amongst those elite groups concerned with decision making for military procurement. Military forces are notorious for their reluctance to accept new technology, especially where this threatens existing missions or roles. There is also plenty of evidence from around the world of resistance by one branch of the armed forces to the acquisition by another of anything which may increase its relative status. Hence, military forces will not necessarily automatically and unanimously support a decision to acquire nuclear weapons. This, again, provides an opportunity for the use of the foreign-linked faction strategy.

Possibilities also exist for encouraging a split between the differing arms of the national military establishment on this issue. A continuous supply of advanced conventional weapons could be offered, on condition that the recipient armed service played its part in delaying a decision to acquire nuclear weapons. Access might also be provided to current Western arguments advocating the replacement of nuclear weapons by advanced conventional weapons in certain roles and perhaps even to their related technology. Moreover, even if the worst came to the worst and nuclear weapons are acquired, it may still be possible to use military foreign-linked factions so as to minimise the resultant dangers by linking them with Western military sources who could advise on PAL mechanisms and other security devices.[21]

These are just two areas to which Kapur's insight might be applied. No doubt others can be thought of. Governments that chose to use these methods as part of their overall non-proliferation strategy would find a variety of means to hand including training programmes and international meetings of one kind or another.

An extension of existing training programmes for nuclear energy professionals, radioactive waste management specialists, radiation hazard experts and more general energy analysts and scientists would enable the build up, over time, of a cadre of specialists imbued with 'Western' ways of viewing their own particular activities. The subsequent involvement of these people in international meetings would maintain, or help to maintain, that orientation. In the diplomatic and arms control sectors, similar schemes could be promoted involving the relevant professionals from the near-nuclear states. The military sector is already well used to such methods of working. Officer training programmes, visits to each other's establishments and participation in exercises are commonplace activities amongst the military brotherhood. The involvement of Latin American and Indian submariners in training for the commissioning of their own nuclear-powered submarines might also be a way of linking those incipient activities to Western interests.

A WORD ON PUBLIC DEBATE

This discussion of deliberate external attempts to influence internal debates through the cultivation of foreign-linked factions raises a loosely related question about the prospects for, and merits of, attempting to influence public debate about the nuclear option in the near-nuclear weapon states. Opinion is divided on the merits of so doing. Kapur points out that public debate is a normal part of the political process in Western democracies, but that it also helps to identify and solidify the bureaucratic constituency and its allies in government, industry and elsewhere. Hence, once positions are taken, it is often felt necessary to reiterate and reinforce them, thus making compromise more difficult.[22] This can slow down the consensus-building process, and it may be concluded that this could have the paradoxical effect of slowing the building of support for both arms control and for a nuclear weapons programme. Kapur also contends that the international debate on non-proliferation during the 1960s led to public debate over an Indian nuclear option, which previously had only been discussed in secret. Poneman agrees that foreign advice can create undesirable consequences because of the suspicions which it can generate. But he also contends that the opposite effect can be created: sometimes foreign advice possesses greater credence than that of domestic agencies, which may be perceived to be less competent and objective.[23]

Each case will probably therefore have to be judged on its merits. Information could be provided in an open way by one government agency for another. Alternatively, funding could be provided for non-governmental organisations that were opposing a potential governmental position that was not desired by Western governments. This might be particularly appropriate in the cases of countries, such as India, where open criticism of both civil and military nuclear programmes is relatively well developed. There may also be scope for creating some sort of international agency analogous to the IAEA in the nuclear field for collecting and disseminating information on energy policy more generally to try to prevent ill-informed decisions about the merits of nuclear policies being taken. The 1985 NPT Review Conference called upon the IAEA to initiate the work of an expert group study on mechanisms to assist developing countries in the promotion of their nuclear power programmes, including the establishment of a financial assistance fund. From the point of view of this proposal, if the phrase 'nuclear power' could be substituted by 'energy', the benefits to non-proliferation might be greater.

CONCLUSIONS

The ideas discussed in this paper are no substitute for the more orthodox instruments of non-proliferation policy. They may, however, augment them usefully in certain circumstances. Moreover, although this discussion has been fairly abstract, so too is much of the more orthodox literature on non-proliferation discussions. This is replete with 'ideal' non-proliferation regimes, schemes for drawing country X or country Y into the NPT system, lists of incentives and disincentives, and speculations about the likely impact upon the prospects for sustaining non-proliferation of movements in oil prices and changes in security environments. Discussion of the possible uses of foreign-linked factions, and of public debate, is not necessarily more abstract or speculative than these writings, though it would undoubtedly be enhanced by much more detailed case study analysis of the near-nuclear weapons states than currently exists. Moreover, the recent relatively successful use, in a different context, of a foreign-linked faction approach in South Africa should be noted. As *The Economist* has suggested:

Demonstrators and politicians round the world have been barking out instructions on how South Africa should change apartheid. In the past, they have not mattered much, because the white Afrikaner government has proved time and again that it will not be dictated to by outsiders, however rich and powerful. Now, at last, it is just conceivable that foreign banks and South African businessmen, acting together, could exert a modicum of influence on President P. W. Botha as they have never done before.[24]

The analogy is not complete, but it is provocative. In the nuclear case, however, we should not lose sight of Dunn's historical observation that:

Where the initial incentives for acquiring nuclear weapons were sufficiently powerful, the disincentives to and complications of acquiring the atomic bomb appear not to have been thoroughly analyzed or taken into account.[25]

Fortunately, the existing world is not that in which the five established nuclear weapons states made their decisions. Going nuclear today, or even simply acquiring the option, is no longer a simple or easy decision, if only because a norm of non-proliferation behaviour now exists. To preserve that norm, there may be room for intervention with the aim of influencing the climate of domestic decision-making and decision-implementation in the near-nuclear weapon states, either by the public debate route or by the use of foreign-linked factions. Both have their dangers: but so do other approaches, as does the underlying problem itself.

NOTES

1. Mitchell Reiss, 'Beyond the 1985 NPT Review Conference: Learning to Live with Uncertainty', *Survival*, vol.xxvii, no 5, (September–October 1985), 229.
2. Ashok Kapur, *International Nuclear Proliferation: Multilateral Diplomacy and Regional Aspects* (New York and London, Praeger, 1979).
3. Rodney W. Jones (ed.), *Small Nuclear Forces and US Security Policy: Threats and Potential Conflicts in the Middle East and South Asia* (Lexington, Mass., Lexington Books, 1984).
4. Jones, *Small Nuclear Forces*, p. 249.
5. R. Betts, 'Incentives for nuclear weapons', in Joseph A. Yager (ed.), *Non-Proliferation and US Foreign Policy* (Washington, DC, The Brookings Institution, 1980), at p. 136.
6. Yager, *Non-Proliferation*, p. 409.
7. Lewis A. Dunn, *Controlling the Bomb: Nuclear Proliferation in the 1980s* (New Haven and London, Yale University Press, 1982), p. 46.

8. Ibid., pp. 45–8.
9. Harald Müller, 'A Theoretical Approach to Non-proliferation Policy', in William H. Kincade and Christoph Bertram (eds.), *Nuclear Proliferation in the 1980s: Perspectives and Proposals* (London, Macmillan, 1982), at pp. 53–4.
10. Kapur, *International Nuclear Proliferation*, p. 41.
11. Ibid., p. 31.
12. Ibid., p. 33.
13. Ibid, p. 221.
14. Ibid., p. 211.
15. Ibid., p. 213.
16. Ibid., pp. 271–8.
17. Ibid., p. 220.
18. Ibid., p. 222.
19. Daniel Poneman, *Nuclear Power in the Developing World* (London, Allen & Unwin, 1982), p. 173.
20. Ibid., p. 191.
21. Jones, *Small Nuclear Forces*, p. 249.
22. Kapur, *International Nuclear Proliferation*, pp. 21–2.
23. Poneman, *Nuclear Power*, p. 209.
24. 'Flight from South Africa', *The Economist* (7 September 1985), 15.
25. Dunn, *Controlling the Bomb*, p. 18.

Part 4: Extending the nuclear non-proliferation regime beyond 1995: issues and prospects

Overview

The Nuclear Non-Proliferation Treaty provides that at some point in the middle of 1995, there shall be a conference to decide on the length of time that the Treaty will continue in operation. The reasons for this provision are buried in the detailed negotiating history of the NPT, and those West European states which originally insisted on its insertion may yet regret their lack of foresight in doing so. Yet the fact remains that the international community is presented with a major problem as a consequence of this provision and strategies will have to be evolved to deal with it.

The situation which will confront delegates in 1995 is examined in considerable detail by David Fischer in Chapter 11. The conference has the option of either extending the Treaty indefinitely or for a fixed period or periods. Although it does not have on its agenda the question of termination of the NPT, any extension for a single period only will result in it ceasing to be operative once that period had expired. Fischer also considers the question of the voting rules applicable to the conference, and points out the problems which they pose for reaching an agreement on an extension.

Other issues which will be on the agenda in 1995 include attempts to amend the Treaty as part of the bargaining process surrounding the extension conference and whether or not a review of the Treaty should be conducted as part of that conference. The existence of these many uncertainties and issues leads Fischer to conclude that there will be considerable scope for procedural wrangling over the conference, which could lead to major difficulties over its management.

Two extreme scenarios exist for the outcome of the NPT Extension Conference. One is that the Treaty will be extended indefinitely: another is that no extension will be agreed upon and the Treaty will crumble in the face of differing interpretations of its status. Alternatively, there may be an extension for a very short period of time, followed by the termination of the Treaty. The second and third chapters in Part 4 attempt to speculate on the consequences of a breakdown in the non-proliferation regime, and in so doing explore many of the latent reasons why it is vitally important that the NPT be extended for a prolonged period of time in 1995.

Joseph Pilat examines in Chapter 12 the nature of a world lacking the foundations for the nuclear non-proliferation regime provided by the NPT. He concludes that although many of the elements of that regime would remain intact, their impact would be much reduced and the regime as a whole would gradually lose credibility. An important element in this judgement is the fate of IAEA safeguards. This issue is examined in detail by Charles N. van Doren in Chapter 13. He explores the complex question of whether the safeguarding arrangements arising out of the NPT would continue in force if the treaty itself were to lapse. His conclusion is that they would remain operative, despite the uncertainties over the legal situation. He also discusses the scope for other technical means to limit the opportunities for proliferation in the 1990s, and concludes that although policies of technical denial must continue, political restraint will remain the core of any non-proliferation regime.

Finally, in Chapter 14, John Simpson draws upon the discussions of draft chapters for this volume at the Sarnia Symposium to summarise and examine further the major issues raised by those chapters and offer some conclusions and policy recommendations concerning non-proliferation policies in the 1990s. His overall conclusion echoes the views of Mohamed Shaker on the 1985 Review Conference: that extensive preparation and considerable goodwill are going to be required to overcome the difficulties inherent in holding an NPT Extension Conference in 1995.

II The 1995 Nuclear Non-Proliferation Treaty Extension Conference: issues and prospects

David Fischer

INTRODUCTION

Article X.2 of the NPT reads:

Twenty-five years after the entry into force of the Treaty, a conference shall be convened to decide whether the Treaty shall continue in force indefinitely, or shall be extended for an additional fixed period or periods. This decision shall be taken by a majority of the Parties to the Treaty.

In theory, at least, this conference in 1995 might decide to extend the Treaty for a fixed period of up to one year, after which, presumably, it would terminate. Such a turn of events is, however, very unlikely. Judging by the strong support that most countries gave to the NPT at the 1985 Review Conference, they would regard the Treaty's demise as a disastrous setback to international security and peaceful nuclear commerce and one to be avoided at any cost. It is almost certain that the supporters of the Treaty could muster enough votes to avert its demise, unless a calamitous decline in international relations occurs before 1995.

There is a more serious risk that disappointment about the Treaty's achievements might make it difficult, perhaps impossible, to get the agreement of 'a majority of the Parties' to any particular proposal for extension. But there seems to be a good chance, too, of avoiding such an impasse.

SETTING THE STAGE FOR 1995

Obviously the political climate of the early 1990s will strongly influence the way in which the conference approaches the formal constitutional choices and procedures open to it. It would be rash to predict what the climate will be. Since 1980, however, certain trends have emerged which,

155

if confirmed, might do much to affect it. One is the almost total decline of the 'peaceful' uses of nuclear explosives, the benefits of which were promised by Article V of the NPT. Only the Soviets still seem to have some interest in this ambiguous technology, though interestingly it was at the proposal of a Soviet ally that the 1985 Review Conference took note of this decline.[1]

A more significant trend is the apparently shrinking interest in the transfer of peaceful nuclear technology under Article IV of the NPT. Many developing countries would stoutly deny that there is any such trend but today, at least, the facts say otherwise. All the nuclear power programmes in developing countries have been curtailed. Those in Mexico, Brazil and Iran have stopped; the ones in Argentina, India, Pakistan, Taiwan and even South Korea have slowed down while those in Egypt and China have had difficulty in getting off the mark.

The delays, cancellations and other difficulties faced by developing countries are no worse than those in certain industrial countries. But the nuclear programmes of Third World countries face problems specific to those countries, such as escalating costs driven higher by long construction times,[2] high foreign exchange components adding to already staggering international debts and the lack of the infrastructure needed to ensure efficient and safe operation.

At the 1985 Review Conference there was far less discussion than in 1980 of the transfer of nuclear technology and also much less complaint about the export restrictions imposed by the suppliers, including those contained in the Nuclear Suppliers Group guidelines and the United States Nuclear Non-Proliferation Act of 1978. In fact the conference's recommendations about the transfer of technology and technical assistance were largely based on a United Kingdom initiative, rather than a Third World one. Amongst the developing countries, only Egypt actively pressed for more aid by seeking to revive a 20-year-old idea of a fund to finance nuclear power plants in developing countries.

Conversely, the recent conference put much more stress, in unusually forthright terms, on the NPT's contribution to regional and international security and on stopping the spread of nuclear weapons. It was certainly no less concerned than in 1980 about the nuclear arms race and about nuclear testing, but Third World and some neutral delegates demonstrated much greater concern than in the past about the health of the NPT. Less encouraging was the rising impact of regional issues, such as Israel, Iraq, Iran and South Africa. If these trends are maintained they will have much influence both on the attitude of the parties towards the extension of the

NPT and the procedures that the 1995 Conference should follow in considering this question.

Unless the developing countries again begin to see nuclear power as vital to their economies, interest in the NPT as a means of securing foreign aid seems unlikely to revive. For many of them the main questions would then be the same as those now asked by the industrialised world. Does the NPT effectively serve our security? Does it lessen the danger of a nuclear arms race in our region or reduce the nuclear threat from countries like Israel and South Africa? Does it reduce the risk of a global nuclear war that would engulf us all in its aftermath?

Besides the NPT's contribution to security one must not forget that it, and the IAEA safeguards that it underpins, are the indispensable framework for peaceful nuclear transactions between states. If either were to fail, nuclear commerce and cooperation would suffer a grievous blow. In this regard, they serve the interest of the industrial as well as the developing countries and of non-parties such as France and China, Argentina and Brazil, as well as of parties.

THE RULES OF PROCEDURE AND THE MECHANICS OF VOTING AT THE 1995 CONFERENCE

If the mood of 1995 is for a long extension of the NPT this will affect the attitude of the parties to procedural matters. It will encourage the search for a consensus and procedures designed to attain a consensus. If no consensus is in sight it may be necessary to rely on the mechanics of voting and seek a formula that will attract the support of the 'majority of the Parties'.[3] This may be no easy task.

It is possible but unlikely that every party will attend the 1995 Conference. How would less than total participation affect the workings of the conference in the light of the requirement that decisions be taken by a majority of the parties? Table 5 shows how many votes would have been needed to take a decision on extension if the matter had been before one of the previous review conferences.

It will be seen that to get a 'majority of the parties' on any proposal, more than three-quarters of the parties actually attending the conference would have to vote for it. Moreover, in 1985 twenty-one abstentions or negative votes would have prevented any proposal being implemented. Of course, the poor turn-out at previous Review Conferences may not be a good guide to what will happen at the much more vital 1995 Conference.

The NPT requires that any amendment to the Treaty be subject to

Table 5. *Numbers of votes needed to obtain a majority of NPT parties at review conferences*

(1) Year of review conference	(2) No. of parties	(3) No. attending conference	(4) No. of votes needed for a decision	(5) (4) as a % of (3)
1975	96	58	49	84%
1980	113	75	57	76%
1985	130	86	66	77%

ratification and that an amendment be binding only on the parties that ratify it. However, a decision of the 1995 Conference to extend the Treaty will need no ratification. Whatever decision is taken will be binding presumably on *all* parties, even on those that might have voted against it, although the Treaty itself is silent on this matter. It may be argued that any state which ratifies the NPT, accedes to it or succeeds to it thereby agrees to be bound by the decision of the majority of the parties on this particular matter; in other words, that the state has delegated this particular decision to the 1995 Conference. Moreover, states, that might find the decision of the conference unpalatable, always have the option of withdrawal from the Treaty on three months' notice, under Article X.1.[4]

Not unnaturally the Treaty is silent on what happens if no proposal gains support from a 'majority of the parties'.[5] But if the conference is unable in 1995 to agree on any decision for its extension, what happens to the Treaty? Does it automatically expire at the end of the year? Or does it remain in force while negotiations continue? All this points to one conclusion. If the issue of extension is still contentious when the conference meets, it may well be difficult to rally enough support for any proposal except a provisional or short extension, followed by another conference of the same kind.[6] For as Table 5 shows, the poorer the turn-out, the larger will be the proportion of the votes of those attending that will be needed for any decision.

The depositary governments and other strong supporters of the Treaty may be faced with a dilemma in this regard. If they successfully encourage the largest possible turn-out, the majority of those attending will be 'non-aligned' developing countries. This is the group that, on the whole, has been most critical of the Treaty, of the failure of both the exporting parties to implement Article IV, and of the nuclear weapon states to implement their Article VI obligations. It also contains those parties that feel threatened by the 'nuclear capability' of Israel and South Africa and that have accused some OECD countries of breaching their NPT obligations by helping these states to attain such capability. This group might be most reluctant to agree to an unqualified extension of the Treaty and would probably demand a high price on these issues in return for their support. On the other hand it is precisely this group whose esteem for the NPT, as a component of their own security, seems to be growing and whose change of attitude did as much as anything to ensure the success of the 1985 Conference.

In considering the impact of a larger turn-out in 1995 it is of interest to see which parties stayed away in 1985. Of the forty-four parties that were absent in 1985, twenty were small Central American, Caribbean and Pacific island countries, nine of which had become parties by succession through accepting the ratification of their former colonial rulers, usually the United Kingdom. A further twenty were smaller African countries, eleven of them francophone, which has led some to see the hand of Paris in their absence, though it is unlikely that France would have intervened in this way. The remaining four were Laos, Kampuchea, Kuwait and Singapore. All absentees were developing countries, almost all were non-aligned and none had any nuclear programme. Almost all would probably vote in favour of any non-aligned position if they were to attend the 1995 Conference. If three months before the conference is due to convene it is clear that no consensus is in sight, it might be desirable to seek informal agreement on procedures to deal with this contingency.

THE NATURE OF ANY EXTENSION PROPOSALS

The conference will have to decide not only how long the NPT should be extended for but also, unless an indefinite extension is agreed upon, what provision should be made for a subsequent extension. Presumably no conference decision will be needed to make provision for further Review Conferences. Assuming that the conference decides to extend the Treaty beyond the year 2000, Article VIII.3 appears to provide adequately for the holding of quinquennial reviews, though it would be open to the conference to seek more or, for that matter, less frequent ones. That, however, might require amendment of the Treaty.

When the Treaty was being drawn up in the Eighteen Nation Disarmament Committee, the United States and the Soviet Union wanted it to be of indefinite or unlimited duration like the PTBT. The Western Europeans, particularly West Germany and Italy, opposed this idea and it was dropped.[7] It is highly unlikely that the international community would accept today or in 1995 an indefinite and perhaps permanent division of the world into five nuclear weapon states and a vast and growing number of non-nuclear weapon states. The best that one could reasonably hope for would be a 25-year term ending, presumably, in another extension conference in 2020. If this proves feasible, the NPT might by 2020 become so much a part of the international structure as to be virtually a fixture. The price sought for such an extension of the Treaty might be its amendment. But, as is shown below, this is well-nigh impossible unless all significant countries agree.

Another question that remains to be answered is what is implied by 'shall be extended for an additional fixed period *or periods.*' Shaker is not able to cast much light on the last two words but quotes K. Narayana Rao as interpreting them to mean that 'the Conference may fix different periods, subjecting them to specified situations'.[8]

Conceivably the conference could decide on an initial extension of X years, and on one or more subsequent extensions, each extension being made contingent on specified progress in nuclear arms control, such as a CTBT, before the preceding extension runs out. It is likely, however, that the depositary governments and other strong supporters of the NPT would vigorously resist any such contingent extension unless the alternative were no extension at all.

A 1995 REVIEW AND AMENDING CONFERENCE?

Article VIII.3 of the NPT could allow a majority of the parties to demand that a fifth Review Conference be held in 1995, presumably before the Extension Conference, so as to examine the way the parties had implemented the Treaty during the period 1990 to 1995 and perhaps propose changes in the light of its twenty-five years of operation. However, if there were specific proposals for amendment it seems more likely that they would be proposed well in advance of the 1995 Extension Conference, perhaps at the Fourth Review Conference, so that action could be taken or, at least, attempted before the parties extend the Treaty. Also, the parties probably will use the Extension Conference itself as a forum for giving their views on how the Treaty has been implemented. In other words, the 1995 Conference would serve simultaneously as a Review, Extension and possibly Amending Conference.

Article VIII of the Treaty provides that:

I. Any Party to the Treaty may propose amendments to this Treaty. The text of any proposed amendment shall be submitted to the Depositary Governments which shall circulate it to all Parties to the Treaty. Thereupon, if requested to

do so by one-third or more of the Parties to the Treaty, the Depositary Governments shall convene a conference, to which they shall invite all the Parties to
the Treaty, to consider such an amendment.

II. Any amendment to this Treaty must be approved by a majority of the votes of
all the Parties to the Treaty, including the votes of all nuclear-weapon States
Party to the Treaty and all other Parties which, on the date the amendment is
circulated, are members of the Board of Governors of the International Atomic
Energy Agency. The amendment shall enter into force for each party that
deposits its instrument of ratification of the amendment upon the deposit of
such instruments of ratification by a majority of all the Parties, including the
instruments of ratification of all nuclear-weapon States Party to the Treaty and
all other Parties which, on the date the amendment is circulated, are members
of the Board of Governors of the International Atomic Energy Agency. Thereafter, it shall enter into force for any other Party upon the deposit of its
instrument of ratification of the amendment.

The length of these provisions and the complexity of the procedures they
prescribe makes the Treaty, as was doubtless intended, practically unam-
endable except in the unlikely event of a virtually unanimous desire of the
parties to change it. Yet each party can insist on having proposals for
amendment formally circulated by each of the three depositary states. In
this way a party may formally place on record its views as to the way in
which the Treaty should be changed and, in recognition of the difficulty of
pressing the matter any further, leave it at that. It is perhaps surprising
that no party has yet taken such a step.

After that, the proposed amendment, somewhat like an enemy missile
in the idealised scenario of Star Wars, must penetrate three barriers before
reaching its target. First,

the Party proposing the amendment must, in effect gain the support of at least one-
third of all the Parties for convening a conference to consider the amendment. This
could probably be done during some other international meeting, for instance a
Review Conferences when bloc support could be sought. Conceivably the Fourth
Conference or the 1995 Conference could also serve the purpose of considering an
amendment if one-third or more of the Parties so requested.

Second,

at the 'Amendment Conference' the amendment must receive the approval of the
majority of the Parties. This majority must include all the nuclear weapon states that
are then Party to the NPT. This, provision like the identical provision in the PTBT of
1963, also safeguards the position of China and France in the event that they accede.
The majority must also include every Party that is a member of the IAEA's Board of
Governors when the amendment is circulated. About twenty-five of the Parties
(including the three nuclear weapon states) are, as a rule, members of the IAEA Board
and each can thus veto the amendment by voting against it or abstaining.

Third,

even if a proposed amendment penetrates this barrier, it will not enter into force until it has been ratified by a majority of the NPT Parties including those who are members of the IAEA Board of Governors. Experience shows that even if a State votes for an amendment to a Treaty there may be a long delay before it completes the procedures needed to implement its ratification: indeed, it may never complete them. Thus the dilatoriness, neglect, or change of mind of any of the approximately twenty-five Parties that are also members of the IAEA Board of Governors could block an amendment indefinitely, even if the other twenty-four had ratified it.

If these were not sufficient safeguards for reluctant parties there is yet one more. Even if an amendment has been ratified by the required majorities, it will only enter into force for those parties that have ratified it. For any party that declines to do so, the NPT remains unamended. This would clearly lead to an ambiguous constitutional situation, though the matter is probably academic in view of the difficulty of carrying an amendment.

What does this mean in practical terms? The approximately twenty-five parties that are members of the IAEA Board of Governors now invariably include not only the three nuclear weapon states but also West Germany and two or three other Western European states, three Eastern European states, Japan, Canada, Australia, and some developing states from Latin America, Africa, the Middle East, South and South-East Asia, and the Pacific and the Far East. No contentious amendment is likely to be supported by every one of these diverse parties. Even if it were possible to bring an amendment before the 1990 Review Conference or before a specially convened conference and even if it had wide support, its failure to penetrate the second barrier would serve only to sour the mood of the majority and perhaps of the 1995 Conference. And if it did penetrate the second barrier, some uncertainty about its entry into force would still hang over it.

Beyond these formidable procedural barriers one may ask what purpose, other than a purely formal one, would be served by amending the Treaty. An amendment incorporating a call for any concrete measures of disarmament or nuclear arms control such as a CTBT, a 'Freeze', a cut-off of fissile material production or a fixed timetable of disarmament measures would only stand a chance of success if all the nuclear weapon state parties were to agree to it and vote for it. If they did, such an amendment would hardly be necessary, as in the circumstances the measures sought would have been taken already or would be the subject of serious negotiations.

Likewise an amendment to require Full-Scope Safeguards or to make more explicit the undertakings in Article IV would require the vote and ratification of all the major exporting countries, some of which are invariably members of the IAEA Board. It is very unlikely that either concept would obtain the necessary support but if it could, it would be more likely to take concrete form in an agreement between the suppliers than in a formal amendment of the Treaty.

As for the dead letters, defects or oversights in the Treaty, including Article V, the opaqueness of Article III.1 and III.2, and the absence of any prohibition against the non-nuclear weapon states helping the nuclear weapon states to make nuclear weapons, even if their rectification were non-contentious, it would hardly be worth the efforts, uncertainties and risks of the amendment procedure to remedy them.

PREPARING FOR THE 1995 CONFERENCE

Article VIII.3 of the NPT explicitly provides that five years after the Treaty's entry into force:

a conference of the Parties to the Treaty shall be held in Geneva, Switzerland, in order to review the operation of this Treaty.

It goes on to provide that at five-year intervals after the first Review Conference:

a majority of the Parties to the Treaty may obtain, by submitting a proposal to this effect to the Depositary Governments, the convening of further conferences with the same objective of reviewing the operation of the Treaty.

The Treaty neither prescribes the venue for the 1995 Conference nor provides any explicit mechanism for convening it. Nevertheless for several reasons it seems likely that Geneva will be selected, as it was for the first three Review Conferences, this choice, among other things, making it much easier for delegates to the Conference on Disarmament to participate.

There is also no explicit provision in the Treaty for any preparatory machinery for the 1995 Conference. If the same procedure is followed as for the Review Conferences, a Preparatory Committee will be established and it will consist of representatives of parties that are serving on the IAEA Board of Governors or as members of the Committee on Disarmament. Given the importance of finding a consensus well in advance of the 1995 Extension Conference, it is certainly desirable that formal preparatory machinery should be established well before the conference opens. In fact, to ensure that the parties are kept fully informed of developments in nuclear energy and nuclear arms control and the relevant work of the United Nations and IAEA, and to provide a degree of continuity that has been lacking until now, it might be useful to create a small, perhaps non-official, inter-sessional working group. For one thing is certain: the conference will only serve the objective of reinforcing the non-proliferation regime if it is the subject of extensive preparatory work to ensure that its proceedings do not degenerate into squabbles over procedure, or fail for lack of sufficient consensus, something which cannot be excluded given the procedural and other problems discussed earlier in this chapter.

NOTES

1. The conference noted that 'the potential benefits' of PNEs 'have not been demonstrated and that the IAEA had not received any requests for PNE services since 1980'.
2. Construction times of 12–14 years compared with 6–10 years in France and Japan are also a United States problem, but here they are caused chiefly by environmentalist opposition and consequent licensing and related problems. The Chernobyl disaster will probably have the effect of retarding Third World programmes. In addition, the government of the Phillipines has recently announced that it will not bring into operation its newly completed reactor.
3. This requirement is, of course quite different from the normal decision-making procedure at international conferences where all that is needed is a simple or, on important questions, a two-thirds majority of the votes *of those present and voting. Abstentions and absences are not counted.* Thus at a normal conference if only three votes are cast on an important question, two positive and one negative, while all others abstain, the requirements for reaching a decision are met.
4. A withdrawing state must, however, under Article X.1 of the Treaty, formally notify the Security Council of those developments, related to the subject-matter of the Treaty, that have 'jeopardised its supreme interests', and thereby prompted it to exercise its right to withdraw. Three months' notice is also required. Of course these formalities can be got around.
5. Shaker considers that the conference 'apparently ... is not juridically entitled to terminate the NPT'. Mohamed I. Shaker, *The Nuclear Non-Proliferation Treaty, Origin and Implementation 1959–79* (New York, Oceana, 1980), p. 864.
6. The normal procedure would be to vote first on the proposal for unlimited extension and then to vote in turn on shorter and shorter fixed periods. Presumably those supporting a longer extension would, if it were unattainable, also vote for a shorter one. I am indebted to Paul Szasz, Director of the General Legal Division, United Nations, for this and several other useful pointers.
7. Italy proposed that the NPT be automatically renewed for fixed periods of 25 years. This renewal would apply to all governments that did not give advance notice of an intention to withdraw. West Germany would have preferred a duration of 5–10 years. Shaker, *The Nuclear Non-Proliferation Treaty*, pp. 860–2.
8. Ibid., p. 864.

12 A world without the NPT?

Joseph Pilat

INTRODUCTION

The world we have experienced since the NPT came into force in 1970 has not been the best of all possible worlds; the world without this Treaty would undoubtedly not be the worst of all possible worlds. But is a world without the NPT possible, or probable? How might it come about? In principle, several paths towards it can be envisaged.

A failure of the NPT parties to extend the Treaty in 1995 would be, for legal and political reasons, highly unlikely. However, blatant non-compliance by any party, overt moves by the holdout states to demonstrate their nuclear capabilities, such as nuclear testing, or dramatic nuclear events such as nuclear theft, sabotage or terrorism could indicate to parties that the NPT was irrelevant, or at best a hollow shell, and that its survival was of no interest to them. The occurrence of any such events, however, seem unlikely in the next decade. More probably, the NPT could be undermined by the withdrawal of a large number of member states or, to prevent such a massive withdrawal, amendments or compromises which would diminish the authority, credibility and effectiveness of the Treaty. Even this prospect is not likely, though it is all too easily imagined, particularly since efforts to obtain universal adherence for the Treaty have brought in parties who may not receive, or may not recognise they are participating in, the full benefits of the Treaty.

In the aftermath of one or another of these dangerous possibilities, all of which are held to be equally destructive to the international non-proliferation regime, the resultant world would undoubtedly be worse than one in which a solid and strengthened NPT were in place as the twenty-first century begins. Without predicting the worst, for this is clearly not the most probable outcome, and to demonstrate concretely the importance of a Treaty that is often praised in vague and general terms, this chapter will attempt to delineate the contours of a world in which the NPT was no longer in force or no longer effective. This analysis does not rest on the choice of any one path for the decline or demise of the NPT. Rather, it is based on the assumption that any weakening of the Treaty by external events, withdrawals or amendments would within ten years create conditions equivalent to its total collapse, despite their very different immediate impacts.

It is often argued that the interest in non-proliferation of NPT states parties would survive the erosion or collapse of the Treaty, that IAEA safeguards would continue to apply with continued effectiveness, and that the world would not fundamentally change. This view is not without some degree of validity. However, it assumes a homogeneity and strength of interest among the parties to the Treaty that would be belied by its collapse, and a less than full realisation of how much the regime and all of its elements have been tied to the NPT during the fifteen years it has been in force. It also assumes that those regime structures and principles that survive the collapse of the Treaty could endure indefinitely without the NPT as a buttress. In contrast, it is argued in the following pages that the possible or probable effects of the loss of the NPT on the international regime, international security and international relations would be considerable, and largely unwelcome to parties and non-parties alike.

THE EFFECTS OF A COLLAPSE OF THE NPT ON THE NON-
PROLIFERATION REGIME

In the absence of the NPT, the prospects for the reduction or removal of differences between nuclear-weapon states and non-nuclear weapon states as suggested, if not explicitly demanded, by Articles IV and VI of the Treaty would become even more distant than they are at present. The universal and inalienable right embodied in Article IV would become irrelevant, and reception of nuclear assistance or exports would depend on the greed, goodwill or grand strategy of the suppliers, without whom indigenous development of a nuclear energy programme would be slow, inefficient, difficult and costly. Obstacles to cooperation could be erected haphazardly and efforts to reduce existing obstacles undermined. In addition, experimental efforts by the nuclear weapon states to assume obligations accepted by the non-nuclear weapon states, exemplified by acceptance of voluntary safeguards, would effectively end.

One of the most likely causes of the Treaty's collapse, as Lewis Dunn suggests in Chapter 8, would be efforts by non-nuclear weapon states parties to the Treaty to utilise the NPT as the horse which pulls the cart of arms control and disarmament. It is clear that the NPT has not been successful in creating a world without nuclear weapons. While this objective was envisioned by many states at the time of the Treaty's conclusion in 1968, the NPT cannot be, and was not originally burdened with being, the international instrument to bring about such a sea change. Nevertheless, the NPT is an arms control treaty and without its existence or effective functioning, hopes for arms control would be diminished. The uncertainties created by the existence or prospect of new nuclear weapon states could be expected to inhibit any further movement among established ones to limit or eliminate their nuclear arsenals. It remains true today, as it was at the time that the NPT was concluded, that effective efforts to manage or prevent horizontal proliferation are necessary but not sufficient conditions for an end to vertical proliferation.

A collapse of the NPT, perhaps due to the dynamics of international diplomacy or the conflict of ideologies, would not immediately or necessarily be followed by a decline of non-proliferation as a principle and a predisposition, for the power of the non-proliferation principle has depended on its practical service to security and perceptions of security. Yet these are primarily derived from the confidence-building effects of the NPT and with no substitute means of affecting the reality or perceptions of security, non-proliferation would begin more and more to fade as a vital national and international objective.

Just as the value of non-proliferation would not immediately disappear in the event of the collapse of the NPT, neither would the primary organisational structure supporting the Treaty's objectives, the IAEA, immediately decline. The latter was established long before the NPT entered into force, and it is likely to continue in existence if the NPT should fail. Yet it is difficult to believe that the Agency would not be profoundly affected by the problems of the Treaty that it has been bound to so intimately for so long.

The Agency's safeguards activities would certainly be adversely affected. As Charles N. van Doren recognises in Chapter 13, the obligations of the non-nuclear weapon states party to the NPT under Article III.1 and III.2 would be terminated, along with all safeguards agreements entered into under the Treaty. While van Doren argues that materials and facilities currently under safeguards would remain so, and subsequent generations of special nuclear materials derived from or produced in safeguarded items would be placed under safeguards, he recognises that this is a legal interpretation that may not be generally understood or accepted and which could be challenged. Only with respect to non-NPT safeguards (INFCIRC 66/Rev.2) has the issue of their continuation been resolved. Even if legal ambiguities were removed from NPT safeguards (INFCIRC 153) by 1995 to assure a recognised, formal requirement for their continuation, or if no legal challenges were forthcoming in 1995 or subsequent years, important politically derived challenges might still emerge.

Because IAEA safeguards have become so closely bound to the NPT, the credibility of these safeguards might well be seriously undermined by the Treaty's collapse, for parties and non-parties alike. Indeed, it is difficult to imagine viable IAEA safeguards a decade after the collapse of the Treaty. It is not clear that states would be willing to endow post-NPT safeguards with the role and importance they now possess, since these technical–political–legal creations would be unsupported by the NPT's more expansive political commitments, including its formal no-weapons pledge. Also, the IAEA as an implementing agency would most probably be weakened.

Without a viable NPT, some states would undoubtedly attempt to shore up the IAEA and, lacking real alternatives, strive to maintain existing IAEA safeguards, extend them to new items, and expand their scope. It might be argued by the governments of the United States, the Soviet Union, Sweden and other staunch supporters of non-proliferation that if the Agency and its safeguards system was given greater responsibilities, and had behind it greater political, and perhaps even military authority, it could fulfil the functions that had formerly been the preserve of the NPT. In practice, however, this would be difficult. Once the IAEA became burdened by the trappings of the NPT, whether this occurred formally or informally, it could begin to lose its broad appeal, which is not universal even today. It must be recognised that the critics of the NPT have vented their spleen not only on the Treaty and the Nuclear Suppliers Group; they have also frequently castigated the IAEA, and in particular what they see as its excessive concern over regulatory as opposed to promotional functions.

Exacerbating these difficulties, there could be public and parliamentary challenges to efforts to strengthen the IAEA in the event of the NPT's collapse. The Congress of the United States, for example, might resist dependence on international institutional solutions in such a situation and mandate actions to restrict and perhaps even suspend United States involvement in international nuclear trade. Such actions could include the ending of approvals for reprocessing and plutonium use and other similar measures. Considerable support for such a stance can be anticipated from public interest groups and the public at large in the United States, with perhaps emulative action by other Western parliaments.

Whatever the justification for and the concrete effects of such moves, they can be expected to create an atmosphere in which states seeking to burden the IAEA and its safeguards with additional responsibilities would undoubtedly find their actions to be somewhat ineffective and perhaps even futile. In addition, confidence in IAEA and other safeguards could subsequently decline to a level so low that they would offer few benefits and be as likely to arouse as to allay suspicions of nuclear weapons development among the non-nuclear weapon states.

Any problems with the IAEA and its safeguards would reverberate through other structures of the non-proliferation regime, all of which depend to a greater or lesser extent upon them. If the Latin American NWFZ established by the Treaty of Tlatelolco were fully operative in the mid-1990s, it would be confronted with difficult choices and challenges were the IAEA safeguards so central to its implementation not perceived to be credible. NWFZs in other regions may be difficult to create without the existence of IAEA safeguards as a common and acceptable standard for their functioning. This is probably true even in regions such as the Middle East, where at least some prospective parties have declared that they would require additional, bilateral or regional, safeguards measures.

The activities of the Zangger Committee and the Nuclear Suppliers Group (NSG) would be adversely affected also by any loss of confidence in IAEA safeguards. Unlike Tlatelolco, however, the committee as well as the group would be directly affected by the loss of the commitments established by the NPT itself. In this situation, the committee would probably be disbanded and the gentlemen's agreement embodied in the group could become a mockery. Moreover, if IAEA safeguards were no longer credible, this would reinforce those trends. The confidence of supplier states that others were not using sweeteners to capitalise on those sales opportunities which presented themselves would then deteriorate, rapidly exacerbating existing differences among the suppliers.

Public criticism of nuclear trade in supplier states, and possible action by the United States Congress and perhaps other legislative bodies, would further this process. Battered on every side, the NSG could collapse, although there might be an effort to revive and strengthen it to carry out the functions that are at present fulfilled by the NPT and the Zangger Committee. While the French, among others, are currently hostile to such a move because of concern about Third World reactions, such perceptions might change in the aftermath of the NPT's failure. Unfortunately, given the limits of the NSG consensus and its underpinning in the NPT/IAEA regime, the NSG would be ill-suited for this function. As a consequence, any hopes of creating a body to fulfil the role of the NPT/IAEA regime by formalising the commitments of the NSG through a treaty would be still-born. This would be the case even if proposals for such a treaty included the emerging suppliers.

INTERNATIONAL SECURITY WITHOUT THE NPT

It has been the NPT, the IAEA safeguards specified by the Treaty and the passage of time that have served to dispel fears that we are moving toward life in a nuclear-armed crowd. Without the Treaty and the required safe-guards obligations, this perception could, and probably would, re-emerge. However, unless the collapse of the NPT were brought about by the nu-clearisation of non-parties, or even parties, the world without the NPT would not automatically bristle with new nuclear-weapon states.

A decision by a state to acquire nuclear weapons, discussed by Philip Gummett in Chapter 10, is based on internal assessments of national interests with priority given to whether or not national security would be served by possession of nuclear weapons. For the great majority of states, such considerations have produced decisions to forego nuclear weapons. Although the collapse of the NPT would eventually affect security percep-tions across the globe, it would not be likely in the near term to damage perceptions of security in any regional contexts, primarily because the obvious countries of concern are non-parties. However, some parties might cause immediate concern for their neighbours if they were suddenly released from the obligations that the NPT requires. This concern might be diminished by considerations such as the high cost of nuclear weapons, especially if they are burdened by stagnant economies and exorbitant international debts, and anticipated superpower pressures. But there is little doubt that over time the regional security situation would deterior-ate, as confidence among non-nuclear weapon states that regional adver-saries are not undertaking nuclear weapons programmes, never absolute under the NPT, would decline without this most impressive of confidence building measures. The fear of armed attacks on other states' nuclear facilities could increase, with disastrous consequences for nuclear power programmes within the region and, possibly, an adverse effect on global nuclear energy development.

General political stability within any region, or around the world, could deteriorate relatively rapidly if states were unsure of their neighbours' nuclear intentions. Whether or not pre-emptive military actions were undertaken, the shifting security situation could result in reassessments by all parties of their need to develop nuclear arms, or perhaps more easily accessible chemical and biological weapons, with which they might attempt to deter the perceived existing or imminent nuclear threat. Contingency plans would have to be adapted to take the new situation into account, with the possibility that military preparations, including new weapons acquisitions, changes in operational doctrine, and the like, could appear so threatening to an adversary as to impel it to realise the capability that was originally feared. There could be a self-fulfilling threat–response interaction of a troubling but virtually inevitable kind.

Arguments about the effect of nuclear weapon proliferation for the establishment of stabilising regional deterrence situations are frequently ethnocentric and ahistorical. However, there is no reason to believe that proliferation would dramatically increase the risk of nuclear war. If the number of nuclear weapons should increase, grave concern is warranted but dire predictions of nuclear disaster do not necessarily follow. Regionally, the presence of nuclear weapons in and of itself is unlikely to precipitate a conflict, although there are grounds for concern over such factors as the political instability of a nuclear-armed country and less effective Command, Communications and Control mechanisms than those utilised in current nuclear weapon states. Moreover, should conflict occur, whether or not it is the result of miscalculation, accident or intent, these weapons could be used if they were available.

On the global stage, some of the least compelling scenarios of nuclear war between the United States and the Soviet Union are those which involve deliberate escalation from, or miscalculated reactions to, Nth country nuclear explosions or exchanges. However, such perceptions would follow all too shortly from ambiguity spawned by the Treaty's collapse, and they could develop a life of their own. Clearly, it is likely that contingency measures would be undertaken by the United States and the USSR in the new security situation, in order to assure that they could preserve their interests and influence, and particularly their ability to project power in potential nuclear environments. Some of these measures might increase the dangers of precipitating a nuclear war, although difficulties in anticipating superpower moves make such assessments highly uncertain. However, it is highly unlikely that new nuclear weapon states would fundamentally alter the superpowers' strategic relations unless the perceived security requirements of a proliferated world led to a significant increase in the arsenals of the French, British or Chinese or an apparent or actual movement towards nuclear weapons by certain states or groups of states with strong industrial bases.

THE EFFECTS ON INTERNATIONAL RELATIONS OF A COLLAPSE OF THE NPT

Not only would the decline or demise of the Treaty affect international security, both regionally and globally, but it would profoundly affect international relations. The influence of international mechanisms created to deal with this vital issue could be effectively limited or eliminated, while the prospect of considering non-proliferation in other international bodies would probably decline. Proliferation problems would be forced to an ever greater extent into bilateral and other multilateral channels, thereby creating or exacerbating tensions and divergent interests along East–West, West–West and North–South lines.

The superpowers could in principle re-establish an effective control system based upon their common interests and the threat of common action in the absence of the international non-proliferation regime. In practice, however, such superpower condominium might not be fully effective, if the erosion of the 'blocs' provides any indication of the declining global politico/military influence of the United States and the Soviet Union. More importantly, perhaps, there is no reason to believe that their interests are so common as is frequently assumed. While superpower cooperation in this sphere has persisted through chills and thaws in East–West relations, the most effective and enduring cooperation has involved those technical matters within the purview of the IAEA.

In the absence of the NPT, and assuming a diminished and diminishing confidence in the IAEA and its safeguards system, the activities of allies and client states regarded as potential proliferators would be so politically sensitive that they could remain largely outside the scope of superpower cooperation. Indeed, these more controversial issues would probably come to dominate their relations in this sphere and traditional differences might be exacerbated as either the Soviet Union or the United States sought political advantage. This trend would be reinforced by the very different geopolitical situations of the superpowers, where a threat to one is not necessarily a threat to the other. While nuclear trade questions *per se* might not provoke excessive friction in superpower relations, they will not be without problems, particularly if the Soviets sought to obtain hard currency or to extend their political influence by entering the international market more aggressively in the 1990s. This scenario, of course, assumes that there is a revival of that market; that the Soviets are competitive in nuclear goods and services and that the Chernobyl accident does not close the door to further Soviet nuclear reactor exports.

Shifts in superpower relations would probably not affect activities within the Eastern bloc over nuclear trade and non-proliferation. Barring a dramatic shift in the Soviet Union's position in the world, the other members of the bloc will continue to follow the Soviet lead in this area. By contrast, harmonious relations among the Western states on these issues are far less likely. West–West relations could be adversely affected by the demise or decline of the NPT. Relations between the United States, Australia, Canada, and some others who fully share non-proliferation interests, perspectives and policies would presumably be unchanged. But their relations with other Western states would undoubtedly worsen.

Real differences have emerged in the last decade among the Western states on nuclear cooperation and non-proliferation issues. The consensus among suppliers has been challenged; questions of nuclear supply and of supplier state policy have often appeared at the forefront of the debate over proliferation concerns and non-proliferation policy. Nevertheless, along with the NPT, the NSG guidelines reflect such supplier consensus as exists and are essential for the survival of the supply regime. However, there are differences in the manner in which the Western supplier states implement their nuclear supply undertakings, and even more important differences between their implementation of supply policy and that of the United States. Their requirements for licensing nuclear exports, the nature of their nuclear export licensing review process and their provisions for post-export controls vary widely, reflecting their different political and legal systems, policy perspectives, economic and political pressures and industry–government relationships.

These divergent policies and perspectives are deeply rooted, and are likely to be exacerbated in the event of the NPT's collapse. They not only reflect the specific nuclear trading interests of the major Western suppliers, but also their views of international trade. The European and Japanese suppliers have a greater reliance on international trade than the United States, and tend to see it in terms of political and strategic, as well as economic benefits. The interdependencies created by international commerce are crucial instruments for managing their relations with other states. These include the special strategic trade relationships between each of these states and various countries and regions in the Third World. In the same vein, the approach of all these states to nuclear supply is also shaped by their differing attitudes toward the proliferation danger, which reflect their unique national security, economic and political interests and perspectives.

Non-proliferation is a declared objective of all of these states. Nevertheless, while the European and Japanese suppliers now hold non-proliferation to be in their national interests, they are unlikely to develop a perspective upon non-proliferation identical to that of the United States. Indeed, some of them have perceived themselves to be 'victims' of the non-proliferation policies of the United States. A collapse of the NPT, and with it credible IAEA safeguards, could throw nuclear trade relations into disarray. Faced with this situation, the United States Congress might enact legislation to restrict or terminate United States nuclear trade, and to attempt to exert more stringent controls over United States-origin nuclear materials, equipment and technology.

THE EMERGING SUPPLIERS AND THE DEMISE OF THE NPT

Although the decline or demise of the NPT would have significant effects on East–West and West–West relations, the most profound effects could appear in North–South relations, with the re-emergence of the politicised nuclear trade issues of the 1970s, and the removal of regime restraints on the behaviour and attitudes of holdout states and emerging suppliers. The war of words on international trade in nuclear materials, equipment and technology has been waged for two decades between North and South, between nuclear 'haves' and 'have-nots'. It reveals differences that go beyond trade itself and permeate the full range of relations between these states. These differences could ultimately freeze the current impasse in the CAS, and portend acute difficulties for the 1990 and 1995 NPT Conferences.

If the worst occurred, the most worrisome consequences could involve changes in the behaviour of the NPT holdouts and the emerging suppliers. Even though the NPT does not now have universal adherence, and is unlikely to have it in the foreseeable future, it has still exerted an influence on the behaviour of holdout states through its effects on nuclear exports, and possibly by its moral suasion. In its absence, the Treaty obligation on parties to require IAEA safeguards on all of their nuclear exports would be terminated, and in time the moral and political principles once upheld by the 'ancien regime' might be seen to be increasingly irrelevant. It is true that the emerging suppliers have proffered support for some elements of the existing supply regime, but many have refused to accept either the NPT or the Treaty of Tlatelolco. Without the formal and informal supply structures that depend to a greater or lesser extent on the NPT and the IAEA, it is not clear how the behaviour of the emerging suppliers could be channeled in ways conducive to non-proliferation. Moreover, these states will inevitably perceive the proliferation danger differently from either the

United States or the other major suppliers. Their view of themselves as the victims of the proliferation policies of the nuclear supplier states is especially vivid and they have bitterly denounced the 'nuclear colonialism' of the 'Caucasian Club' and the existence of 'atomic apartheid'. For states like India and Argentina, opposition to the existing non-proliferation regime has become ideological. All of these states have expressed a principled opposition to restrictions on the transfer of all types of technology. For all emerging suppliers, with the exception of those, such as South Korea and Taiwan, with robust domestic power programmes heavily dependent upon imported technology, equipment and material, the preservation of the existing regime is not a matter of concrete economic or commercial interest. Indeed, some of these states might welcome its collapse, hoping to prosper amid conditions in which nuclear commerce, at least to certain states and regions, was perceived as extremely dangerous and avoided by the major suppliers. Most of the emerging suppliers have no military strategy interests beyond the region in which they are located, although states like China, Brazil and India aspire to the status of global power. If these countries perceive a proliferation danger at all, they do so primarily in regional terms. Although the emerging suppliers can be expected to pursue responsible policies towards their own regions, there will be few concrete inhibitions to irresponsible trade with extra-regional states if the NPT/IAEA regime were to collapse. It is true that these states could be influenced by the political reactions of the nuclear-weapon states and other advanced industrial countries with whom they might have military, diplomatic and trade relations. Yet it is unclear whether the great powers would actively intervene to prevent nuclear trade they deemed dangerous and irresponsible. Further, most emerging suppliers have ties to groupings of states, such as the Islamic or non-aligned ones, which could influence their behaviour either through expectations of disapproval and possibly sanctions, or because of an unwillingness to diminish their preponderance in the group by foregoing an area of clear superiority. Membership in these groups might facilitate some irresponsible types of nuclear transfer, as is suggested by perhaps exaggerated fears of Pakistani assistance to the nuclear ambitions of other Islamic states.

CONCLUSIONS

Clearly, the principal lesson of the 1985 NPT Review Conference, as Mohamed Shaker recognises in Chapter 1, is that the parties to the Treaty held the NPT to be in their national interest and were not prepared to see it destroyed or undermined by an acrimonious Review Conference that re-played the tragedy of 1980. While this common interest produced a fragile consensus, there are no guarantees that this consensus will either endure until, or reappear in, 1995. Nonetheless, the vision of a world without the NPT should demonstrate that the decline or demise of the Treaty would pose problems for holdouts or wavering parties, no less than for fully committed ones. To the extent that it does so, it reveals foundations on which to base a firmer consensus in the future and thereby provides an impetus for preserving this essential treaty regime intact.

13 Safeguards and technical constraints in the 1990s

Charles N. van Doren

INTRODUCTION

The starting-point for this analysis of safeguards and technical constraints against proliferation in the 1990s is that, while these tools are essential to an effective non-proliferation regime, they should not be viewed as a complete answer to the proliferation problem. Although they can be among the inhibiting factors considered in the internal decision-making discussed by Philip Gummett in Chapter 10, the greatest challenge to non-proliferation policy is the political one of fostering and preserving the judgement by non-nuclear weapon states that the acquisition of nuclear weapons would not be in their best interests. Technical constraints may reinforce this judgement but are unlikely to be the prime factors producing it. International safeguards against proliferation have a technical component, but it is wrong to think of them as primarily technical constraints. They are such only to the extent that they may limit the amount of fissile material that a state *considers* it has available for use in nuclear explosives or for other military purposes. *This limitation is not a physical one, but a legal and political one.* It is based on:

(1) The fact that each safeguards agreement includes a legal commitment to the international community by the state involved not to use safeguarded material for military or explosive purposes[1] and, in the case of those argrements with non-parties to the NPT,[2] not to transfer it to any non-nuclear weapon state unless it will be under safeguards in the recipient state.

(2) The general reluctance of a state to violate or abrogate such commitments, both because of the damage this would do to its general reputation of adherence to its international legal commitments, and

because it sees value in preserving the benefit of similar safeguards and commitments by other states.

(3) The high risk that a violation of such a commitment would be detected and internationally condemned, and might lead to punitive responses.

Another political function of safeguards, which would be forfeited by violating or abrogating them, is to lessen inhibitions on nuclear trade with the safeguarded country by providing assurances to its prospective suppliers that their nuclear exports to it will not be diverted to military or explosive uses.

The effect of these legal and political constraints can be illustrated by the case of Sweden, whose early flirtation with nuclear weapons development was described in some detail in a Swedish magazine article in 1985.[3] That article showed the lengths to which the Swedish government deemed it necessary to go to avoid utilising materials that were covered by international commitments against their use for military purposes.

As a further illustration of the difference that safeguards can make, compare the situation with respect to two reactors in the State of Israel: the research reactor supplied by the United States, which is under IAEA safeguards; and the Dimona reactor, which is not. In the first case, the international community has been kept fully informed on the operation of that reactor, the quantities and types of fissile materials that are used and produced in it, where those materials are located, and what becomes of them. Thus any diversion of such materials to military or unknown purposes, or any transfer to another location or recipient could readily be detected. Moreover, the United States–Israel–IAEA Safeguards Agreement contains a legal commitment to both the United States and the IAEA not to use the material produced in or fuelling this reactor for any military or explosive purpose. Israel has a very high political stake in the avoidance of a breach of such commitments to its principal financial and political backer.

In the case of the unsafeguarded Dimona reactor, the international community has no solid information on how it has been operated, how much of what kind of nuclear material has been used or produced in it, and what form it may be in or where it may be situated. It thus has no means of detecting its diversion or transfer. Moreover, Israel has assumed no international legal obligation, other than as a party to the Limited Test Ban Treaty, *not* to use it for military or nuclear explosive purposes. Needless to say, it is this unsafeguarded reactor, rather than a safeguarded one, which is the principal focus of concerns about Israel's reputed efforts to develop nuclear weapons.

This serious gap would be filled if Israel were to accept comprehensive, full-scope IAEA safeguards on all its present and future civil nuclear activities, as each of the non-nuclear weapon states parties to the NPT has obligated itself to do. Such comprehensive safeguards could also help reassure potential antagonists and make it less difficult for them to forgo nuclear weapons acquisition themselves.

Against this background, the outlook for safeguards in the 1990s will next be examined. How termination of the NPT in that period could affect them will first be considered, and then a brief look will be taken at the prospects for safeguards and the challenges to them.

HOW NPT TERMINATION COULD AFFECT INTERNATIONAL SAFEGUARDS

David Fischer and Lewis Dunn, in their chapters in this volume, have expressed well-founded optimism that the NPT is likely to be extended beyond 1995. What follows is not intended to question that view, but rather to examine what would happen in the unlikely event that the NPT was terminated for, as yet, unforeseen reasons.[4] The focus will be on the impact of such termination on IAEA safeguards coverage, and what could be done before 1995 to hedge against that impact.

Termination of the NPT would directly affect IAEA safeguards in three ways:

(1) It would terminate the obligation of the non-nuclear weapon parties to the Treaty under Article III.1 to accept IAEA safeguards on 'all source or special fissionable material in all peaceful nuclear activities' under their jurisdiction or control.
(2) It would have the collateral effect of terminating all the safeguards agreements entered into under the Treaty.[5]
(3) It would terminate the obligation of all parties to the Treaty under Article III.2 to require IAEA safeguards on all their peaceful nuclear exports to any non-nuclear weapon state.

The last of these is one of the principal provisions in the Treaty that has an impact on non-parties, who include most of the states of current proliferation concern,[6] since it eliminates the ability of a non-nuclear weapon state not party to the Treaty to obtain unsafeguarded imports from any of its parties.

Duration of NPT safeguards

In assessing the impact of the first two of these points, a key question is what would actually happen if Article III.1 and its associated NPT safeguards agreements did expire. One optimistic interpretation is that while the expiration of Article III.1 would mean that non-nuclear weapon states parties to the Treaty would no longer be obligated to place under safeguards entirely new items that had no connection with previously safeguarded items, any items that were under NPT safeguards would remain so and safeguards would continue to be applied to subsequent generations of nuclear material produced through their use. The expiration of the safeguards agreement would thus mean only that entirely new items could no longer be added to the inventory of safeguarded ones. Safeguards would continue on items already in the inventory or subsequently produced through their use, and would remain in effect until the IAEA determined that such items were no longer usable for any nuclear activity of relevance to the safeguarding system.

Unfortunately other, more pessimistic, interpretations also exist. These suggest that all items currently under NPT safeguards would be released from those obligations unless they were covered by fall-back provisions which would bring other multi- or bi-lateral safeguarding arrangements into operation.[7] Thus considerable uncertainty exists over what would happen to safeguarding obligations in the event of the NPT's expiry: all that can be asserted is that neither interpretation appears to be generally accepted.

With respect to non-NPT safeguards agreements[8] negotiated since 1973, when the IAEA Board of Governors adopted Gov/1621 (see Appendix 2), this point has been clarified. These agreements not only cover the existing inventory but also subsequent generations of materials, and they remain in force until safeguards on items in the inventory are terminated by the IAEA. Thus, for example, the duration clause of the 1981 IAEA Safeguards Agreement with Spain (INFCIRC 291) reads as follows:

This Agreement shall remain in force until safeguards have been terminated in accordance with its provisions, on all nuclear material, including subsequent generations of produced material, subject to safeguards under this Agreement, and all other items referred to in Section 2 [which includes specified nuclear facilities and equipment, nuclear material or equipment transferred by the US to Spain, nuclear material, including subsequent generations of special nuclear material, which is produced or processed or used in or on the basis of or by the use of any item referred to in that section, or any other item required to be listed in the inventory by another section of the agreement] or as otherwise may be agreed between the Agency and Spain.

The United States position appeared to be that this clarification simply stated what had always been the correct interpretation of residual duties under IAEA safeguards agreements, even when not explicitly spelled out. It was obviously better to remove any basis for dispute on this point in all future safeguards agreements by including the clarifying language, and earlier IAEA safeguards agreements should also be interpreted in the same way.

No such explicit clarification has been attempted with respect to NPT safeguards agreements,[9] or those intended to meet the safeguards requirements of the Treaty of Tlatelolco. This is because many of the original agreements required the approval of the national parliaments and, in some cases, this was obtained only with great difficulty. Renegotiating or amending over one hundred agreements would thus be very time-consuming and probably impracticable. The United States position would probably be that a similar legal interpretation to that suggested above for non-NPT safeguards agreements is the correct one even in the absence of any clarifying language.

In this connection the Nuclear Suppliers guidelines, which are the stated policy of most of the major nuclear supplier nations,[10] and which by their terms apply to nuclear exports 'to any non-nuclear weapon State' including one that is a party to the NPT', provide that 'Suppliers should transfer trigger list items only when covered by IAEA safeguards, *with duration and coverage provisions in conformance with the Gov/1621 Guidelines.*' This suggests that all the present subscribers to the guidelines share the view that NPT safeguards agreements, and those pre-1973 safeguards agreements still active, should be construed as consistent with Gov/1621. The same conclusion is suggested by the fact that all new or amended agreements for cooperation with non-nuclear weapon states entered into by the United States since enactment of the Nuclear Non-Proliferation Act of 1978 (including agreements with Australia, Bangladesh, Canada, Colombia, Egypt, Indonesia, Morocco, Norway, Peru, Sweden and Finland), as well as that with the IAEA, were required by statute to contain a guarantee that:

safeguards as set forth in the agreement for cooperation will be maintained with respect to all nuclear materials and equipment transferred pursuant thereto, and with respect to all special nuclear material used in or produced through the use of such nuclear materials and equipment, so long as the materials or equipment remains under the jurisdiction or control of the cooperating party, *irrespective of the duration of other provisions in the agreement or whether the agreement is terminated or suspended for any reason.*[11]

Thus, for example, the United States Agreement for Cooperation with Finland, signed in 1985, provides that:

Notwithstanding the suspension, termination or expiration of this Agreement or any cooperation hereunder for any reason, [specified Articles, including that requiring safeguards on all exports thereunder] shall continue in effect so long as any material, equipment or components subject to these Articles remains in the territory of the party concerned or under its jurisdiction or control anywhere, or until such time as the parties agree that such material, equipment or components are no longer usable for any nuclear activity relevant from the point of view of safeguards.[12]

It would be useful, well before 1995, to try to remove any doubts that residual duties under NPT safeguards agreements should be construed in this manner. One method of doing this would be for the issue to be considered by the IAEA Board of Governors and clarified in the Final Declaration of the 1990 NPT Review Conference.

Fall-back safeguards agreements

In the case of most of the states having nuclear cooperation agreements with the United States, termination of their NPT safeguards agreements would automatically reinstate the trilateral safeguards agreements between the United States, the IAEA and the cooperating country that antedated the NPT safeguards agreement. These were suspended for as long as the NPT safeguards agreement remained in effect. This applies for example to the case of Japan. In the case of the EURATOM countries the fall-back would not be IAEA safeguards but the European organisations own regional safeguards. In the case of those NPT safeguards agreements that also cover obligations under the Treaty of Tlatelolco, the NPT safeguards agreement would presumably remain in force.

Such fall-back safeguards would be far less comprehensive in their coverage than NPT safeguards, except in the case of the EURATOM ones.[13] In most other cases, they would apply only to items transferred by the United States and to special nuclear materials derived from their use, and not to materials, equipment or facilities indigenous to the recipient state or obtained from other sources. Most other supplier states do not have such fall-back safeguards with respect to their nuclear exports. Moreover, in some cases, such as Egypt, Finland, Indonesia and Morocco, there was no antecedent trilateral safeguards agreement, and so this fall-back is not available. Unfortunately, there seems little or nothing that could be done between now and 1995 that would significantly change this picture.

A reversion to bilateral safeguards arrangements in those circumstances would offer few benefits and would probably produce chaos. Take, for example, the case of Canadian uranium, enriched in the United States, fabricated in Japan and used to fuel French-supplied reactors in South Korea. Each of the four supplier countries would presumably insist on safeguards to ensure that the material was not being diverted to military or explosive use. The administrative and financial burden on South Korea of having to submit to four separate bilateral safeguards systems, each with reporting requirements and their own inspection team, and the need for each of those suppliers to staff and fund its own safeguards make this contingency too horrible to contemplate. In addition, such safeguards systems would lack the comprehensive information available to the full-scope IAEA safeguards system.

Article III.2 and nuclear trade

The termination of Article III.2 of the NPT would have the effect of removing from over 130 states, including virtually all the significant suppliers other than France, the Treaty obligation to require safeguards on all their peaceful nuclear exports to non-nuclear weapon states. This is the most fundamental of all nuclear export conditions, and is the principal way in which the NPT affects the non-nuclear weapon states that have shunned that Treaty – notably Israel, South Africa, Pakistan and India.

Fortunately, this norm has now become so well established that it would probably continue to be followed even if the NPT obligation were to end. But the virtue of the NPT is that it has converted into a mutually binding international legal obligation what otherwise would be only a policy preference, susceptible to change or exceptions.

There exist a number of hedges against the loss of this valuable Treaty obligation. One is continuation of the consensus among the states participating in the Zangger Committee[14] that this norm should be applied to all exports on their 'trigger list'. But the Zangger Committee was formed to work out minimum common standards for the implementation of Article III.2 of the NPT, and this raises the question of whether its guidelines would survive the termination of that article. While they probably would, this is not beyond question and it would seem wise to seek guarantees well before 1995, if that can be done without implying that the NPT will terminate in the 1990s.

Another hedge is the existence of a consensus among the subscribers to the Nuclear Suppliers guidelines.[15] These subscribers include France, which is not a party to the Treaty but has declared that it would behave as if it were. Would this consensus be undermined by the termination of Article III.2, which has from the outset provided assurance that the suppliers could count on this norm being followed by all parties to the NPT? Again, it seems probable that this consensus could be sustained, but it is not a certainty, and it might be wise for the nuclear suppliers to make clear before 1995 that they would continue to adhere to the guidelines whatever happens to the NPT.

Another potentially promising opportunity to reinforce the norm of insisting on safeguards as a condition of supply independently of the NPT is the CAS. The prospects seem good that this gathering, which is independent of the NPT, will reaffirm this basic export norm.

Valuable as these back-up mechanisms may be, they cannot fully take the place of the present nearly universal *Treaty* obligation. This is not only because of the general ways in which treaty obligations can reinforce a policy norm, but also because of a peculiarity in NPT safeguards agreements. NPT safeguards agreements differ from non-NPT ones in that they do not contain a provision explicitly requiring that when a safeguarded item is exported it must be subject to IAEA or equivalent safeguards in the recipient state.[16] This was doubtless because Article III.2 of the NPT itself was deemed to create that obligation. But if the obligation under Article III.2 were to come to an end, there would be a serious question, at least in the case of exports of items that were under safeguards in the exporting state but whose retransfer was not subject to prior consent rights of a third country, whether there would be any legal obligation to ensure that such exports would remain safeguarded in the recipient non-nuclear weapon state.

The hedging actions discussed above might partially mitigate the potential damage from the termination of Article III.2 of the NPT. However, it is clear that the paramount objective must be to avoid resorting to them through avoiding a termination of the NPT in the 1990s.

Other challenges and prospects for safeguards

Apart from dealing with the potential problem of NPT termination, the major challenges facing safeguards for the remainder of this century include the following:

(1) Attempting to move further toward universal full-scope safeguards coverage in non-nuclear weapon states. The Final Declaration of the 1985 NPT Review Conference, while reflecting a welcome move-

ment toward the adoption of full-scope safeguards as a condition of new nuclear supply commitments, fell somewhat short of that goal, and continued resistance by states such as India and Argentina must be expected. Yet the states of greatest near-term proliferation concern have still not accepted full-scope safeguards coverage, and the principal focuses of attention in those countries are their unsafeguarded facilities. In seeking this goal, however, the potential risk of relying entirely on an NPT safeguards agreement in a situation where the NPT could be terminated is highlighted.

(2) The application of safeguards to new types of nuclear facilities. The Final Declaration of the 1985 NPT Review Conference fully endorses this goal. A particularly difficult but important challenge, looking toward the introduction of some laser isotope separation facilities in the 1990s, is to develop an effective approach to safeguarding them.

(3) Continuing to address the other institutional, political and operational problems identified and discussed in David Fischer's outstanding recent book on *Safeguarding the Atom*,[17] and in the Final Declaration of the 1985 Review Conference.

TECHNICAL CONSTRAINTS AND DENIAL

Policies of 'denial' are regularly denigrated at international gatherings. There is no doubt that they can be overdone, that they can be in tension with the NPT, and that they can be counterproductive. But they can still make a significant, if limited, contribution to non-proliferation, even in the 1990s. Five areas where denial will be particularly important are:

Weapons design information

The continued classification and denial of information on how to design and manufacture nuclear weapons or other nuclear explosives is clearly not in conflict with the NPT. In fact, the non-nuclear weapon states parties to that Treaty undertook to accept that they would be denied nuclear explosives, and the nuclear weapon states parties have an obligation 'not in any way to assist, encourage, or induce any non-nuclear weapon state to manufacture or otherwise acquire nuclear weapons or explosive devices'. The latter obligation would be violated if they assisted such a state by giving it access to information on weapons design and manufacture that was not otherwise available to it. Moreover, the non-proliferation advantages of a comprehensive test-ban treaty would be largely nullified if the detailed results of past testing programmes by the nuclear weapon states were made freely available to non-nuclear weapon states.

The only question is whether so much information about nuclear weapons design has already been published that the protection of design data and know-how has become pointless, or will be so in the 1990s. Though extensive information about the basic design of first-generation fission explosives is widely available, there is and will continue to be an appreciable body of information whose disclosure could both facilitate and accelerate the acquisition of nuclear weapons by non-nuclear weapon states and whose protection is thus warranted. At the very least, the withholding of such information can help prevent a state, including one that knows how to make a first-generation fission weapon, from developing more advanced nuclear devices, such as thermonuclear, boosted or miniaturised weapons. The lamentable indiscretions of Howard Morland[18] do not change this conclusion, for they fell far short of providing all the information that would be needed to make a thermonuclear bomb.

Nuclear explosive testing

Also clearly compatible with the NPT are constraints on nuclear explosive testing by its non-nuclear weapons states parties, who obviously could not conduct a test without having violated their undertaking 'not to manufacture or otherwise acquire nuclear weapons or other nuclear explosive devices'. Most of them are also parties to the PTBT and both in that treaty, and in the NPT itself, have affirmed their determination to achieve a true CTBT which could place some meaningful constraints on non-nuclear weapons states not parties to the NPT.

There is some validity in the contention that a state could acquire a first-generation fission bomb, and have some degree of confidence that it would work, without testing. But without testing, a state could not *demonstrate* that it had achieved a nuclear explosive capability; its leaders could not be *certain* that it had achieved such a capability; it would have greater difficulty and uncertainties in taking the further steps necessary to 'weaponise' that explosive design, for example to verify its compatibility with particular designs of delivery vehicles, or tailor it for use in others; it would lack some of the data necessary to make improvements in the design; and it would be unable to develop advanced thermonuclear, boosted or miniaturised weapons. These observations are likely to remain valid in the 1990s. Moreover, at least some of the non-parties to the NPT that are of special proliferation concern might be persuaded to join a CTBT which also prevented further testing by the superpowers. Such a treaty is thus one of the most promising ways to strengthen the international non-proliferation regime.

Sensitive nuclear materials, facilities and technology

In the past, attempts to deny a state nuclear materials, equipment and technology, which it claims are solely for peaceful uses, have aroused much controversy. There exists considerable tension in this area over Article IV of the NPT which promises the 'fullest possible exchange of equipment, materials and scientific technological information for the peaceful uses of nuclear energy' among its parties. Yet this undertaking can hardly be used by non-parties to the NPT to buttress their case for acquiring such items.

Moreover, the promise must clearly bc implemented in a manner that does not undermine the basic objectives of the Treaty or defy common sense. Thus, for example, few would contest the right of an NPT party to decide against supplying Gaddafi with large quantities of highly enriched uranium or separated plutonium, despite his citation of Article IV of the NPT to which Libya is a party. Nor should they deny the right of a state to prohibit the export to NPT parties of items whose use in its own country it had banned as unsafe.

There has recently been a considerable lessening of opposition to the provisions in the Nuclear Suppliers guidelines which specify that 're-straint', but not necessarily denial, should be exercised in the export of highly enriched uranium and separated plutonium, the enrichment and reprocessing facilities that produce them and the technology to construct such facilities. This also applies to the provisions that:

For a transfer of an enrichment facility, or technology therefore, the recipient nation should agree that neither the transferred facilities, nor any facility based on such technology will be designed or operated for the production of greater than 20% enriched uranium without the consent of the supplier nation, of which the IAEA should be advised;

that:

Suppliers should encourage the designers and makers of sensitive equipment to design it in such a way as to facilitate the application of safeguards;

and that:

Suppliers should make every effort to support the IAEA in increasing further the adequacy of safeguards in the light of technical developments.

There has been a clear decline in the expected demand for highly-enriched uranium for peaceful purposes. Power reactors requiring such fuel have become obsolete, and considerable progress has been made in adapting research reactors to the use of lower enriched fuel. In these circumstances it seems both feasible and desirable to carry the guidelines one step further: to seek the explicit dedication of new enrichment facilities to the production of low-enriched uranium only, and to introduce additional new technical means to verify that such commitments are being kept. Though the number of countries with laser isotope separation facilities is likely to be fairly limited, even in the 1990s, there is an urgent need in the interim to develop appropriate safeguards techniques for such plants. This is likely to be a formidable challenge.

The problems presented by separating plutonium and by the reprocessing facilities and technology needed to perform this task will be more difficult to resolve to everyone's satisfaction. There is no counterpart here to the dedication of enrichment facilities solely to the production of low-enriched uranium, although the possible limited availability of laser isotope separation processes in the 1990s should be accompanied by some means of ensuring that they are not used to convert reactor-grade plutonium into plutonium better suited for weapons use.

As for plutonium demand, there is no longer expected to be widespread use of commercial breeder reactors in the 1990s, and the recycling of plutonium in thermal reactors is likely to be limited, because of economic considerations, to those relatively few highly industrialised states who entered into commercial reprocessing contracts in the 1970s and want to salvage that investment. These states will have to face up to the problems of providing adequate physical protection for the separated plutonium, and deciding what to do with the high-level wastes resulting from such reprocessing.

Progress may also be made in evolving an effective international plutonium storage system. The possibilities were thoroughly identified and examined by an IAEA expert group, but action by the Board of Governors and by the principal states concerned is still needed. Support for such development was expressed in the Final Declaration of the 1985 NPT Review Conference, which also endorsed the development of safeguards techniques applicable to new nuclear technologies.

Nuclear export controls

The mechanism for exercising the 'restraint' referred to above is national nuclear export controls, coupled with international efforts to ensure that minimum common standards for them are adopted by all potential suppliers. These can be helpful both in ensuring that any nuclear material or facility resulting from exported items of technology will be safeguarded, and in making it possible to delay and impede its acquisition of access to sensitive materials or equipment for its production where an applicant poses a particular proliferation risk. While the circumstances necessary for the effective use of this approach may well be present in a decreasing number of cases, there will still be some scope for its use in the 1990s in particularly sensitive cases.

Sub-national and terrorist groups

Technological constraints must not be aimed solely at the acquisition of nuclear explosives by national governments. They must also help cope with the risk of acquisition of nuclear explosives or sensitive nuclear materials or equipment by sub-national or terrorist groups. The NPT, international safeguards and other political strategies are of little or no help in preventing this. Reliance must be placed almost entirely on limiting both targets and opportunities, on providing adequate physical protection and, at least in the case of actual weapons, on the existence of mechanisms designed to deny their unauthorised use. Policies must also be aimed at securing international cooperation in identifying potential threats, quickly recovering stolen materials and deterring, apprehending and punishing those who may be involved.

Even in the absence of a major hijacking, theft or seizure, it seems inevitable that there will be growing concern about these risks, with attention being particularly focused on shipments of large quantities of weapon-usable materials. If such a seizure does occur in the next fifteen years, this concern will be greatly intensified and public demands for increased precautions will be loud and clear. In this connection, the glacial pace at which most of the industrial countries have approached the International Convention on the Physical Protection of Nuclear Material,[19] the only international mechanism currently designed to address this problem, is to be deplored. Yet it seems likely that most of them will have joined it by the 1990s. Valuable as this will be, it needs to be accompanied by further efforts to minimise targets of opportunity and to promote the achievement of significant improvements in physical security measures.

CONCLUSIONS

In looking ahead to the 1990s, this chapter has highlighted the need to extend the duration of the NPT because of the impact of failing to do so on the valuable commitments and reassurances offered by international safeguards agreements, and the desirability of taking steps in the meantime to hedge against the possibility of such failure. After briefly reviewing other safeguards challenges to be faced, it has examined the limited but necessary contributions that technical constraints can make in that period, noting that they must constrain sub-national and terrorist groups as well as governments. In general, the prognosis is cautiously optimistic if enough constructive attention can be directed to preserving and keeping up to date the international non-proliferation regime, while at the same time pursuing political approaches aimed at reducing the motivation to acquire nuclear explosives.

NOTES

1. The commitment in NPT safeguards agreements is against diversion to use in nuclear weapons or other nuclear explosive devices; that in pre-NPT agreements is against use to further any military purpose; and that in most safeguards agreements entered into in recent years with non-parties to the NPT is against diversion for either of these purposes.
2. i.e., those concluded with non-parties to the NPT pursuant to INFCIRC 66/Rev.2.
3. Christer Larssen, 'Build a Bomb!', *Ny Teknik* (25 April 1985).
4. Exactly how its termination might come about is a complicated question treated by David Fischer in Chapter 11. The analysis offered here of the impact of termination of the Treaty also applies to a situation where a particular party's obligations under the Treaty were terminated by its exercising its right of withdrawal under Article X.1.
5. INFCIRC 153 provides that the safeguards agreements entered into pursuant to the NPT will 'remain in force as long as the State is a party to the Treaty on the Non-Proliferation of Nuclear Weapons', and each such agreement contains a duration clause to that effect.
6. The other principal provision affecting non-parties is the undertaking of the nuclear weapon states parties to the Treaty in Article I 'not to transfer to any recipient whatsoever nuclear weapons or other nuclear explosive devices or control over such weapons or explosive devices, directly, or indirectly' and 'not in any way to assist, encourage, or induce any non-nuclear weapon State to manufacture or otherwise acquire nuclear weapons or other nuclear explosive devices or control over such weapons or explosive devices'.
7. This interpretation is implicit in comments on this question contained in J. Simpson 'Ploughshares into swords? The International Nuclear Non-Proliferation Network and the 1985 NPT Review Conference', *Faraday Discussion Paper* no 4 (Council for Arms Control: London, 1985).
8. i.e. those concluded with non-parties to the NPT pursuant to IAEA INFCIRC 66/Rev.2.
9. i.e. those concluded with NPT parties, in accordance with IAEA INFCIRC 153.
10. The following states have announced that their nuclear export policies are in conformity with the guidelines which were published in 1977 in IAEA INFCIRC 254: the United States, the United Kingdom, the Soviet Union, France, the Federal Republic of Germany, Canada, Japan, Belgium, Czechoslovakia, the German Democratic Republic, Italy, the Netherlands, Poland, Sweden, Switzerland, Australia, Finland, Denmark, Greece, Luxembourg, Ireland, Bulgaria and South Africa. It is expected that Spain and Portugal, which joined EURATOM on 1 January 1986, will also follow the guidelines, in keeping with the decision of all other members to do so as a matter of common policy.
11. Sec. 123(1) of the United States Atomic Energy Act of 1954, as amended by the Nuclear Non-Proliferation Act of 1978.
12. Article 14(2) of the United States–Finland Agreement for Cooperation.
13. While EURATOM safeguards are comprehensive in scope, they do not apply to materials

that a member state declares are to be used in a military programme. But this option is not open with respect to items transferred from another country under a peaceful use guarantee. This includes all items transferred from the United States under the US agreements for cooperation with EURATOM.

14. The current adherents include: Australia, Austria, Belgium, Canada, Czechoslovakia, Denmark, FRG, Finland, GDR, Greece, Hungary, Ireland, Italy, Japan, Luxembourg, Netherlands, Norway, Poland, Soviet Union, Sweden, Switzerland, United Kingdom, United States of America.

15. See note 10 above.

16. Sec.28 of INFCIRC 66 Rev.2 provides that 'No safeguarded nuclear material shall be transferred outside the jurisdiction of the State in which it is being safeguarded until the Agency has satisfied itself that one or more of the following conditions apply: . . . (c) Arrangements have been made by the Agency to safeguard the material in accordance with this document in the State to which it is being transferred; or (d) The material will be subject, in the State to which it is being transferred, to safeguards other than those of the Agency but generally consistent with such safeguards and accepted by the Agency.' Thus, for example, Sec.9 of the 1971 trilateral safeguards agreement between the United States, the IAEA and India provides that 'The two Governments shall jointly notify the Agency of any transfer of materials, equipment or devices subject to this Agreement to a recipient which is not under the jurisdiction of either of the two Governments. Such materials, equipment or devices may be transferred and shall thereupon cease to be subject to this Agreement, provided that:

    (a) Such materials, equipment or devices are subject to Agency safeguards; or
    (b) The materials, equipment or devices are subject to safeguards other than those applied by the Agency under this Agreement, but generally consistent with such safeguards and accepted by the Agency.'

    INFCIRC 153, on the other hand, deals with international transfers simply by requiring that the safeguards agreement provide that the states concerned shall make suitable arrangements to determine the point at which the transfer of responsibility betwen the exporter and the recipient will take place: that the IAEA be notified in advance of any such shipment, and that 'if the nuclear material will not be subject to Agency safeguards in the recipient State [which, even under Article III.2 of the NPT, could be the case if the recipient were a nuclear weapon state], the exporting State shall make arrangements for the Agency to receive, within three months of the time when the recipient State accepts responsibility for the nuclear material from the exporting State, confirmation by the recipient State of the transfer'. (Sec.94).

17. David Fischer and Paul Szasz, *Safeguarding the Atom: A Critical Appraisal*, edited by Josef Goldblat (Taylor and Francis: London for Stockholm International Peace Research Institute, 1985).

18. Morland was the author of a notorious article in the *Progressive* magazine in the late 1970s that disclosed some previously unpublished information about the design of thermonuclear weapons. The United States government tried unsuccessfully to prevent the publication of this article.

19. This Convention entered into force in early 1987 for those states, such as the United States and the Soviet Union, which had previously ratified it.

14 Nuclear non-proliferation in the 1990s: an agenda of issues and policy choices

John Simpson

INTRODUCTION

Each year, at least one large international conference is held under the auspices of the United Nations. These conferences can be divided into two categories: those which are intended to establish an international consensus on a particular area or issue and those intended to institute programmes of action to reinforce and exploit such a consensus. In theory, conferences to review or extend existing treaties should be of the latter type: in practice they often become amalgams of the two, with arguments about aims and objectives becoming inextricably intertwined with differences over implementation. The conferences associated with the NPT are no exception to this general rule.

The arguments over objectives and implementation at the 1995 NPT Conference are likely to take place in several contexts. One is the evolution and future significance of those substantive matters which in the past have dominated discussions at NPT Review Conferences. Another involves the procedural questions which will need to be resolved either before or during the Extension Conference.

The substantive matters which have dominated NPT Review Conferences can be divided for the purpose of analysis and exposition into three issue areas. The first of these is the possession of nuclear weapons by China, France, the United Kingdom, the United States and the Soviet Union. This situation has generated anxiety and apprehension in the community of states and stimulated numerous attempts to manage and/or physically destroy and ban their devices. The relevance of this issue area to the NPT is that many states see one object of the Treaty as the disarmament of the existing nuclear weapon states. The second issue area concerns the working of the international regime to prevent the acquisition of nuclear weapons by additional states; an integral part of this regime is the trading relationships between supplier and recipient countries. The third issue area is the search for guarantees that the civil exploitation of nuclear technology is safe from diversion to military purposes by either states or non-state actors.

These three issue areas, the management of nuclear armaments, the prevention of the proliferation of nuclear weapons and the safeguarding of nuclear energy activities are based upon similar bodies of scientific knowledge. They are also concerned with the production and use of the same chemical elements, plutonium and uranium. Whether these areas are linked in a similar organic way in the political arena, however, seems likely to continue to be a major source of international disagreement.

The procedural issues surrounding the 1995 Extension Conference have been extensively discussed by David Fischer in Chapter 11. These are not easy to think through in advance, as so many alternative possibilities appear to exist. They are made even more complex by the interaction between substantive and procedural conflicts that will undoubtedly occur at the 1995 Conference. For some will seek to exploit these procedural uncertainties in their attempt to achieve substantive aims, making the conference very difficult to manage and its outcome uncertain.

In the sections which follow, an attempt will be made to summarise and evaluate the substantive and procedural issues surrounding the 1995 NPT Conference, in an attempt to alert states and statesmen to the need to address them now rather than immediately before the conference convenes. At the same time, some ideas for dealing with these problems will be explored. The result will be a tentative agenda for non-proliferation policy in the 1990s.

THE MANAGEMENT OF NUCLEAR ARMAMENTS IN THE 1990S

Fundamental disagreements over the norms and principles underlying international arrangements for managing nuclear energy, and more especially those underlying the NPT, have been endemic ever since those arrangements were first envisaged. Many states regard the NPT as a Treaty whose prime objective is the total elimination of all nuclear weapons from the globe. Others see it as having the much more restricted task of dissuading further states from acquiring nuclear weapons. Fortunately, this second objective is an integral component of the first one, as is the need for guarantees and safeguards against the use of nuclear energy facilities in non-nuclear weapon states for military purposes. This fortuitous overlap is the pragmatic basis for the existing regime.[1]

193

A key question for the 1990s, however, is whether some of those states and statesmen who regard the prime norm of the NPT as global nuclear disarmament may feel so strongly about achieving it that they would be prepared to risk the future of the existing nuclear non-proliferation regime, and more specifically the NPT, in pursuit of their objective. A supplementary issue is the degree of risk they would feel they could accept in pursuit of that objective. Linked to this is the danger that in the course of a process of political bargaining nominally intended to achieve global nuclear disarmament, diplomatic miscalculations will inadvertently result in a weakening of the non-proliferation regime.

This situation would present no danger to the existing regime if there were excellent prospects that in the 1990s the objective being sought could be achieved and nuclear weapons would be eliminated from the globe. This is an issue where significant differences exist between what many decision-makers within nuclear weapon states realistically believe is possible and the aspirations for global nuclear disarmament articulated by many individuals and states.

These differences and their relationship to the NPT can only be fully understood in their historic context. The facilitation of negotiations on nuclear disarmament and General and Complete Disarmament (GCD), as well as a CTBT, was specifically mentioned in the preamble to the NPT. Achieving agreement on these objectives still appeared realistic in the early 1960s when negotiations on an NPT commenced, as nuclear weapon technology and nuclear power programmes were in their infancy. The amount of fissile material of weapon grade that had been produced was limited, there had been relatively few explosive nuclear weapon tests involving fissile material and the numbers of nuclear powered submarines were small. But by the 1980s total nuclear disarmament by the superpowers appeared to many in nuclear weapons laboratories and in positions of responsibility in governments as technically unrealistic, whatever the content of discussions on the subject between the leaders of the United States and the Soviet Union in Iceland or elsewhere.

The reasons for this pessimism were not hard to find. The favourable conditions of the 1960s had long ceased to exist, and after several decades of unmonitored national activities it was believed it would be almost impossible to verify with credibility any figures for production and stockpiles of fissile materials and bombs provided by nuclear weapon states to each other. Without such guarantees, it was unrealistic to expect that the United States (to mention just one nuclear weapon state) would be prepared to abandon both its offensive nuclear systems and any defensive

capabilities it had against such systems while it had acute political differences with other nuclear weapons states.

Several consequences emerged from this situation. There existed a large
gap between what some of those in weapon laboratories and nuclear
establishments believed was technically possible and what much of the
world's population and many of its governments were seeking to achieve.
This was not unusual, as aspirations and beliefs in the political realm and
what is physically possible are often radically different. Thus the government of the Soviet Union was pursuing publicly the disarmament objectives of the 1960s with the avowed aim of achieving GCD, despite the
practical problems that appeared to preclude the full implementation of
that aim. The government of the United States, by contrast, was seeking a
logical, technical solution to its security problem by developing the SDI,
and in doing so had radically altered the political agenda for superpower
arms control negotiations. If its future deployment could be linked to
cooperative arms control measures which would significantly reduce the
numbers of offensive systems, this held out the prospect of making detailed
verification of both stockpiles of weapon materials and the destruction of
offensive nuclear weapons less relevant.

Whether a watertight defence of the United States against ballistic
missiles would ever be technically feasible was, of course, open to debate.
Moreover, the United States position was based on the assumption that
nuclear weapons would continue to be needed into the indefinite future
to sustain United States and NATO security by deterring a Soviet attack if
effective defences could not be developed against them. Political aims and
what many specialists saw as technical reality thus appeared to be in
conflict in the policies of both the United States and the Soviet Union.
The significance of these differences for the future of the NPT was that
the Soviet position conformed to the wishes of much of the population
and many of the states of the world while that of the United States did
not.

For a number of reasons the negotiation of a CTBT has become the
battleground between these two positions. This has also made it a key area
of conflict influencing the future of the NPT. Its significance derives not
only from it being specifically mentioned in the preamble to the Treaty, but
also from the history of the trilateral negotiations concerning it which
started in the late 1970s. They are widely regarded as having made
considerable progress[2] when first events in Afghanistan and then a new
American Presidency led to their suspension. The immediate cause of the
breakdown in negotiations was overtly political, rather than technical, for

the Reagan administration did not choose to justify its refusal to restart them on the grounds that a CTBT could not be effectively verified.

This reversal of United States policy has made negotiations on a CTBT symbolic of the attitude and committment of the Reagan administration towards nuclear disarmament negotiations. The United States stance is also seen as a breach of the promise contained in Article VI of the NPT that it would negotiate in good faith on nuclear disarmament. This symbolism is reinforced by the stubborn refusal of the United States to even discuss talks on an agreement which is widely regarded as relatively easy to conclude. The Soviet Union's unilateral moratorium on nuclear testing and the lack of any overt United States reciprocal response has compounded this situation. As a consequence, negotiations on a CTBT have acquired a political symbolism within the international community which gives them a significance independent of the concrete advantages that might flow from the Treaty.[3]

The current prospects for a CTBT thus seem more dependent upon the resolution of basic superpower differences in attitude and declaratory policy towards nuclear disarmament than more instrumental questions of the need to develop power systems for the SDI's X-ray lasers. If disarmament is believed to be a near-term prospect, then foregoing the ability to validate changes in nuclear weapon designs for purposes of modernisation, enhancing safety features or correcting stockpile degradation can be accepted. If disarmament is seen as technically unrealistic, or at best a long-term possibility, then retaining the option to engage in nuclear explosive testing will continue to be seen as essential for national security. Admittedly, a new administration in the United States in 1989 or 1993 could theoretically result in both a change in attitude towards a CTBT and real prospects that any agreement would be ratified by the Senate, but at the time of writing this seems a rather remote possibility.

Having the ability to test is thus non-negotiable as far as the current United States government is concerned, though there may be scope for agreements which would limit the frequency of underground tests and the size of their yields. This posture and the political symbolism that other states invest in a CTBT suggests that negotiating this treaty and fulfilling the commitment contained in Article VI of the NPT will remain a major area of contention at both the 1990 Review Conference and the 1995 Conference. Moreover, the international and domestic debates over nuclear weapons still seem likely to be conducted in terms of political aspirations instead of what many would see as practical possibilities. The dangers inherent in these differences in perspective on nuclear disarmament and the impasse over a CTBT arise from the risks that both state and non-state proponents of nuclear disarmament are prepared to take with the future of the NPT and the viability of the nuclear non-proliferation regime in their attempts to press for the negotiation of nuclear disarmament agreements. This in turn will depend on how skilled they will be at this form of diplomatic brinkmanship.

The basic disagreements over the principles and aims of the NPT thus seem likely to remain central to discussion and negotiation throughout the 1990s. The only changes which would radically alter this situation would be either a diminution in international demands for nuclear disarmament or the advent of a United States administration and Congress prepared to move towards a nuclear disarmed world in the absence of either a technically credible verification regime or strategic defences. In the absence of such developments, conflict and bargaining over nuclear disarmament is destined to remain a permanent feature of NPT conferences. The uncertainties reside in the impact these activities will have upon the commitment of non-nuclear weapon states to both the NPT and to the other elements of the nuclear non-proliferation regime and in the ability of states to limit the damage to the treaty arising from such conflict.

THE NUCLEAR NON-PROLIFERATION REGIME IN THE 1990S

The international nuclear non-proliferation regime comprises several interlocking elements, including the NPT, the IAEA and its safeguards system, the Nuclear Suppliers Group and the nuclear trading guidelines, EURATOM and its safeguards, the nuclear weapon-free zone in Antarctica, the Partial Test Ban Treaty and national export control procedures. In addition, there also exist a number of treaties which are not yet fully in force, including the Treaty of Tlatelolco creating a nuclear weapon-free zone in Latin America and a similar treaty covering the South Pacific. These elements cover a very comprehensive range of activities and as a consequence the scope or need for new organisations or for amendments to existing agreements is problematic. Rather, what appears to be required is to enhance the functioning of existing institutions and implement fully the agreements under which they were created and operate.

The NPT plays a pivotal role in the non-proliferation regime both because it embodies unique commitments by states not to acquire or assist in the acquisition of nuclear weapons and because it makes full-scope safeguards mandatory for all its non-nuclear weapon parties. Increasing the number of signatories is an obvious way of strengthening its effects, though this could also result in an increase in the divisions between parties at NPT conferences. The states whose signatures would most enhance its geographic scope are relatively few in number: Argentina, Brazil, China, France, India, Israel, Pakistan and South Africa. The motives of these states in staying outside of the NPT are diverse, as each has a different political system and unique political imperatives. As a consequence, there is little evidence to suggest that changes to the NPT or other measures with universalist consequences would cause them all to become signatories. For the key changes which might lead to the accession of most of these states are not in the Treaty itself but in the implementation of certain of its existing articles or in the resolution of regional disputes which threaten their national security.

This suggests concentrating on non-proliferation policies tailored to a state's individual circumstances. Such policies might include inducing these states to participate in alternative arrangements to the NPT. These could include unilateral declarations that they will act as though they were Treaty members, declarations that they will use nuclear materials for peaceful purposes only and the negotiation of regional and bilateral arrangements to reduce the pressure upon them to acquire nuclear weapons.

Such a strategy could serve as a response to the noticeable rise in the prominence of regional disputes during the three NPT review conferences between 1975 and 1985. One explanation for this is that many states now see the NPT as a security Treaty rather than a disarmament one. This may ease disputes over nuclear disarmament in the 1990s, but it may also result in states wishing to use it to articulate their specific security concerns. For African states, the most pressing threat from nuclear weaponry is perceived to emanate from South Africa rather than from one of the existing nuclear weapon powers. Regional disputes will thus continue to be seen by many states as the core non-proliferation issues and it seems likely that political brinkmanship of the type that persisted between Iran and Iraq at the 1985 Review Conference will continue to be experienced during future NPT conferences. Yet unless the states involved in these regional disputes choose to acquire nuclear weapons themselves, the NPT remains essential for their national security and logically they cannot afford to see its effectiveness decline. At the same time, the NPT itself cannot resolve any of the political conflicts which give rise to these regional problems. There thus seems no obvious method of preventing such issues playing a central role in NPT discussions in the 1990s.

Nuclear weapon free zones are one method of tackling these regional problems in the context of the nuclear non-proliferation regime, and appear to be the most promising method of doing this in South Asia, Latin America and perhaps the Middle East. Such a belief rests on the assumptions that the major motivations for nuclear proliferation arise out of the local or regional context and can best be dealt with there. Yet this will still leave some scope for both active external support for regional activities and offers of external mediation to help resolve disputes. An issue for further exploration is whether a permanent mediation and conflict resolution organisation might be created and promoted under the auspices of the United Nations rather than the IAEA. It could be given the task, among other things, of actively encouraging local and regional non-proliferation efforts.

The 1985 NPT Review Conference saw a marked reduction in complaints about the lack of economic benefits to developing states from membership of the Treaty. A mixture of a glut of oil on world markets, low oil prices and the political consequences of the Chernobyl disaster seems likely to restrain global demands for access to nuclear energy into the foreseeable future. In such circumstances, the supplier guidelines will be easier to justify and sustain, thus helping to limit the scope of the nuclear non-proliferation problem.

Although attempts will continue to be made to address the question of the financing of nuclear power plant in developing countries, there seems no simple institutional way in which this can be linked to the NPT and used as a device to make membership of the Treaty more attractive. The NPT does confer international legitimacy on its members' national nuclear energy programmes, but it is not linked to any financial provisions which would allow states to more easily fund such programmes. Moreover, although the IAEA is the international institution which has the specific task of promoting nuclear power, its predominant roles are now monitoring and technical assistance. Many states regard this as a basic flaw in the NPT and it may result in these issues of financing legitimate activities having a greater predominance in the 1990 and 1995 NPT Conferences than they did in 1985.

Access to finance thus seems likely to continue to be a key element restraining nuclear energy programmes outside of the OECD countries. In addition, there may be increasing reluctance to provide states with finance for nuclear programmes, even where the conditions attached include entry into the NPT, if the alternative appears to be the prevention of such developments by apparently non-discriminatory financial means. Such denial may be contrary to the 'spirit' of Article IV of the NPT, but there is nothing in the Treaty which compels its parties to fund nuclear programmes in other states.

Policies of denial through financial constraint are one aspect of a broader international strategy of using supplier controls to hinder nuclear proliferation. There seems little possibility that the supplier guidelines, which are at the core of this strategy, will be strengthened in future by making all exports conditional upon acceptance of FSS by recipients. However, insistence on safeguards over exported materials and facilities will continue to be a most effective way of denying proliferation options to states outside the NPT. Similarly, it might be counterproductive to change the requirement to exercise restraint over the export of sensitive plant and materials into an absolute prohibition, as this would remove the ability to discriminate between problem and non-problem countries. This situation would also be strengthened if the IAEA Committee on Assurances of Supply could produce a set of pragmatic guarantees that states would have access to fuel supplies for their power programmes. One possibility here would be to revive and fully implement the IAEA's powers to act as a supplier of fissile materials in its own right.

An area in need of greater investigation is cooperation in drawing up national export regulations, particularly those covering dual-use technologies, so as to minimise problems arising from the wording, substance and implementation of national regulations. This is a continuous task, for the new technological possibilities provided by centrifuge and laser-enrichment techniques will make it necessary to ensure that access to them remains restricted during the 1990s. In addition, there is a need to coordinate other national actions designed to deny relevant technologies and equipment to a potential proliferator. One area of concern here is to regulate the export of components necessary for the construction of nuclear devices. Another is to restrain the export of ballistic missiles, cruise missiles and advanced attack aircraft which would serve as potent nuclear weapon delivery systems. It has to be accepted, however, that this latter restraint may lead to acute dilemmas in cases where a state made the provision of modern offensive weapons a condition for *not* proliferating.

Two major potential threats to supplier arrangements seem likely to emerge during the 1990s: the growth of new suppliers and of a 'grey market'. Indeed the new suppliers might, under some circumstances, be the only suppliers remaining in the market. They will be those states that have built up an indigenous technological base which is not subject to the IAEA safeguards system. Coupled to this, they will be both anxious to obtain a return for this investment and among the most vociferous opponents of the alleged inequalities inherent in the NPT.

Formal or informal methods will have to be devised to bring such states within the system of supplier guidelines, including persuading them to either publicly accept the guidelines or pledge that they will act in accordance with them. This may be rather easier than it appears. Once they have attained supplier status they are unlikely to want to assist regional rivals in acquiring a similar capability to their own. The more difficult relationships to regulate will be those between states in different regions or continents, such as India or China with Argentina. This may require the opening of dialogues designed to assimilate these states into the global system of restraints, perhaps through a revived series of informal Suppliers Group consultation meetings. There seems every prospect that such dialogues would be very fruitful, as trade already seems to be taking place between states such as China and Argentina on the basis that acceptance of IAEA safeguards is a condition of supply.

The 'grey market' problem is more difficult to tackle because states involved in covert trade outside of the supplier guidelines are unlikely to welcome any publicity for their actions and will make active efforts to conceal their activities. This problem may only be capable of being dealt with through diplomatic channels and quiet persuasion.

These arrangements to restrain the dissemination of sensitive nuclear capabilities and materials form the visible and tangible part of the non-proliferation regime: the practical programmes. The less visible part is the maintenance of a global consensus against nuclear proliferation based upon agreed principles and norms. This is one reason why it is desirable for the existing nuclear weapon states to be seen to be actively committed to their own nuclear disarmament during the 1990s, as otherwise a clear logical conflict will exist between their position and the policies they are attempting to impose on the rest of the world: a case of 'do as I say, not as I do'.

One substantive basis upon which the limited global consensus against nuclear proliferation appears to rest is a belief that nuclear weapons are not relevant to the security problems faced by the majority of states. A major reason for this is that such weapons are perceived by the majority of states as incapable of performing any direct or useful normal military functions: they are essentially political bargaining instruments or punitive weapons to deter the total destruction of the state. This basis for consensus is reinforced by the case studies that exist of those states, such as Sweden, which have in the past considered acquiring nuclear weapons but rejected this course of action on grounds of lack of military utility and cost-effectiveness. It is also strengthened by the lengthy period of time that has elapsed since the emergence of China as the fifth nuclear weapons state. The longer this period is extended, the stronger will be the case for arguing that nuclear weapons acquisition offers few benefits to the average state. On the other hand, this lengthening period may also increase the impact made upon the international community by any state that chooses to proliferate.

One method of reinforcing this intangible international consensus against proliferation might be to promote the acceptance by all states of a formal no-first-use commitment in respect of nuclear weapons. This would serve to further strengthen the view that nuclear weapons have little positive military utility. The nuclear weapon states have already made a collective commitment of this type in respect of individual non-nuclear weapon states acting alone, but not in respect of other nuclear weapon states or their non-nuclear weapon allies. The main barrier to extending this collective commitment is the conflict between it and current NATO doctrine. This is one area where development and deployment of the new conventional weapons technologies discussed in an earlier chapter would have a direct effect upon the nuclear non-proliferation regime, if they were able to free NATO states from reliance upon a deterrent doctrine which included use of nuclear weapons in response to non-nuclear attack.

Any decision by a non-nuclear weapon state to acquire nuclear weapons will be taken through a process of decision-making unique to that state. This makes the nature of state decision-making processes and their accessibility to external influences of crucial importance if international pressures are to be mobilised to prevent proliferation. Yet such intervention would have to be carefully managed, for the circumstances under which overt breaches of the rule against interference in other states' internal affairs are legitimate and the degree to which such intervention might be counterproductive will be crucial elements in producing a successful outcome. This area for potential action seems likely to be the most difficult part of the nuclear non-proliferation regime to manage in the 1990s. Yet at the same time it cannot be ignored if domestic elites are to be prevented from using nuclear weapons activities as partial solutions to internal political difficulties.

Any attempt to evaluate the overall state of the global non-proliferation regime in the context of the 1990s therefore has to deal with two contradictory considerations. On the one hand it can be optimistically predicted that considerable stability seems likely within the institutions and processes of the regime itself, with consolidation and expansion of existing activities being the normal mode of action rather than the pursuit of radical new initiatives. On the other hand, it has to be pessimistically recognised that the ability of the regime to survive an act of proliferation remains open to question. No attempt has been made to plan in advance detailed international responses to such an event. Yet it merely takes a decision to proliferate by the leadership or even just the leader of a single state in possession of a nuclear weapons option for the regime to be thrown into crisis. Moreover, such a decision and its implementation might not be accessible to external influence. As a consequence, when viewed from this perspective, the non-proliferation situation both now and in the 1990s appears very fragile.

Creating a strategy to prevent such proliferation decisions in the 1990s may necessitate advance planning and coordination of both the sanctions to be imposed upon a proliferator and other actions to be taken to deal with the situation. This could be done on both a global and regional basis, the latter involving consultations within organisations such as the EEC. Substantive issues that may need to be discussed would include, for example, provision of security assistance to prevent or offset any act of proliferation and the form that any sanctions against the proliferator would take.

The nuclear non-proliferation regime will never be perfect. Yet its imperfections will become obvious only when its objectives are put into question by an act of proliferation. This is why any agenda for the 1990s will have to include attempts to reach consensus on the norms and principles of the regime, efforts to reinforce its practical programmes and a willingness to plan responses in the event that proliferation does occur. It may also involve many non-proliferation activities at both local and regional levels that do not fit conveniently into a global framework. Finding means of coordinating such national actions and ensuring that they do not clash with each other and the workings of the global regime could be a major issue for the 1990s.

SAFEGUARDING NUCLEAR ENERGY ACTIVITIES

The system of international safeguards administered by the IAEA is not intended to physically prevent states from diverting materials and facilities to military activities. Rather, it aims to provide political reassurance both through the probability that diversion of safeguarded materials would be retrospectively detected and through the potential diverters being deterred from acting by the likelihood of discovery. The scope of IAEA safeguarding activities is circumscribed by the organisation having no ability or legal power to actively search for undeclared materials and facilities, although it does have a right to demand a special inspection if it obtains information that undeclared facilities or materials exist. An issue for the 1990s is whether the IAEA safeguards system could be linked to enhanced international facilities for obtaining information upon which these special challenge inspections could be based, such as satellite photography. Given current political attitudes, however, such a development seems most unlikely to be agreed or implemented.

Another issue which seems destined to continue to be on the nonproliferation agenda in the 1990s is the safeguarding of nuclear energy activities in nuclear weapon states. The prime aim of such safeguards is the symbolic one of accepting equivalent restrictions upon their nonmilitary activities to those imposed on non-nuclear weapon states: the 'equality of misery principle'. Suggestions have been made that IAEA safeguarding activities in nuclear weapon states should both become mandatory and be based upon similar principles to those underlying EURATOM safeguards. This latter move would mean that all nuclear materials would be automatically subject to safeguards unless they were withdrawn from the arrangements for military purposes.

Such a change is open to several objections. The most damaging is that if a EURATOM-type system were to apply to all states, it would legitimise the use of some fissile materials in weapons. For the basis of the current NPT/IAEA system is that such use is illegal. Thus if all INFCIRC 153 arrangements were renegotiated on the EURATOM basis, non-nuclear weapon states would acquire a right to withdraw materials from safeguards for unspecified military purposes. This would effectively undermine the whole basis of the NPT, unless this system was only to apply to the nuclear weapon states. However, if that was the case it would not deal with accusations of discrimination resulting from operating two different systems of safeguards. In addition, the costs of such a change would be considerable and the benefits not easily assessed.

The IAEA safeguarding system will also have to respond in the next decade to the challenges presented by changes in materials production technologies and the increase in shipments and use of plutonium. Some of these matters are discussed in greater detail in Appendix 3. The ability to enrich uranium to weapons grade in relatively low-technology centrifuges which make small demands on space and electrical power will make it imperative that safeguarding techniques be developed to ensure that both feed materials and technology are not diverted to such uses. The suggestion contained in Appendix 3 that reactor grade plutonium could also be enriched in this way makes it even more important to safeguard this technology, as well as all stocks of plutonium. The same imperatives will be reinforced when laser enrichment techniques become more widely available.

These problems will be compounded if substantial quantities of plutonium become readily available from the reprocessing of thermal reactor fuel. This may lead to the view becoming dominant that it makes more economic sense to recycle the resultant plutonium through thermal reactors than store it for eventual use in fast reactors. Given current uranium prices, such a development appears unlikely, but if it were to occur it would place an added burden on the safeguarding system.

Three sets of activities would help to enhance the ability of the IAEA safeguards system to meet the challenges posed by these technological developments. First, pressure could be placed on all non-signatories to subscribe to the Convention on the Physical Protection of Nuclear Material. Second, records of stocks of safeguarded plutonium could include details of isotopic composition, as is already the case with uranium. In this way, stocks of the most sensitive grades of the material could be readily identified for safeguard purposes and appropriate action taken. Finally, the question of whether the IAEA should follow the lead of EURATOM and insist on import safeguards for yellowcake (U_3O_8) could be addressed. While these moves would not guarantee that the type of activities outlined in Appendix 3 could be prevented, they would make them much more difficult to undertake.

The 1990s will also see the availability of more efficient remote monitoring equipment for safeguarding both stores of fissile materials and the operation of nuclear facilities. Technically, this holds out the possibility of relaying data on global nuclear energy activities back to either regional safeguarding centres or the IAEA headquarters in Vienna on a real-time basis. Key issues will be whether states would be prepared to accept such direct and immediate surveillance of their nuclear energy activities and whether they will be prepared to finance the equipment and running costs involved in such a system. There is also the political problem posed by the tacit understanding that the IAEA's safeguarding and technical assistance budgets should be roughly equal. A positive attempt to overcome these problems would make a major contribution to enhancing the political reassurance role of IAEA safeguards in the 1990s. One innovation might be to use EURATOM states as the trial ground for such equipment; another to incorporate the equipment in both the design of facilities and their purchase price.

Chapters 12 and 13 discussed the consequences for the IAEA safeguards system of the NPT not persisting beyond the end of the 1990s. The immediate causes of any termination of the NPT would probably affect the functioning of the IAEA also, and might even lead to states withdrawing from it, thus weakening even further the non-proliferation regime. At the same time, major conflicts will probably arise over differing national interpretations of the status of the IAEA safeguards applicable to them. Ways of evading this difficulty would be for states to attempt to obtain authoritative clarification of the legal situation well before 1995 and for supplier states to insist that fall-back safeguard provisions should be written automatically into all future NPT INFCIRC 153 safeguards. Unfortunately, it is almost certainly too late for this to be done retrospectively for existing agreements. However, this problem may be less significant than it appears, as only Canada, Sweden and the East European states are not covered by fall-back INFCIRC 66 safeguards.

These safeguarding questions are crucially dependent upon the state of international demand for energy during the 1990s and the role played in meeting this demand by nuclear power. In a world experiencing low oil prices, as well as grappling with the uncertain consequences of the Chernobyl disaster and anticipating little expansion in plans to construct new nuclear energy facilities, there is a danger that these safeguarding issues will be accorded a low priority. Conversely, the next decade may offer a unique opportunity to strengthen the safeguards system while the pressures to cope with a rapid expansion of nuclear energy facilities are low. A major issue for the 1990s is thus going to be how to ensure the necessary political support for attempts to reinforce activities in this area.

THE 1995 EXTENSION CONFERENCE

The conference that will convene in 1995 to consider the extension of the NPT will be crucially dependent for its success upon the efforts made to resolve many of the issues and problems raised in earlier parts of this chapter. Equally important, however, will be the ability of the states involved in the conference to resolve a large number of procedural questions. The only opportunity to do this or to set up procedures for doing so will probably be the NPT Review Conference in 1990. It thus seems essential to identify these central procedural issues well in advance of that meeting, in order to allow governments and others time to consider and consult about them.

The first issue is whether there should be a separate NPT Review Conference in 1995 or whether it should be incorporated in the mandatory Extension Conference. One consequence of holding a separate review conference is that it might allow the Extension Conference to concentrate on the issue of the period of extension of the Treaty without it becoming involved in bargaining and trade-offs linking this question to other matters such as regional issues and nuclear disarmament. But this would deprive those states giving greater priority to these latter issues of a valuable bargaining lever, and will be actively opposed by them. Moreover, if this matter is addressed at all in 1990, it will have to occur in the context of negotiations over the wording of the Final Document of the 1990 Review Conference. For it is traditional to make a recommendation concerning the next review conference in the Final Document of the previous one.

Decisions on the content of final documents of NPT Review Conferences are taken by consensus if this is at all possible, rather than by majority voting (see Appendix 4). The pressure to reach decisions by consensus is such that it will be difficult to stop any attempt by developed states to clarify issues of procedure related to the 1995 Conference becoming entangled in the general bargaining over the wording of the Final Document from the 1990 Review Conference. The choice that may face many Western governments in these circumstances will be between accepting a merged review and extension conference in 1995 as the price for the neutral and non-aligned group agreeing to the 1990 Final Document or agreeing to leave the matter to be decided by consultation and negotiation at a later date.

A theoretical possibility also exists for some states to propose the holding of a conference to amend the Treaty in 1995. Their motive in proposing this could be to attempt to trade changes in the Treaty for an agreement on its extension. Such an exercise would be difficult, to say the least. For, as David Fischer has described in Chapter 11, the process of ratifying amendments is both complex and lengthy, and there could be no guarantees that any changes in the Treaty would overcome the barrier presented by the ratification rules. In addition, a number of contributors have made the point that the key problems over the NPT concern implementation of the existing Treaty. Changing its wording is unlikely to alter this position.

Moreover, most potential amendments serve little positive purpose, as Harald Müller has demonstrated in Chapter 9. Finally, the political effect sought by amendments can probably be obtained by linking to the Treaty protocols or resolutions passed at a review conference. This is another reason why the question of whether the 1995 Extension Conference will also double as a review conference is likely to be so central to its outcome. Despite this, it would not be surprising to see some neutral and non-aligned states being urged to seek the convening of an amendment conference in 1995, if only to acquire additional bargaining leverage over the developed states in the context of the extension conference.

The NPT contains no indication of how the extension conference should be structured or conducted: by contrast there now exists a well-established framework of events and set of procedures in relation to review conferences. If a review conference were to be incorporated into the extension conference, a number of possible ways of handling the recommendation for extension would exist, some of which would overlap. These could include:

(1)   Creating a fourth main committee to handle it during the second half of the review conference;
(2)   Making it the responsibility of the drafting committee or the president. A working group could be convened to attempt to agree a proposal to put to the plenary under their auspices;
(3)   Incorporating it in the Final Document of the Review Conference;
(4)   Dealing with it in a separate document, protocol or resolution.

The range of these possibilities suggests some very fertile grounds for debate and disagreement if any attempt were to be made to agree on how the extension conference was to be handled prior to 1995.

The 1995 Extension Conference would have before it many alternatives when it came to attempting to agree a recommendation on the future of the NPT. It could include recommending:

(1)   An indefinite extension;
(2)   An extension for an infinite number of fixed periods (e.g. five years) linked to a negative procedure for extending the Treaty. Such a procedure could, for instance, involve the Treaty being automatically extended for a further period unless a vote on termination was requested;
(3)   An extension for an infinite number of fixed periods linked to a positive procedure for continuation by an affirmative majority vote at the end of each period;

(4)   An extension for a single fixed period which could be anything from three months to twenty five years. At the end of this fixed period, the Treaty would either automatically lapse or be extended following a further conference.

It is probable that those states satisfied with the functioning and value of the Treaty will argue for an indefinite extension, or at the very least for an extension for an infinite number of fixed periods linked to a procedure for automatic extension in the absence of a request for a vote on termination. Those states who see the NPT as a source of political leverage, for whatever purpose, are likely to opt for a single, short extension linked to a procedure making further extensions conditional upon a positive vote of the parties. In the absence of such an affirmative vote, the Treaty would automatically lapse. In this way these states would simultaneously increase both the number of opportunities for using the NPT as a bargaining forum and their potential leverage over other states during such negotiations.

These many and varied options for handling the extension issue increase the importance attached to the voting procedures described by David Fischer in Chapter 11. One consequence may be to place a great premium on a consensus decision, if the consequences of voting are unclear and there is a fear among all groups of an unintended outcome. Equally, if the conference decides to vote upon a number of alternatives in succession, there is a danger that the conference could eventually be confronted with the choice between a single extension for a very short period or no majority decision on extension at all. This outcome becomes more likely if a relatively low number of parties attend the extension conference. In these circumstances some attempt to agree in advance on the legal status of the Treaty in the event of a non-decision would seem prudent.

AN AGENDA FOR THE 1990S

The implication of this discussion of the likely substance of the 1995 NPT Extension Conference suggests that parties are going to be confronted by a very complex and confusing situation. This could result in considerable manoeuvering over those procedural issues which appear to preclude or reinforce the possibility of agreement on substantive questions. It is clear that the president of the conference will face a daunting task, and that delegations and the secretariat may have to rely heavily on the services of their legal advisers. Yet all the issues are capable of resolution given time, preparation and good will.

Three conditions thus seem necessary for a productive NPT Extension Conference in 1995: adequate preparation, a positive commitment on the part of all delegations to the importance of the Treaty and goodwill in negotiating agreed conditions for an extension. The preparations for the conference should take many forms. There should be the prior negotiation of insurance agreements against the possibility of the conference failing to produce a result; there should be an effort to agree legal interpretations of documents and procedures in advance of 1995 and there should be an attempt to nominate key personnel well in advance of the convening of the conference to allow them adequate time for consultation and preparation. Much of this work could be set in train at the 1990 Review Conference, which could also agree on the relationship between the 1995 Extension Conference and any review conference that it recommended should be held in that year. One innovation to assist in these tasks could be the creation of a small secretariat with the responsibility for identifying potential problems well in advance and with powers to consult on solutions to them.

The creation by 1995 of an atmosphere supportive of resolving some of the substantive problems may be a more difficult task than resolving the procedural issues, for no amount of preparation will overcome a relative lack of commitment to the Treaty arising out of conflicts over substance. This problem can only be tackled by a broad approach of seeking solutions to regional problems, by the nuclear weapon states being seen to have a positive commitment to nuclear disarmament and by seeking to strengthen the non-proliferation regime in a gradual and incremental way over the next decade.

Ensuring the strengthening and survival of the NPT into the next century will not be an easy matter: neither is it something which will automatically occur. It will require considerable foresight, creative problem-solving and commitment. This chapter represents a first attempt to identify some of the major difficulties that are likely to confront the Treaty in the 1990s and some tentative policy options for addressing them. If this chapter and those which preceded it result in these matters being seriously addressed by governments and researchers in the years before the 1990 NPT Review Conference convenes, then it will have succeeded in its major aim.

Concern over the outcome of the 1995 NPT Conference should be placed in perspective, however. The problem states in the non-proliferation context are almost all non-signatories of the NPT. Its existence reduces the concern that its parties will become problem states, but it does not directly restrain these non-signatories from proliferating. Strengthening the regime associated with the NPT will provide needed public reassurance that proliferation is unlikely to occur, but it will not necessarily have any effect upon the decision of a non-signatory to acquire nuclear weapons. Thus while it remains vital that the NPT should be extended and the regime strengthened, the fragility of the global non-proliferation situation will persist so long as key states continue to maintain options to proliferate. Extending the NPT may be a necessary condition to enhance the non-proliferation regime in the 1990s, but it is a sobering thought that it will not be a sufficient condition to prevent nuclear proliferation during this period.

NOTES

1. For a more extensive treatment of this issue of the norms and objectives of the non-proliferation regime see J. Simpson, 'The Nuclear Non-Proliferation Regime as a Model for Conventional Armament Restraint', in M. Brzoska and T. Ohlson (eds.), *Third World Arms Control*, SIPRI, Ch.17, forthcoming.
2. Although substantial elements of a CTBT had been agreed, the issues that remained to be resolved when negotiations were terminated were regarded by many as very intractable. In particular, no agreement had been reached on either the principles underlying the verification system or the numbers of remote seismic stations in each state. Thus while the treaty might have been 95% complete in terms of its wording, a much lesser percentage of the differences between the parties had been resolved.
3. This symbolism also derives from a CTBT being the longest-running item on the international arms control agenda, having been first discussed in the mid-1950s. Agreement on it would thus indicate that real progress was occurring in disarmament negotiations.

Appendices

Appendix 1 Treaty on the Non-Proliferation of Nuclear Weapons (NPT)

The States concluding this Treaty, hereinafter, referred to as the 'Parties to the Treaty',

Considering the devastation that would be visited upon all mankind by a nuclear war and the consequent need to make every effort to avert the danger of such a war and to take measures to safeguard the security of peoples,

Believing that the proliferation of nuclear weapons would seriously enhance the danger of nuclear war,

In conformity with resolutions of the United Nations General Assembly calling for the conclusion of an agreement on the prevention of wider dissemination of nuclear weapons,

Undertaking to cooperate in facilitating the application of International Atomic Energy Agency safeguards on peaceful nuclear activities,

Expressing their support for research, development and other efforts to further the application, within the framework of the International Atomic Energy Agency safeguards system, of the principle of safeguarding effectively the flow of source and special fissionable materials by use of instruments and other techniques at certain strategic points,

Affirming the principle that the benefits of peaceful applications of nuclear technology, including any technological by-products which may be derived by nuclear-weapon States from the development of nuclear explosive devices, should be available for peaceful purposes to all Parties to the Treaty, whether nuclear-weapon or non-nuclear-weapon States,

Convinced that in furtherance of this principle, all Parties to the Treaty are entitled to participate in the fullest possible exchange of scientific information for, and to contribute alone or in cooperation with other States to, the further development of the applications of atomic energy for peaceful purposes,

Declaring their intention to achieve at the earliest possible date the cessation of the nuclear arms race and to undertake effective measures in the direction of nuclear disarmament,

Urging the cooperation of all States in the attainment of this objective,

Recalling the determination expressed by the Parties to the 1963 Treaty banning nuclear weapon tests in the atmosphere, in outer space and under water in its Preamble to seek to achieve the discontinuance of all test explosions of nuclear weapons for all time and to continue negotiations to this end,

Desiring to further the easing of international tension and the strengthening of trust between States in order to facilitate the cessation of the manufacture of nuclear weapons, the liquidation of all their existing stockpiles, and the elimination from national arsenals of nuclear weapons and the means of their delivery pursuant to a Treaty on general and complete disarmament under strict and effective international control,

Recalling that, in accordance with the Charter of the United Nations, States must refrain in their international relations from the threat or use of force against the territorial integrity or political independence of any State, or in any other manner inconsistent with the purposes of the United Nations, and that the establishment and maintenance of international peace and security are to be promoted with the least diversion for armaments of the world's human and economic resources;

Have agreed as follows:

ARTICLE I

Each nuclear-weapon State Party to the Treaty undertakes not to transfer to any recipient whatsoever nuclear weapons or other nuclear explosive devices or control over such weapons or explosive devices directly, or indirectly; and not in any way to assist, encourage, or induce any non-nuclear-weapon State to manufacture or otherwise acquire nuclear weapons or other nuclear explosive devices, or control over such weapons or explosive devices.

ARTICLE II

Each non-nuclear-weapon State Party to the Treaty undertakes not to receive the transfer from any transferor whatsoever of nuclear weapons or other nuclear explosive devices or of control over such weapons or explosive devices directly, or indirectly; not to manufacture or otherwise acquire nuclear weapons or other nuclear explosive devices; and not to seek or receive any assistance in the manufacture of nuclear weapons or other nuclear explosive devices.

ARTICLE III

1. Each non-nuclear-weapon State Party to the Treaty undertakes to accept safeguards, as set forth in an agreement to be negotiated and concluded with the International Atomic Energy Agency in accordance with the Statute of the International Atomic Energy Agency and the Agency's safeguards system, for the exclusive purpose of verification of the fulfilment of its obligations assumed under this Treaty with a view to preventing diversion of nuclear energy from peaceful uses to nuclear weapons or other nuclear explosive devices. Procedures for the safeguards required by this Article shall be followed with respect to source or special fissionable material whether it is being produced, processed or used in any principal nuclear facility or is outside any such facility. The safeguards required by this Article shall be applied on all source or special fissionable material in all peaceful nuclear activities within the territory of such State, under its jurisdiction, or carried out under its control anywhere.

2. Each State Party to the Treaty undertakes not to provide: (a) source or special fissionable material, or (b) equipment or material especially designed or prepared for the processing, use or production of special fissionable material, to any non-nuclear-weapon State for peaceful purposes, unless the source or special fissionable material shall be subject to the safeguards required by this Article.

3. The safeguards required by this Article shall be implemented in a manner designed to comply with Article IV of this Treaty, and to avoid hampering the economic or technological development of the Parties or international cooperation in the field of peaceful nuclear activities, including the international exchange of nuclear material and equipment for the processing, use or production of nuclear mater-

ial for peaceful purposes in accordance with the provisions of this Article and the principle of safeguarding set forth in the Preamble of the Treaty.

4. Non-nuclear-weapon States Party to the Treaty shall conclude agreements with the International Atomic Energy Agency to meet the requirements of this Article either individually or together with other States in accordance with the Statute of the International Atomic Energy Agency. Negotiation of such agreements shall commence within 180 days from the original entry into force of this Treaty. For States depositing their instruments of ratification or accession after the 180-day period, negotiation of such agreements shall commence not later than the date of such deposit. Such agreements shall enter into force not later than eighteen months after the date of initiation of negotiations.

ARTICLE IV

1. Nothing in this Treaty shall be interpreted as affecting the inalienable right of all the Parties to the Treaty to develop research, production and use of nuclear energy for peaceful purposes without discrimination and in conformity with Articles I and II of this Treaty.

2. All the Parties to the Treaty undertake to facilitate, and have the right to participate in, the fullest possible exchange of equipment, materials and scientific and technological information for the peaceful uses of nuclear energy. Parties to the Treaty in a position to do so shall also cooperate in contributing alone or together with other States or international organisations to the further development of the applications of nuclear energy for peaceful purposes, especially in the territories of non-nuclear-weapon States Party to the Treaty, with due consideration for the needs of the developing areas of the world.

ARTICLE V

Each Party to the Treaty undertakes to take appropriate measures to ensure that, in accordance with this Treaty, under appropriate international observation and through appropriate international procedures, potential benefits from any peaceful applications of nuclear explosions will be made available to non-nuclear-weapon States Party to the Treaty on a non-discriminatory basis and that the charge to such Parties for the explosive devices used will be as low as possible and exclude any charge for research and development. Non-nuclear-weapon States Party to the Treaty shall be able to obtain such benefits, pursuant to a special international agreements or agreements, through an appropriate international body with adequate representation of non-nuclear-weapon States. Negotiations on this subject shall commence as soon as possible after the Treaty enters into force. Non-nuclear-weapon States Party to this Treaty so desiring may also obtain such benefits pursuant to bilateral agreements.

ARTICLE VI

Each of the Parties to the Treaty undertakes to pursue negotiations in good faith on effective measures relating to cessation of the nuclear arms race at an early date and to nuclear disarmament, and on a Treaty on general and complete disarmament under strict and effective international control.

ARTICLE VII

Nothing in this Treaty affects the right of any group of States to conclude regional treaties in order to assure the total absence of nuclear weapons in their respective territories.

ARTICLE VIII

1. Any Party to the Treaty may propose amendments to this Treaty. The text of any proposed amendment shall be submitted to the Depositary Governments which shall circulate it to all Parties to the Treaty. Thereupon, if requested to do so by one-third or more of the Parties to the Treaty, the Depositary Governments shall convene a conference, to which they shall invite all the Parties to the Treaty, to consider such an amendment.

2. Any amendment to this Treaty must be approved by a majority of the votes of all the Parties to the Treaty, including the votes of all nuclear-weapon States Party to the Treaty and all other Parties which, on the date the amendment is circulated, are members of the Board of Governors of the International Atomic Energy Agency. The amendment shall enter into force for each Party that deposits its instrument of ratification of the amendment upon the deposit of such instruments of ratification by a majority of all the Parties, including the instruments

of ratification of all nuclear-weapon States Party to the Treaty and all other Parties which, on the date the amendment is circulated, are members of the Board of Governors of the International Atomic Energy Agency. Thereafter, it shall enter into force for any other Party upon the deposit of its instrument of ratification of the amendment.

3. Five years after the entry into force of this Treaty, a conference of Parties to the Treaty shall be held in Geneva, Switzerland, in order to review the operation of this Treaty with a view to assuring that the purposes of the Preamble and the provisions of the Treaty are being realised. At intervals of five years thereafter, a majority of the parties to the Treaty may obtain, by submitting a proposal to this effect to the Depositary Governments, the convening of further conferences with the same objective of reviewing the operation of the Treaty.

ARTICLE IX

1. This Treaty shall be open to all States for signature. Any State which does not sign the Treaty before its entry into force in accordance with paragraph 3 of this Article may accede to it at any time.

2. This Treaty shall be subject to ratification by signatory States. Instruments of ratification and instruments of accession shall be deposited with the Governments of the Union of Soviet Socialist Republics, the United Kingdom of Great Britain and Northern Ireland, and the United States of America, which are hereby designated the Depositary Governments.

3. This Treaty shall enter into force after its ratification by the States, the Governments of which are designated Depositaries of the Treaty, and forty other States signatory to this Treaty and the deposit of their instruments of ratification. For the purposes of this Treaty, a nuclear-weapon State is one which has manufactured and exploded a nuclear weapon or other nuclear explosive device prior to January 1, 1967.

4. For the States whose instruments of ratification or accession are deposited subsequent to the entry into force of this Treaty, it shall enter into force on the date of the deposit of their instruments of ratification or accession.

5. The Depositary Governments shall promptly inform all signatory acceding States of the date of each signature, the date of deposit of each

instrument of ratification or of accession, the date of the entry into force of this Treaty, and the date of receipt of any requests for convening a conference or other notices.

6. This Treaty shall be registered by the Depositary Governments pursuant to Article 102 of the Charter of the United Nations.

ARTICLE X

1. Each Party shall in exercising its national sovereignty have the right to withdraw from the Treaty if it decides that extraordinary events, related to the subject matter of this Treaty, have jeopardized the supreme interests of its country. It shall give notice of such withdrawal to all other Parties to the Treaty and to the United Nations Security Council three months in advance. Such notice shall include a statement of the extraordinary events it regards as having jeopardized its supreme interests.

2. Twenty-five years after the entry into force of the Treaty, a Conference shall be convened to decide whether the Treaty shall continue in force indefinitely, or shall be extended for an additional fixed period or periods. This decision shall be taken by a majority of the Parties to the Treaty.

ARTICLE XI

This Treaty, the English, Russian, French, Spanish and Chinese texts of which are equally authentic, shall be deposited in the archives of the Depositary Governments. Duly certified copies of this Treaty shall be transmitted by the Depositary Governments to the Governments of the signatory and acceding States.

IN WITNESS WHEREOF the undersigned, duly authorised, have signed this Treaty.

DONE in triplicate, at the cities of London, Moscow and Washington, the first day of July one thousand nine hundred and sixty-eight.

Appendix 2 Duration and Termination of Iaea INFCIRC 66 Agreements, GOV/1621 of 1973

Item 1(b) of the provisional agenda (GOV/1620)

SAFEGUARDS
(B)   THE FORMULATION OF CERTAIN PROVISIONS IN
AGREEMENTS UNDER THE AGENCY'S SAFEGUARDS SYSTEM
(1965, AS PREVIOUSLY EXTENDED IN 1966 AND 1968)

Memorandum by the Director-General
1.   A substantial number of Governors have urged that there should be a
greater degree of standardization than in the past with respect to the
duration and termination of such agreements as may henceforth be
concluded under the Agency's Safeguards System (1965, as Provi-
sionally Extended in 1966 and 1968) for the application of safeguards
in connection with nuclear material supplied to States by third parties. To achieve this, it is recommended that the following two concepts should be reflected in these agreements:
(a)   That the duration of the agreement should be related to the
period of actual use of the items in the recipient State: and
(b)   That the provisions for terminating the agreement should be
formulated in such a way that the rights and obligations of the parties
continue to apply in connection with supplied nuclear material and
with special fissionable material produced, processed or used in or in
connection with supplied nuclear material, equipment, facilities or
non-nuclear material, until such time as the Agency has terminated
the application of safeguards thereto, in accordance with the provisions of paragraph 26 or 27 of the Agency's Safeguards System.
A short exposition with respect to the application of these concepts is
annexed hereto.

2. The proposed standardization would appear likely to facilitate the uniform application of safeguards measures. It is furthermore to be noted that the combined operation of the two concepts would be consistent with the application of the general principle embodied in paragraph 16 of the Agency's Safeguards System.

Requested action by the Board

3. In bringing this matter to the Board's attention, the Director General seeks the views of the Board as to whether it concurs with the two concepts set out in paragraph 1 above.

ANNEX

1. In the case of receipt by a State of source or special fissionable material, equipment facilities, or non-nuclear materials from a supplier outside that State, the duration of the relevant agreement under the Agency's Safeguards System would be related to the actual use in the recipient State of the material or items supplied. This may be accomplished by requiring, in accordance with present practice, that the material or items supplied be listed in the inventory called for by the agreement.

2. The primary effect of termination of the agreement, either by act of the parties or effluxion of time, would be that no further supplied nuclear material, equipment, facilities or non-nuclear material could be added to the inventory. On the other hand, the rights and obligations of the parties, as provided for in the agreement, would continue to apply in connection with any supplied material or items and with any special fissionable material produced, processed or used in or in connection with any supplied material or items which had been included in the inventory, until such material or items had been removed from the inventory.

3. With respect to nuclear material, conditions for removal are those set out in paragraph 26 or 27 of the Agency's Safeguards System; with respect to equipment, facilities and non-nuclear material, conditions for removal could be based on paragraph 26. A number of agreements already concluded have prescribed such conditions in part, by providing for deletion from the inventory of nuclear material, equipment and facilities which are returned to the supplying State or transferred (under safeguards) to a third State. The additional provisions contemplated would stipulate that items or non-nuclear material

could be removed from the purview of the agreement if they had been consumed, were no longer usable for any nuclear activity relevant from the point of view of safeguards or had become practicably irrecoverable.

4. The effect of reflecting the two concepts in agreements would be that special fissionable material which had been produced, processed or used in or in connection with supplied material or items before they were removed from the scope of the agreement, would remain or be listed in the inventory, and such special fissionable material, together with any supplied nuclear material remaining in the inventory, would be subject to safeguards until the Agency had terminated safeguards on that special fissionable and nuclear material in accordance with the provisions of the Agency's Safeguards System. Thus, the actual termination of the operation of the provisions of the agreement would take place only when everything had been removed from the inventory.

Appendix 3 The problem posed by anonymous proliferation

Norman (Ned) Franklin

Norman (Ned) Franklin

INTRODUCTION

Nuclear proliferation is normally defined as the extension of ownership or control of nuclear weapons to additional sovereign states. Such states are assumed to be seeking a significant number of reasonably efficient weapons of dependable performance which are both capable of being stockpiled for periods of years and are designed and weaponised for use by advanced aircraft or missile delivery systems. Great significance is therefore attached to the detectability and attribution of tests of nuclear explosives, as it would be difficult for a state to develop these types of weapon without such tests.

At the other end of the spectrum of proliferation is nuclear theft. Systems for safeguarding the physical security of fissionable materials are responses to this concern, as are similar security measures surrounding nuclear weapons themselves. Yet the potential remains for a non-sovereign group of extortionists, terrorists or freedom-fighters to claim to have constructed or stolen a nuclear device and to threaten to explode it.

In the middle of this spectrum there is at least one intermediate case that has so far been largely ignored, that of 'anonymous proliferation'. This would be a situation where a nuclear device was constructed by a nominally non-nuclear weapon state in region A and transferred to a terrorist group in region B who then exploded it.

MOTIVES FOR 'ANONYMOUS PROLIFERATION'

The drive to eliminate nuclear weapons from the globe originates in emotive fears and anxieties over the consequences of their use. These concerns produce a wish to be reassured both that nuclear relationships are in a stable state and that nuclear proliferation is not going to take place. If circumstances existed in which this belief in the stability and continuity of the status quo was destroyed, it would threaten the existing public perception in many countries that non-proliferation is the best course for their governments, as well as others.

At least four sets of circumstances could produce a degradation in perceptions of nuclear stability. The first would be the conduct of the nuclear weapon states. In particular, the state of United States–Soviet Union relations influences people's expectation of limits being placed on levels of nuclear arms, which in turn they associate with a reduced risk of the use of these weapons. A second circumstance would be if a non-nuclear weapon state were to choose to declare publicly its intention to acquire a stockpile of nuclear weapons. If a weapon test was identified as having been undertaken by such a state, the stability of relations in its region would be significantly affected.

A third circumstance would be if an act of nuclear terrorism were perpetrated in a state. This would be likely to significantly alter perceptions of security and attitudes to nuclear weapons on both a regional and global basis. Linked to this is a fourth circumstance where a state believed it had a direct interest in destabilising a region, which would not necessarily have to be the one of which it was a geographical part. Any detonation in such a region of a primitive, low-yield nuclear weapon would have the most severe consequences. If the manufacturer of such a primitive nuclear device could arrange to be an 'anonymous proliferator' he would not need to produce a substantial number of weapons nor to test them: an undetected misfire would merely call for a second try. This would substantially increase his chances of achieving anonymity. Suicidal fanatics could probably be found to detonate such a weapon in an offshore boat or aircraft.

CREDIBILITY AND FEASIBILITY

The chances of 'anonymous proliferation' occurring depend on two factors: the existence of national leaders with an overwhelming interest in destabilisation and the technical feasibility of this course of action. History and recent events suggest that it is not inconceivable that fanatical national leaders could act in this way. Its technical feasibility is more difficult to discuss, as the more detailed and persuasive the analysis the more it may encourage adoption of such policies. What follows will thus seek only to establish in general terms that the likelihood of the case is sufficiently high to justify more detailed investigation.

'Anonymous proliferation' would seem to be technically feasible if the detonation of a first-generation device lacking 100% reliability and high performance will achieve the objectives of the 'destabiliser'. Either uranium or plutonium could be used in the construction of such a device. The use of highly enriched U-235 would offer a high probability of achieving its calculated yield, thus negating the need for a prior explosive test. Some 25 kg of U-235 would be sufficient for this purpose.

A low-technology centrifuge plant could be used to produce the necessary quantities of U-235. A plant made up of units producing no more than 1 kg SWU per year would require 4,000 centrifuges and a feed of 10 tons a year of uranium in the form of UF6, the production of which is a pilot-scale operation. The power requirements of such a plant would only be 200 kw, the heat disposal load the same and the floor area perhaps $2,500 \text{ m}^2$. Such a plant would not be detectable in operation except by espionage. It would involve the use of high-strength aluminium alloys as tubes or forgings and a degree of expertise in this area which would depend upon the speed and therefore machine output required. Many countries could probably procure or manufacture these alloys without raising suspicions. The development of such a low-technology non-commercial plant would be a medium-size technological challenge, but could be accomplished in many countries without expatriate assistance over a five year period.

The use of weapons grade plutonium in the device would offer a relatively lower probability of attaining the intended yield and impose greater demands upon its designer and the performance of its non-nuclear components. This situation would worsen quantitatively as the proportion of higher plutonium isotopes increased. Some 10–15 kg of plutonium would be required for this purpose.

A low-technology plant to separate plutonium from irradiated fuel on a small scale could be used to produce the necessary quantities of this material. That fuel would either be diverted from safeguarded facilities or produced in an unsafeguarded reactor. A study carried out at Oak Ridge in 1977 stated that: 'We have looked at a facility capable of isolating 10 kg of plutonium and converting it to metal buttons. Actually we estimate that it will take 4 to 6 months to start operations with the first 10 kg of plutonium metal one week later. We have assumed one PWR fuel element per day throughput [about 5 kg of plutonium a day]. Much of the equipment can be improvised of stainless steel 55-gal drums, but all can be easily fabricated in a small metal working shop. It is probable that most equipment will be available from local industries, requiring, at most, minor alterations.' Although those involved in this study were experienced chemical engineers, the quantities involved may be a little optimistic. Such a plant would only have a limited life and the operators would have to be motivated to accept radiation doses of tens of rads per year for a limited period.

One additional technological option for the future is plutonium isotope separation. Laser separation of uranium atomic vapour appears feasible and it may be a commercially competitive process. It has been suggested that the same method may also be usable to separate plutonium isotopes. Contemporary judgements are that restrictions for non-proliferation purposes on laser isotope separation should be easier to implement than those on gas centrifuges, because low-technology versions do not seem feasible. The single unit difference in mass number of Pu-239 and Pu-240 means, however, that the separative work output from the same low-technology centrifuge machine would be an order of magnitude lower for a plutonium feed than a uranium one. On the other hand an examination of tables of separative work as a function of product and feed concentrations shows that the separative work required to produce military grade plutonium from civil plutonium feed is two orders of magnitude less than to produce weapon grade U-235 from natural uranium feed. A much smaller plant would therefore be required for this purpose. It could not operate for an extended period of time, however, because the PuF_6 would be decomposed by particle collisions and plutonium would be plated out as unattractive and hazardous solid fluorides.

CONCLUSION

There exists a need to give more thought to the possibility that states may not aim for a significant stockpile of advanced weapons when they engage in nuclear proliferation, but may instead engage in the small-scale production of one or a few simple nuclear devices. One motivation for this could be to implement a policy of 'anonymous proliferation'. If it is accepted that this is a political possibility, policies to combat it will need to focus upon preventing the operation of pilot scale heavy isotope separation processes using laser or centrifuge technologies. In the cases of both low-technology centrifuge enrichment and plutonium reprocessing plants, controlling the export of special items may be inadequate to prevent such developments. On the other hand, if their existence was uncovered, the patently uncommercial nature of such plants would make it difficult for a state to claim that they were civil facilities.

Appendix 4 NPT/III/41
NPT Review Conference: 1985
Rules of Procedure

Rule 24

Proposals and substantive amendments shall normally be submitted in writing to the Secretary-General of the Conference, who shall circulate copies to all delegations. Unless the Conference decide otherwise, proposals and substantive amendments shall be discussed or decided on no earlier than 24 hours after copies have been circulated in all languages of the Conference to all delegations.

WITHDRAWAL OF PROPOSALS AND MOTIONS

Rule 25

A proposal or a motion may be withdrawn by its sponsor at any time before a decision on it has been taken, provided that it has not been amended. A proposal or a motion thus withdrawn may be reintroduced by any representative.

DECISION ON COMPETENCE

Rule 26

Any motion calling for a decision on the competence of the Conference to adopt a proposal submitted to it, shall be decided upon before a decision is taken on the proposal in question.

RECONSIDERATION OF PROPOSALS

Rule 27

Proposals adopted by consensus may not be reconsidered unless the Conference reaches a consensus on such reconsideration. When a proposal has been adopted or rejected by a majority or two-thirds vote, it may not be reconsidered unless the Conference, by a two-thirds majority of the members present and voting, so decides. Permission to speak on a motion to reconsider shall be accorded only to two speakers opposing the motion, after which it shall be immediately put to the vote.

VI. VOTING AND ELECTIONS

ADOPTION OF DECISIONS

Rule 28

1. Decisions on matters of procedure and in elections shall be taken by a majority of representatives present and voting.

2. The task of the Review Conference being to review the operation of the Treaty with a view to assuring that the purposes of the preamble and the provisions of the Treaty are being realized, and thus to strengthen its effectiveness, every effort should be made to reach agreement on substantive matters by means of consensus. There should not be voting on such matters until all efforts to achieve consensus have been exhausted.

3. If, notwithstanding the best efforts of delegates to achieve consensus, a matter of substance comes up for voting, the President shall defer the vote for 48 hours and during this period of deferment shall make every effort, with the assistance of the General Committee, to facilitate the achievement of general agreement, and shall report to the Conference prior to the end of the period.

4. If by the end of the period of deferment the Conference has not reached agreement voting shall take place and decisions shall be taken by a two-thirds majority of the representatives present and voting, providing that such majority shall include at least a majority of the States participating in the Conference.

5. If the question arises whether a matter is one of procedure or of

substance, the President of the Conference shall rule on the question. An appeal against this ruling shall immediately be put to the vote and the President's ruling shall stand unless the appeal is approved by a majority of the representatives present and voting.

6. In cases where a vote is taken in accordance with paragraphs 1 and 4 above, the relevant rules of procedure relating to voting of the General Assembly of the United Nations shall apply, except as otherwise specifically provided herein.

VOTING RIGHTS

Rule 29

Every State Party to the Treaty shall have one vote.

MEANING OF THE PHRASE 'REPRESENTATIVES PRESENT AND VOTING'

Rule 30

For the purposes of these rules, the phrase 'representatives present and voting' means representatives casting an affirmative or negative vote. Representatives who abstain from voting are considered as not voting.

Index